Sport and Exercise Science

Active Learning in Sport – titles in the series

Coaching Science	ISBN 978 1 84445 165 4
Personal Training	ISBN 978 1 84445 163 0
Sport Sociology	ISBN 978 1 84445 166 1
Sport and Exercise Science	ISBN 978 1 84445 187 6
Sport Management	ISBN 978 1 84445 263 7
Sport Studies	ISBN 978 1 84445 186 9

To order, please contact our distributor: BEBC Distribution, Albion Close, Parkstone, Poole, BH12 3LL. Telephone: 0845 230 9000, email: **learningmatters@bebc.co.uk**. You can also find more information on each of these titles and our other learning resources at **www.learningmatters.co.uk**

Sport and Exercise Science

*Joanne Thatcher, Rhys Thatcher, Melissa Day,
Matthew Portas and Simon Hood*

LearningMatters

First published in 2009 by Learning Matters Ltd

British Library Cataloguing in Publication Data
A CIP record for this book is available from the British Library

ISBN: 978 1 84445 187 6

Cover design by Toucan Design
Text design by Code 5 Design Associates Ltd
Project Management by Swales & Willis Ltd, Exeter, Devon
Typeset by Swales & Willis Ltd, Exeter, Devon
Printed and bound in Great Britain by TJ International Ltd, Padstow, Cornwall

Learning Matters Ltd
33 Southernhay East
Exeter EX1 1NX
Tel: 01392 215560
E-mail: info@learningmatters.co.uk
www.learningmatters.co.uk

FSC
Mixed Sources
Product group from well-managed
forests and other controlled sources
Cert no. SGS-COC-2482
www.fsc.org
© 1996 Forest Stewardship Council

Contents

Acknowledgements

We would like to thank a number of people who provided helpful comments on earlier drafts of some of the chapters in this book: Glen Davison, Ruth Hughes, David Lavallee, Rachel Rahman, Les Tumilty and Bernadette Woods.

Chapter 1

Introduction

Joanne Thatcher, Rhys Thatcher,
Matthew Portas and Simon Hood

Sport and exercise science

Sport and exercise science is one of the most exciting ways to study and apply science and has never been more important than in today's society. We're never too far away from a major sporting event: Wimbledon, the Olympics and Paralympics, the cricket, rugby and football World Cups, the Ryder Cup in golf, Badminton horse trials . . . the list is almost endless. Sport scientists have an increasingly prominent role in contemporary sport, working with athletes, coaches and officials to help them to optimise performance and ensure that their involvement in competitive sport is a rewarding and positive experience.

On the opposite side of the coin, we are faced with increasing levels of obesity and physical inactivity in our society, contributing to physical and mental ill health in adults, and, worryingly, in children. Exercise science plays a critical role in understanding these problems and offering solutions aimed at optimising physical activity levels and the health benefits that we know can be gained from physical activity.

We can see, then, that there's a fundamental difference between sport science and exercise science. The main aim of sport science is to optimise the mental and physical preparation, performance and overall experience of competitive sports participants, from amateurs to Olympic champions, including athletes, coaches, officials and so on. The main aim of exercise science is to optimise physical activity levels, experiences and benefits in the general population. This fundamental difference aside, there is, of course, a great deal of overlap between the two areas. For instance, the same theories can be used to understand why people are motivated to take part in both competitive sport and health-related physical activity. Many of the same physiological factors limit physical performance whether it is an elite athlete running at 20km/hour or a previously physically inactive person who is jogging at 6km/hour. The same can be said of biomechanics, where the theories and laws of physics that underpin the subject apply to a person slowly jogging around a park to keep fit or an elite runner speeding through Central Park at the end of the New York Marathon. These examples also introduce us to the three key sub-disciplines within sport and exercise science: psychology, physiology, and biomechanics.

Sport and exercise psychology

As well as being a sub-discipline within sport and exercise science, sport and exercise psychology is a sub-discipline within the field of psychology, alongside other areas such as clinical psychology, counselling psychology and educational psychology. As such, its main concern mirrors that of other fields of psychology: to understand, explain, predict and change people's behaviours, emotions and thought processes.

Sport and exercise psychology therefore involves the application and use of psychology within sport and exercise settings. The box below presents some of the key questions and issues that sport and exercise psychologists are interested in.

- What psychological strategies will help an athlete to stay focused during competition?
- How can we develop cohesion in competitive sports teams?
- What motivates teenage girls to do physical activity and exercise?
- Can exercise help to prevent mental ill health, such as anxiety and depression?

Sport and exercise physiology

Physiology is the study of the function of biological systems. In sport and exercise physiology we are interested in how the body responds to exercise and physical activity, what limits physical performance, and how training can be used to improve health and performance. For instance, we examine how the heart functions to deliver blood to muscle and how muscle functions to produce force. Other areas covered in sport and exercise physiology include the effects of diet on health and performance. The box below presents some of the key questions and issues that sport and exercise physiologists are interested in.

- How can an individual change their diet to improve their health and their ability to compete in sport?
- How can an athlete train to improve their athletic performance?
- What physical factors can limit an athlete's sporting performance?
- What does an athlete need to do to stay healthy while they are training hard?

Sport and exercise biomechanics

Biomechanics is the application of the laws and principles of physics to biological systems (e.g. a human being). When studying biomechanics you will encounter *clinical* (generally gait analysis and injury rehabilitation) and *applied biomechanics*, both of which rely on understanding the basic concepts of forces and principles of bodily motion. For example, if a person experiences pain in their shins when they try to jog (known as shin splints), biomechanists can examine the motion of the person's legs during running and work out how forces produced by the movement pass through the body. They then make adjustments to the runner's technique to try to stop them experiencing pain. The box below presents some of the key questions and issues that biomechanists are interested in.

- How can we analyse the techniques used in different sport skills to help athletes become quicker and more powerful?
- How can we increase efficiency of human movement so that elderly people are steadier on their feet?
- How do we design sports equipment such as golf clubs that make the ball travel further with less human effort or footballs that travel through the air with less resistance?

The aims of this book

With our book, we aim to try to achieve five things:

1   To introduce you to key topics within each of the sub-disciplines of sport and exercise science.
2   To introduce you to the methods that are used by sport and exercise scientists to research questions like those listed above.
3   To encourage you to think about, use and develop study skills to help you to get the most out of reading this book and your future learning.
4   To encourage you to be an active learner as you work through this book.
5   To help you to enjoy studying sport and exercise science.

Aim 1: Introducing sport and exercise science

In the chapters on sport and exercise psychology, Joanne Thatcher and Melissa Day discuss motivation in sport and exercise, stress, anxiety and coping in sport, the dynamics of teams and achieving team cohesion and the psychological effects of exercise participation. In the chapters on sport and exercise physiology, Rhys Thatcher examines the role of diet and nutrition before moving on to discuss muscle function and the role of the cardiovascular system in physical performance.

In the biomechanics chapters, Matthew Portas and Simon Hood explore how key anatomical terminology relates to biomechanics before going on to introduce Newton's Laws of Motion. They then consider some of the key principles surrounding the study of forces and human movement, and conclude by discussing the principles and terms that are related to the motion of the body in straight lines and during rotation.

Aim 2: Introducing sport and exercise science research

As with all academic disciplines, the knowledge we have about sport and exercise science is based on research. Theories, for example, about what motivates people to take part in sport and exercise, and the practical strategies we use to enhance sport and exercise performances and experiences (e.g. drinking carbohydrate drinks), are all tested in research. Knowing how to conduct research and being able to distinguish between poor quality and good research is therefore an important part of developing into a sport and exercise scientist. So, the chapters on research methods introduce you to what we mean by research and the different approaches to research that we can use. In these chapters, Joanne and Melissa also discuss the key issues involved in planning research and how to conduct research using the two major types of research employed in sport and exercise science: quantitative and qualitative.

Aim 3: Studying smart

In our view, one of the key factors that distinguishes students who learn effectively and do well from those who don't, is their use of appropriate study skills and their ability to reflect on their own learning and development. We have, therefore, provided an additional chapter on the internet, focusing on how to study. Our aim in doing so is to make the chapter truly interactive, so you can complete activities online whenever and wherever you like (unless you're on top of a mountain without internet access, of course, but in that instance you may have other things on your mind).

   In this additional chapter, we encourage you to think about the ways that you learn best and alternative approaches that might help to make your learning more effective. We offer some strategies to help you make your learning more effective, encourage you to reflect on your learning and set targets to improve the effectiveness of your learning in the future.

   Throughout each chapter of the book we indicate links to this internet-based chapter, where we hope you will hop on to the internet to try out some of the strategies we offer to help you to better understand the material we cover and to find out which strategies work best for you. The links to the internet resource provide, we hope, ways to develop your study of sport and exercise science. We should emphasise, however, that it is certainly not necessary to have internet access in order to learn from this book, which is designed to work effectively as a standalone resource too.

Aim 4: Learning through doing

In our experience, people tend to really learn and understand things when they're *active learners*. If you don't take our word for it, consider the wisdom of the ancient Chinese philosopher, Confucious:

   I see and I forget
   I hear and I remember
   I do and I understand.

   So by simply reading through this book we don't feel you'll get the most out of it; you need to do something with or to the material we discuss to really get to grips with it.

The study skills activities we've placed on the internet are one of the ways we hope you can achieve this. We've also included a number of activities in each chapter (e.g. reflecting on personal experiences and relating them to what we discuss, critical thinking exercises, practical activities) to help you to become active learners as you work your way through the book. Where appropriate, in some chapters we have highlighted key points to emphasise important definitions and ideas.

Aim 5: Enjoy it

We (Jo, Matt, Mel, Rhys and Simon) are all incredibly lucky to spend our working lives doing something we enjoy and we hope that our passion and enthusiasm for sport and exercise science, particularly helping others to learn about the topic and develop into sport and exercise scientists, is conveyed to you. We have written each chapter with you, the student, in mind and our aim is that the ways in which we present the material encourage you to be active learners and develop your study skills. We also aim to help you enjoy studying sport and exercise science.

Of course, only you can be the judge of whether or not we have met our final aim but we hope you enjoy reading our book as much as we have enjoyed writing it.

Chapter 2

Understanding research

Joanne Thatcher and Melissa Day

Chapter focus

This chapter focuses on understanding what we mean by research and the two main paradigms that are used in sport and exercise science:

- positivist paradigm;
- interpretative paradigm.

We first of all consider what we mean by research and research paradigms and explain the paradigms most often used in sport and exercise science research: the positivist and interpretive paradigms. Often students find research methods quite difficult to grasp, so activities are included to try to help you to think about the ideas presented and see how they apply in real-life research examples.

Learning outcomes
This chapter is designed to help you be able to:
1 Understand what is meant by research and the different elements of the research process;
2 Explain what we mean by a paradigm;
3 Explain the key characteristics of research conducted using the positivist paradigm;
4 Explain the key characteristics of research conducted using the interpretative paradigm.

What is research?

- An exercise instructor provides positive feedback to motivate the exercisers in her class.
- A marathon runner includes a warm-up and a cool-down in his training sessions.
- A tennis player visualises her best shots to improve her self-confidence before her match.
- A cyclist uses a carbohydrate drink during long training and competition rides.

The practices listed above are familiar to most of us who are interested in sport and exercise, but what do they have in common? They are all based on the results of research that suggests that these practices can be beneficial to athletes and exercisers, either psychologically or physiologically. The fact that they're beneficial is great, but the important point here is *how* we know this: because somewhere, at some point, sport and exercise scientists have conducted research to see if they are worthwhile practices. In fact, all of what we know and do in sport and exercise science is underpinned by research (Hyllegard et al., 1996). It's important, therefore, that when you read or hear information about sport and exercise science, you first ask yourself, 'Is there any *evidence* to support this?' and that's a good start to thinking critically about the information you receive. The next step is to look at the type and quality of any evidence presented to you, asking yourself questions like, 'Was an *appropriate research approach* used to gather this evidence?' and, 'Was this high *quality* research?' Your critical evaluation process should go something like that shown in Figure 2.1.

Before we get into the nitty gritty of what different kinds of research are possible and how we can make sure that the research we conduct and read is high quality, we ought to be sure of what we mean by 'research'.

Figure 2.1: Critical evaluation process in research

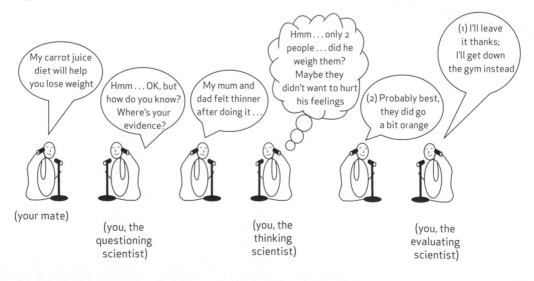

(your mate)

(you, the questioning scientist)

(you, the thinking scientist)

(you, the evaluating scientist)

Burton and Bartlett (2005) have offered some ideas to answer these questions, some of which will probably be included in your own lists. You've also probably listed some answers that aren't included here, so take them to your next research methods class to share with your tutor and fellow students.

Looking down the first list in Table 2.1, we can see that research is all about asking questions in a structured, methodical, logical and organised way (*systematic inquiry*). As we mentioned before, research helps us to understand and develop knowledge about something, like sport and exercise (*the foundation of knowledge*) but its purpose goes beyond developing knowledge, to providing answers to real-life problems and improving our practice as sport and exercise scientists (*problem solving, which is key to reflective practice*). For instance, a coach may want to know the most beneficial type of training to help develop an 800m runner's sprint finish or a sport psychologist may want to know how best to improve the quality of her work with young athletes. Understanding what motivates and demotivates people to attend an exercise class, to stick with an exercise programme and to work hard to achieve their goals are all questions that exercise psychologists have researched and continue to do so; and, in doing so, they are trying to *make sense of the world* (or at least a small part of it). But, of course, the more problems we try to solve and the more questions we research, the more questions we tend to produce (*problem creating*), meaning that the process of research becomes a continuous cycle (like the one shown in Figure 2.2, which we'll return to later on).

And finally, Burton and Bartlett (2005) suggest that research involves both *formal* and *informal inquiry*, and of course they're right. We're all constantly carrying out informal research, answering questions such as those shown in Figure 2.3.

Table 2.1: The nature and purpose of research (Burton and Bartlett, 2005)

What is research?	Why do we need research?
Systematic inquiry	To advance knowledge
The foundation of knowledge	To solve practical problems
Problem solving	To underpin practice
Problem creating	To make a difference
The key to reflective practice	To stimulate new research
A way of making sense of the world	
Informal and formal inquiry	

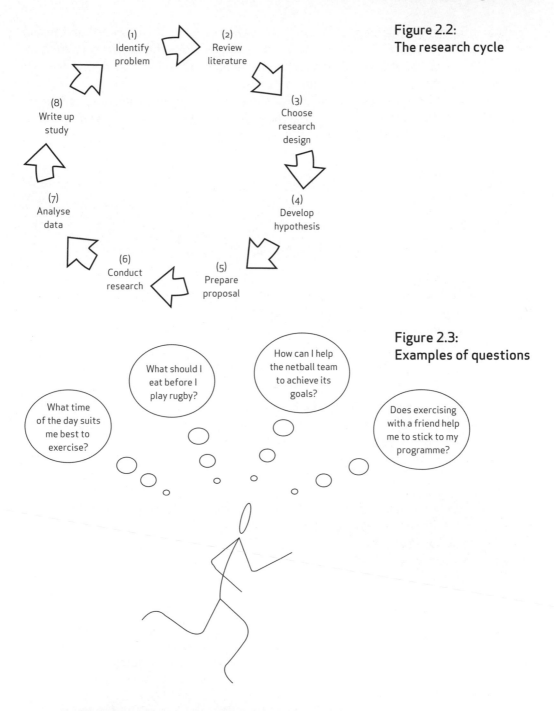

Figure 2.2:
The research cycle

(1) Identify problem
(2) Review literature
(3) Choose research design
(4) Develop hypothesis
(5) Prepare proposal
(6) Conduct research
(7) Analyse data
(8) Write up study

Figure 2.3:
Examples of questions

What time of the day suits me best to exercise?

What should I eat before I play rugby?

How can I help the netball team to achieve its goals?

Does exercising with a friend help me to stick to my programme?

Personal reflection 2.1

Jot down a few questions that have occurred to you whilst you've been exercising, coaching, playing or preparing for sporting competition.

This informal questioning is obviously less rigorous and structured than formal, systematic research but helps us to find answers to questions that are important to us personally and quite often can lead sport and exercise scientists to develop research questions that they then investigate more formally.

Looking down the second column in Table 2.1, it's no surprise that the purpose of research links very closely to what research is, so I won't go back over this list in detail but leave you to check through it on your own.

> Research . . . is a disciplined attempt to address or solve problems through the collection and analysis of primary data for the purpose of description, explanation, generalisation and prediction.
>
> (Blaxter et al., 2005, p. 5)

Hopefully, that's got you thinking about what research is and why we need it but we have yet to discuss what we mean by a paradigm.

See Study Skills Activity 2.1 in the internet chapter for an additional activity.

What is a paradigm?

To answer this question, I'm first going to ask you to engage in a little self-reflection. Think about how you'd answer the questions listed in the box below – you don't need to reveal your answers to anyone but yourself so you don't need to write them down; just take a moment to reflect.

- What is your religion?
- What political party would you vote for?
- Do you agree with private schooling?
- Do you believe in charity?
- Do you support corporal punishment?
- Do you support equal rights?

Okay, now forget about your answers to the questions and look back at the questions themselves and have a go at the next activity.

Critical thinking activity 2.2

Try to describe what these questions are asking you to reflect on and what your answers represent.

What are these questions trying to tap into? Some students I've taught in the past have given answers like, 'If you're narrow-minded!', or, 'If you're prejudiced!' and they're right of course, but these things tell us only about your responses to specific questions from the list. What we're interested in here is *collectively* what your answers represent. We could say they represent your way of looking at things, your philosophy on life (an answer from a very reflective student I taught) or your way of looking at the world. And, essentially, this is what a *paradigm* is: it's a general view of the world, of how it works, of what things are important and unimportant and what the right and wrong ways are of doing things (see Burton and Bartlett, 2005). Our view of the world might influence our attitudes and behaviours; for example, whether or not an athlete thinks that it's right to take performance-enhancing drugs, and refuses or takes them when they're offered. Think about how your 'world view' or 'life philosophy' influences your attitudes and behaviours.

That's all fine, but how does this relate to research? Well, in research we have different paradigms, or ways of doing research. Each paradigm emphasises a specific way of looking at the things we're interested in and a specific way of carrying out the research, because different things are important within different paradigms (Burton and Bartlett, 2005). This probably sounds a little vague and confusing at the moment, but once we've had a look at two of the key paradigms used in sport and exercise science (*positivist* and *interpretative*), it should hopefully become clearer. There are other research paradigms, such as action research, but these are used less widely in sport and exercise science, so we won't look at them here. You can, however, find out more about them in the Further Reading at the end of the chapter.

> [A paradigm] is used to describe how scientists work within accepted (usually unquestioned) ways of defining, assigning categories, theorising and procedures within disciplines . . . particular world views that are taken as knowledge, and are used as standard forms of solutions to problems, of explaining events and of undertaking research.
>
> (Hart, 2003a, p. 126)

See Study Skills Activity 2.1 in the internet chapter for an additional activity.

The positivist paradigm

So, now we know what a paradigm is, we can have a look at the positivist paradigm (a nice example of alliteration, like *pickled pepper* or *pied piper*), or, the positivist way of looking at research: what's important in research and how we should conduct research to develop knowledge and understanding. Let's use a recent research study to do this.

Research focus one

Osterberg et al. (2008) used the positivist paradigm to compare the effects of two sports drinks (one with added protein and one with no added protein) on cycling performance. They hypothesised that the added protein would have no extra performance benefit to drinking only a carbohydrate drink (contrary, in fact, to the suggestion of some previous researchers).

A group of 13 male trained cyclists each completed three trials of cycling in the laboratory (a two-hour ride, followed by a two-minute time trial). They completed the trials in random order.

The only thing that differed between the trials was the type of drink the cyclists drank: (1) a carbohydrate drink; (2) a carbohydrate plus protein drink; and (3) a placebo drink with no protein or carbohydrate. Neither the cyclists nor the researchers knew which drink each cyclist was drinking during each trial until after the study. This is known as a *double-blind* protocol (Hyllegard et al., 1996).

Everything else about the trials was kept the same: the athlete's workload, the length of the trial, the volume drunk and frequency of drinking, the laboratory where the trials took place, the temperature and humidity in the laboratory, and the athlete's diet the day before the trial.

The researchers carried out statistical comparisons of all the cyclists' performances in the three trials and their results supported their expectations – adding protein to a carbohydrate drink provides no additional benefit for endurance cycling performance.

Now we've got a summary of the study, let's consider the key features of this research that used the *positivist paradigm* (Thomas and Nelson, 2001).

- The researchers began their study with a *hypothesis* – a statement of what results they expected to find – and their study was then designed to test this hypothesis.
- The researchers conducted an experiment to test their hypothesis (a process known as *empirical verification*) and observed the effects of their experiment (a process known as *discovering laws through observation*).
- The researchers did not want their expectations about the results to influence their findings, so they used a double-blind protocol to allow them to stay *objective* or *detached* from the results.
- The researchers ensured that they standardised each trial so that they could *control* anything (like pre-trial diet) that could affect their results instead of the drinks they gave the cyclists. By ruling out these other factors, they were able to test for *cause and effect*. In other words, they could see if the type of drink *caused* a change in performance. Also, by standardising conditions and ensuring the researchers didn't influence the results, they aimed to produce findings that are *generalisable*. So, if other researchers conducted the same study, they would find the same results.
- The researchers wanted to identify an objective answer to their question about which drink most benefited performance: they were not interested in which drink the cyclists *thought* was most beneficial. Instead, they focused on finding an *objective* answer that was unrelated to the athletes' opinions of the drinks.
- The researchers collected a fairly *large sample of numerical data* (39 trials' worth in total), which they *analysed statistically*.
- The researchers conducted their study in controlled, laboratory conditions, an approach that has its foundation in the *natural sciences*, such as biochemistry or physics.

These highlighted characteristics in the list above (which we'll return to in Chapters 3 and 4) are all the main features of the positivist paradigm and this study has done a really good job of showing us what these features are. One feature that hasn't been mentioned is that studies that use the positivist paradigm are *based on theories or models*. The box below summarises the features of the positivist paradigm.

Characteristics of the positivist paradigm (Kuhn, 1970).

- Grounded in the natural sciences
- Objective view of reality
- Objective/detached researcher
- Controlled
- Theory driven
- Laws discovered through observation
- Establish general principles
- Empirical verification
- Hypothesis testing
- Establish cause and effect
- Large samples and statistics

To summarise this paradigm we can draw on a definition from scientific philosophers that clearly explains the way of thinking that underpins the positivist paradigm (the highlights are mine to emphasise the key points of this definition), as shown in the box below.

. . . our beliefs [experimental results] may be determined by *nothing human*, but by some *external permanency* – by *something upon which our thinking has no effect* . . . The method must be such that *the ultimate conclusion of every man shall be the same*. Such is the method of science. Its fundamental hypothesis . . . is this: *there are real things, whose characters are entirely independent of our opinions about them* . . .

(Buchler, 1955, p. 18; cited by Kerlinger, 1973, p. 6; my addition in brackets)

Critical thinking activity 2.3

Try to write a paragraph that summarises what you understand about the positivist paradigm. Make sure you use your own words to explain as much as you can about this approach to research. Compare your paragraph with the one below.

Example paragraph to describe the positivist paradigm

Using the positivist paradigm, researchers conduct research studies to test hypotheses that are based on theories or models of how things work. They control any things that may influence the results, including themselves, so that they can generalise their findings and demonstrate that one thing has an effect on another. This means that they are able to demonstrate cause and effect. They are interested in finding out one objective answer to their research question that is the same regardless of who conducted the study or collected the data. They generally collect large sets of numerical data, which they analyse statistically to see if their hypothesis is supported.

The interpretative paradigm

Now that you have checked your understanding of the positivist paradigm, let's move on to the interpretative paradigm. You will notice as we discuss this paradigm that there are many contrasting features between the interpretative and positivist paradigms. Try to see how many contrasts you can spot as we go along. There will be time to test yourself on this at the end of this section.

Research focus two

Rees et al. (2003) investigated the influence of social support on the lives of men who had sustained a spinal cord injury and become disabled through playing sport. They used a four-factor model of social support (Rees and Hardy, 2000) as a framework for their study. The aim was not to test this model, but to use it as a guide for interview questions and structure.

Participants were six males who all defined themselves as disabled. These men took part in life history interviews. After the first interview with each participant, the researchers made suggestions for questions in subsequent interviews. Each participant took part in at least two interviews.

The interviewer kept a reflexive journal and used his co-authors as critical friends during the data collection process. This meant that he was able to reflect on the difficulties of research and become aware of his own subjectivity. The research paper also highlights the need for good rapport and trust to be built up during the interviews.

The interviews were transcribed verbatim (word for word) and categorical content analysis was used. This means that Rees et al. used the four factors from the model of social support to categorise statements from participants.

In the results section, direct quotes were used from participants to illustrate the findings. Rees et al. (2003) stated that the results and discussion should provide the reader with a better understanding of the experiences of these men and how social support operates in their world.

Now that we have an overview of this research, let's look at how it uses the interpretative paradigm.

- The researchers began their study with a model of social support. They did not attempt to test this model but instead used it to guide their interview questions.
- There were only six participants in this study. Interpretative research uses smaller sample sizes than positivist research.
- The researchers used interviews to collect data. Data collection techniques such as interviews, case studies and ethnographies are frequently used in interpretative research.

- The researchers acknowledged their subjectivity and used a reflexive journal and critical friend to gain awareness of this. They acknowledged that they would have pre-determined beliefs and ideas and that recognising these in the research process is important.
- This paper highlights the need for rapport and trust between researcher and research participants. It is often said that these are the most important aspects of interviewing since they will encourage participants to be more open and disclose information that may be sensitive.
- Content analysis was used to analyse the data. This is a common technique for analysing interview data and involves identifying themes within the data.
- Direct quotes were used within the results section. This is because interpretative researchers are interested in understanding the world of the participant. The participant's own words are very important to illustrate this.
- The researchers stated that the results aimed to promote understanding. They were not trying to find laws of behaviour or make generalisations.

The study by Rees et al. (2003) shows us the key components of interpretative research. You may want to look up this study to gain a more in-depth understanding of how research findings are presented in interpretative research. The box below summarises the key characteristics of the interpretative paradigm.

Characteristics of the interpretative paradigm (Kuhn 1970).

- Understanding the world from the participant's point of view
- Knowledge can never be certified as absolute truth
- Subjective view of reality
- Focuses on how individuals make sense of the world around them
- Researcher as a research instrument
- Interviews, case studies and ethnography are methods used for data collection
- Small sample size
- Includes research questions not hypotheses
- Participants are observed in their natural settings
- Illustrative quotes from participants

To summarise this paradigm we can draw on a definition from Sparkes (see the box below). The highlights are mine to emphasise key characteristics of the interpretative paradigm.

Since humans beings are thinking, conscious, feeling, language- and symbol-using animals, interpretative researchers do not feel drawn towards the natural science approaches for understanding the social world ... *knowledge is a human construction*, which means that it *can never be certifiable as ultimately true* but rather it is problematic and ever changing ... there can be no data that is free from interpretation ... *we can not hope to see the world outside of our place in it.*
(Sparkes, 1992, pp. 25–27)

Critical thinking activity 2.4

Based on the information that you have gained from our discussions of the positivist and interpretative paradigms, you will probably have noticed that there are a number of contrasts between the two. Use this information to try to summarise the differences between the positivist and interpretative paradigms. See if you can come up with at least four differences in the way that research is conducted using each of these perspectives. One example is provided below.

Positivist	Interpretative
1. Large sample size	1. Small sample size
2.	2.
3.	3.
4.	4.

You can find some example answers by clicking on the link to Critical Thinking Activity 2.4: Example Answers in the internet chapter.

See Study Skills Activity 2.2 in the internet chapter for an additional activity.

Review

In this chapter we've seen that research involves systematic inquiry and can be represented as a research cycle, spanning from identifying the research problem to completing and writing up the study (Learning Objective (LO) 1). We looked at the different paradigms used in sport and exercise science research and began by defining a paradigm as a general way of viewing the world. This provides guidelines on the important things to consider when conducting research using different paradigms (LO 2). We then identified the key characteristics of the positivist and interpretative paradigms (LOs 3 and 4). Positivist research is based on theories or models and the aim is to conduct controlled studies to find out objective answers to research questions that will tell us if our hypotheses are supported or not. The central concern of the interpretative paradigm is to understand human experiences. It does not aim to test hypotheses or theories or construct laws of behaviour. Instead, it seeks to understand the subjective meanings that individuals attach to social actions and how they make sense of the world around them.

Work through the review questions in Study Skills Activity 2.3 in the internet chapter for an additional activity.

Further reading (understanding research)

Baumgartner, TA, Strong, CH and Hensley, LD (2002) *Conducting and reading research in health and human performance*, 3rd edition, pp. 4–13. Maidenhead: McGraw-Hill.

This section provides an easy introduction to the concept of research and discusses the research cycle. It does introduce some ideas we haven't touched on (inductive and deductive reasoning) and so should help to expand your knowledge about research beyond this chapter.

Thomas, JR and Nelson, JK (2001) *Research methods in physical activity*, 4th edition, pp. 10–13. Leeds: Human Kinetics.
These pages provide a good summary of how to recognise things that cannot be classified as scientific research, which should help to reinforce what scientific research is.

Burton, D and Bartlett, S (2005) *Practitioner research for teachers*, pp. 18–21, 37–41. London: Paul Chapman.
Don't be put off by the title – this is a clear explanation of the positivist paradigm and the second set of pages provides an overview of action research for those of you who are interested in finding out what this is.

Sparkes, A (1992) *Research in physical education and sport: exploring alternative visions*. Oxford: Routledge.
The first chapter in this book is especially useful for explaining the interpretative paradigm.

Chapter 3

Planning research

Joanne Thatcher and Melissa Day

Chapter focus

This chapter focuses on key issues in planning research:

- reviewing literature;
- research questions and problems;
- research hypotheses;
- selecting a study sample;
- conducting a pilot study.

When we defined research, we identified that this is a process of systematic inquiry (Hyllegard et al., 1996), which should suggest to you that planning is an essential ingredient of good quality research. You may have identified an exciting research question and be keen to get on and collect some data (information) to answer this question – but beware. If you don't plan your study in detail beforehand – what you'll measure, how and where you'll measure it, who will take part, etc. – you could end up with poor quality or useless evidence.

In this chapter we look at the main activities involved in planning research (Baumgartner et al., 2002; Neutens and Rubinson, 2002):

- reviewing literature;
- defining the research question/problem;
- identifying a hypothesis;
- choosing the research design;
- selecting the study participants;
- conducting a pilot study.

As we consider each of these activities, look back to Figure 2.2 in Chapter 2 illustrating the research cycle and see where they fit into this process.

Reviewing literature

Before we conduct research, we need to read similar studies that other researchers have conducted previously and become familiar with different theories or models that have been used to guide their studies and the development of their questions.

We may also consider alternative theories or models that we think would provide a better explanation of what we're researching. This review of previous research, theories and models is called a *literature review* (Hart, 2003a).

Critical thinking activity 3.1

Note down a few reasons why you think we need to conduct a literature review.

Check your answers against those listed in Table 3.1, and if you've come up with anything that's not included, check your answers with your tutor.

What do the answers to the questions listed in the first column in Table 3.1 provide? And what's the aim of the questions in the second column? You've probably worked out that the questions in column one are about identifying a reason for conducting your study by showing that it will ask a significant question. In other words, using the

Table 3.1: The purposes of a literature review (Hart, 2003a, 2003b; Neutens and Rubinson, 2002)

Why conduct a literature review?	Why conduct a literature review?
To see if this is a worthwhile question: • Has this topic has been studied before? • Is this a new study or research question? • Does this study improve on previous research? • Will this study help to develop or understand a theory or a model? • Will the study produce results that can be applied in real-life situations?	To help plan your research: • What has previous research found? • What theory or model will I use? • How has previous research addressed the topic (e.g. which paradigm was used)? • What is the research question? • What do I need to measure or observe? • What do I expect to find?

literature review to consider these questions helps to provide a *rationale or justification* for your study, highlighting the weaknesses and limitations of previous research, comparing the results from these studies and identifying a gap in our knowledge that your research will fill (Baumgartner et al., 2002). Think of ways that a study could be novel and add new knowledge to what we already know; some are listed in Figure 3.1.

These are just some examples of how we can develop a *novel* study. There may be others, such as changing the way the study is carried out to improve on the weaknesses of previous research or, of course, asking a totally new question that no one has examined before. It's important to remember that, even though your question may be novel, it may not be worthwhile, so there has to be a good reason for using a novel sample or environment not just because no one has done so before.

Looking down the second column in Table 3.1, we can see that these questions are geared towards developing your own understanding of the area you intend to research and your own study. Presenting the background to the study helps to show how it fits into the area and adds to our knowledge. Discussing different theories or models helps you to decide which one you will use to underpin your research. And, looking at the way that other studies were carried out and what they found helps you to decide how you will conduct your research and what your questions will be (Hart, 2003a; Neutens and Rubinson, 2002). Putting all this together, we can see how we arrive at the definition of a literature review.

Figure 3.1: Example ways of developing a novel research question

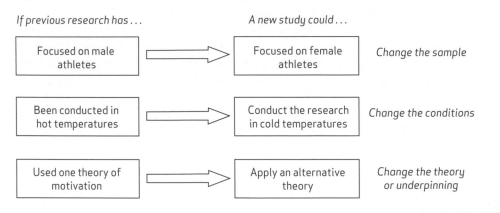

A literature review is a critical summary of previous research and theory that provides a rationale for and a background to the research you are conducting.
(Synthesised from Burton and Bartlett (2005) and Williams and Wragg (2004))

Further reading (reviewing literature)

Williams, C and Wragg, C (2004) *Data analysis and research for sport and exercise science*, Chapter 2. London: Routledge.
Contains some practical advice on writing a literature review which we haven't had time to cover here.

Your literature review will include a statement of the research problem/question in your study. Sometimes we have already decided on our research question before we conduct our literature review and sometimes we decide this after we've read through the background literature.
See Study Skills Activity 3.1 in the internet chapter for an additional activity.

Research questions and problems in the positivist paradigm

A research problem/question is:

> An interrogative statement that asks: what relation exists between two or more variables?
>
> (Kerlinger, 1973, p. 17)

Stating a clear research question or problem is important as this helps us to identify the *purpose of the research*: what we are trying to achieve and what our research will and won't focus on (Neutens and Rubinson, 2002). The research question/problem, alongside the literature review, helps us to start to plan the research – what paradigm should we use? How should we carry out the research? Who should our study participants be? What variables (things) should we measure or observe? This helps us to decide if the research question is realistic (do we have the time, equipment, expertise, participants, etc. needed to address the question?). Identifying a research question helps us decide whether it's a worthwhile question to ask – will it help to develop new knowledge, test a theory or improve practice with athletes or exercisers? And, as with anything in life, if we don't know the problem we're trying to solve, we don't know how to solve it.

Critical thinking activity 3.2

Consider the following questions. Which ones do you think can be examined using the positivist paradigm; which would be difficult to examine using this paradigm, and why?

1   Can exercise participation increase self-esteem?
2   Is competitive sport an enriching experience for children?

> **Critical thinking activity 3.2 continued**
>
> 3 Does a carbohydrate drink help improve endurance performance?
> 4 Will positive feedback increase motivation in exercisers?
> 5 Is fartlek training better than endurance training?
> 6 Will video instruction improve coaches?
> 7 Should boxing be banned?

If you said that numbers 2, 5, 6 and 7 are difficult to address using the positivist paradigm, well done. But what was your reasoning behind your answers? Let's look at the questions that would be difficult to examine using the positivist paradigm and see why – see Table 3.2.

The remaining questions could be examined using the positivist paradigm. Having looked at examples of inappropriate research questions, if we look at those remaining (1, 3 and 4), we can see what makes good research questions. They:

- are phrased clearly and unambiguously as a question;
- include expected outcomes (e.g. self-esteem, motivation, performance);
- include variables that can be measured.

Once we have identified a worthwhile research question, the next step in planning research using the positivist paradigm is to identify the study's hypothesis.

Table 3.2: Inappropriate research questions for the positivist paradigm

Rejected question	Reasons to reject
'Is competitive sport an enriching experience for children?'	'Enriching' is a term that is too vague to quantify and measure objectively.
'Is fartlek training better than endurance training?'	This includes a cause (the type of training) but no effect. We don't know what fartlek training is supposed to be 'better' for (sprinting, endurance running etc.).
'Will video instruction improve coaches?'	Similar to the question above: this question doesn't tell us what we should expect to see improved in coaches and what we mean by improvement.
'Should boxing be banned?'	This question involves obtaining *subjective opinions*, so the positivist paradigm would be unsuitable.

The research hypothesis

A research hypothesis is a statement of what we expect to find in our study. We can apply the same principles for identifying good research questions to develop good scientific hypotheses.

A hypothesis should:

- be clear and unambiguous;
- refer to the relationship between two or more variables that can be objectively measured;
- be based on previous theory, models or research findings.

Because hypotheses are based on theories, models or previous research findings, they fulfil some of the criteria of positivist research. First, the research is based on *theory* or *scientific understanding*, so, hypotheses contribute to the criterion of *objectivity*: they are not based on our subjective opinions of what we expect to find. By stating what we expect to find in a hypothesis before we conduct our research, we have increased confidence that the results are due to our research and not to any chance happenings or random occurrences.

Different types of hypotheses

Traditionally, positivist researchers have stated two hypotheses: a *null* and a *research hypothesis*. The null hypothesis states that there will be no effect and the research hypothesis states that there will be an effect (Williams and Wragg, 2004). For example, in a study that examines the effects of exercise participation on self-esteem, here are the null and research hypotheses:

Null   There will be no effect of exercise participation on self-esteem.
Research   Exercise participation will lead to increases in self-esteem.

Another example is a study that examines the relationship between pre-competition anxiety and sports performance, with the following null and research hypotheses:

Null   Pre-competition anxiety and sports performance will not be related.
Research   Pre-competition anxiety will be related to sports performance.

We could refine this research hypothesis by stating the *direction* of the expected results:

Higher levels of pre-competition anxiety will be related to lower levels of sports performance.

Table 3.3: Null and research hypotheses

Null hypothesis	Research hypothesis
Imagery use will have no effect on self-confidence.	
	Pre-exercise stretching will result in greater levels of flexibility.
Strength training will not be related to higher muscular power output.	
	Goal setting will be related to higher levels of motivation.

Try stating the null and research hypotheses in Table 3.3 and check your answers at the end of the chapter.

Nowadays, researchers only report the research hypothesis (and you should too) but it's a good idea to be aware of the null hypothesis when you read more advanced texts and start to statistically analyse your results.

Critical thinking activity 3.3

Find six journal articles that have used the positivist paradigm to examine research questions in sport and exercise psychology, physiology and biomechanics. Identify the research questions that were examined in these studies. Explain *why* these were good questions. Find each study's hypothesis and read through the introduction section of the article to see how the researchers arrived at their hypothesis.

Research questions and problems in the interpretative paradigm

Unlike the positivist paradigm, the interpretative paradigm does not state a hypothesis at the start of the research. Interpretative researchers do not design a study to 'test out' pre-set hypotheses. Instead they follow a more exploratory approach that is based on research questions. Mason (1998) suggests that using research questions entails formulating questions to be explored or developed. This is more fluid than using hypotheses that must be tested by or against empirical research or theory. Interpretative research questions are generally open-ended but state the purpose of the study in specific terms.

A research question is a question which the research is designed to address and, taken together, your research questions should express the essence of your enquiry.

(Mason, 1998, p. 15)

Earlier in this chapter you were asked to identify questions that could be examined using the positivist paradigm. Now try to see if you can identify the questions from the list below that would be suited to an interpretative study.

1   Why do elite athletes have higher levels of motivation than recreational athletes?
2   What are the experiences of athletes returning to training after Olympic success?
3   How might choking under pressure be described and interpreted by athletes who have experienced it?
4   Should boxing be banned?

If you answered that questions 2 and 3 were suited to interpretative research, you were correct: these questions examine individuals' experiences and interpretations. Interpretative research often uses questions such as 'what' and 'how'. There were two questions (1 and 4) that would be rejected as interpretative research questions, as explained in Table 3.4.

You can check the quality of your interpretative research question using the following checklist.

Does my research question:
• express the problem that I would like to explore?
• address one point per question?
• 'fit together' to express the problem I would like to explore?
• make sense (can other people understand it)?
• ask something new that has not yet been researched?

Table 3.4: Inappropriate research questions for the interpretative paradigm

Rejected question	Reasons to reject
'Why do elite athletes have higher levels of motivation than recreational athletes?'	Interpretative research does not usually ask 'why' a phenomenon occurs; it cannot provide an answer as it does not examine cause and effect relationships.
'Should boxing be banned?'	This question was also deemed unsuitable for the positivist paradigm since it was too subjective. Although it is a suitable topic for interpretative research, the question is not specific, as it does not tell us whose opinion is being sought. It would be a suitable interpretative research question if it was rephrased to read: What is the general public's perception of boxing?

Further reading (problems and hypotheses)

Neutens, JJ and Rubinson, L (2002) *Research techniques for the health sciences*, 3rd edition, Chapter 2. San Fransisco: Benjamin Cummings.

Although it focuses on health, this chapter includes some good examples of how to develop research problems and hypotheses. They touch on the research proposal and, although some of the information may not be relevant for you, do complete the suggested activities as they are a useful way of reinforcing your knowledge.

Selecting the study participants in the positivist paradigm

Once we have identified our study rationale and question or hypothesis, we need to know who will take part in our study. Sampling is vital in any research because, as Miles and Huberman comment:

> 'You can not study everyone everywhere doing everything.'
>
> (1994, p. 27)

Therefore every researcher has to make decisions about whom they choose to sample. Let's look at this by beginning with an imaginary example, where I want to conduct a study to examine the effects of exercise on weight loss. I've decided on my topic and my hypothesis, so now I need to find some people to take part in the study (the *study sample*). I've got a group of friends and family who are keen to lose weight, always willing to help me and want to see my research go well. So, I recruit them into the study. But is this a good idea? Reflect on anything you think that might be wrong with this approach to selecting a sample for my study.

You've probably outlined quite a few reasons why this is not an ideal approach to selecting a sample; specifically, doing so would contradict two of the key characteristics of positivist research. See Figure 3.2. Clearly, using this approach in positivist research is inappropriate. Instead, we use an approach known as *probability sampling* which allows us to select a *non-biased sample* that is *representative of the population* it was taken from. Let's check we're clear on what's meant by a sample and a population:

Figure 3.2

This approach lacks *objectivity*: my friends and family are too familiar; they know what I want to achieve with my research and are keen to help me achieve it. This may mean that they act in ways to ensure I get the results I expect, or to 'help' my study may not be honest when I ask them questions about their behaviour.	This approach limits how much I can generalise the results of my study (*establish general principles*) as the group is biased. They belong to a specific group (people I know), have selected themselves to be involved and are motivated to participate and see the results turn out as I expect.

- the population is the whole group of people from which we could select our sample;
- the sample is the specific group of people, taken from the population, which takes part in our study.

(Holmes et al., 2006)

Now we know the difference between a sample and a population, how can we use probability sampling to select our sample from our accessible population?

In a probability sample, everyone in the accessible population has an equal chance (*probability*) of being included in the study sample. The most common way to use probability sampling to select a sample is *random sampling*, where we select participants at random (Neutens and Rubinson, 2002). This is just like the way the weekly lottery numbers are chosen in the UK – a machine picks six numbered balls (sample) at random from a total of 49 balls (population). Each ball has an equal chance of being chosen, so, believe it or not, a lottery draw of 1, 2, 3, 4, 5, 6 is equally as likely as a draw of 3, 17, 21, 29, 36, 4.

Critical thinking activity 3.4

Return to the characteristics of the positivist paradigm in Chapter 2 and identify some reasons why probability sampling is essential when using this paradigm. The key reasons you might have identified are that positivist research should display:

- *Objectivity:* a random sample prevents the researcher influencing the sample selection;
- *Control:* a random sample prevents the nature of the sample influencing the results;
- *Generalisability:* a random sample is representative of the population so we can generalise our results to the population.

There are other types of probability sampling (systematic, stratified and cluster sampling) but these are less widely used in sport and exercise science, so we'll restrict our discussion to random sampling. Consult the Further Reading to find out more about these other kinds of probability sampling.

Sampling in the interpretative paradigm

An interpretative researcher has a number of things to consider when making decisions about sampling. To highlight these, let's use an example of an interpretative study where you want to look at the sources of stress experienced by university athletes to examine the research question: *What do university athletes perceive as the main sources of stress they have experienced?* What do you think are your main considerations when choosing this sample? Check and see if your answers match those below.

Consideration one: sample size

Your first consideration may have been the sample size you are going to use. Interpretative research sample sizes tend to be smaller than those used in positivist research. Think about the following examples of samples: which do you think may be suitable for conducting an interpretative study and which may be more problematic?

1   Ten of my friends at university who play on the same team as me.
2   All of the players on the university netball first team.
3   One athlete who is on a sports scholarship at the university.
4   Three athletes from each of the 12 university sports teams.
5   As many university athletes as possible.

You may have said that numbers 1, 4 and 5 would be the most problematic samples to use in interpretative research. Although ten people (sample 1) is a manageable size, it may be difficult to conduct research such as interviews with people who are already friends. Just like the positivist paradigm, interpretative research will be problematic if you rely on the help of your friends as suggested by sample 1. Sample 4 may also be problematic, depending on how you conduct your research. If you choose to use interviews, you may find it difficult to conduct these with all 36 individuals in this sample. Similarly, sampling as many people as possible (sample 5) is not the aim of interpretative research. Often interpretative researchers try to examine commonalities in the data that are generated, which would be difficult with the large sample sizes in samples 4 and 5.

The examples of suitable samples were 2 and 3. You may decide that you want to use a homogenous sample so, rather than sampling from all the university teams, you focus on one team that is likely to have shared experiences within this sport. You may not have selected sample 3 because you felt the sample size was too small. However, it is important to remember that case studies are frequently used in interpretative research and can give in-depth insight into the experiences of this participant.

> A homogenous sample means that there is group similarity. In this case, all the players are from one sports team.

You could consider an alternative approach to choosing a sample size by waiting until you have achieved *theoretical saturation*. Here, you would analyse your data after interviewing or observing each participant. Using our study on sources of stress as an example, let's say that the first five participants have identified six main sources of stress (these are the themes in your analysis). See Figure 3.3.

You then interview and analyse the data of participant six and find that, as well as these themes, a further source of stress is 'diet'. You add this into the overall analysis, producing six themes for your six participants. See Figure 3.4.

Since participant six added new information to your analysis, you interview another participant. However, after interviewing and analysing data obtained from participant seven, no new themes emerge. Participant seven only discusses those six themes

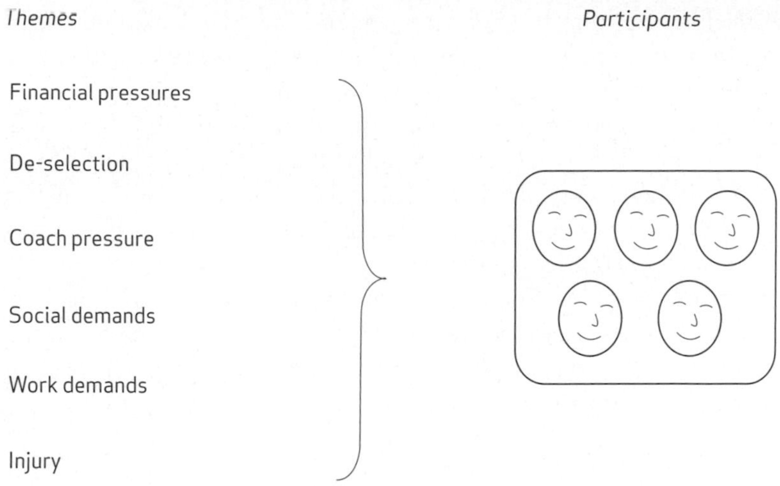

Themes   Participants   **Figure 3.3**

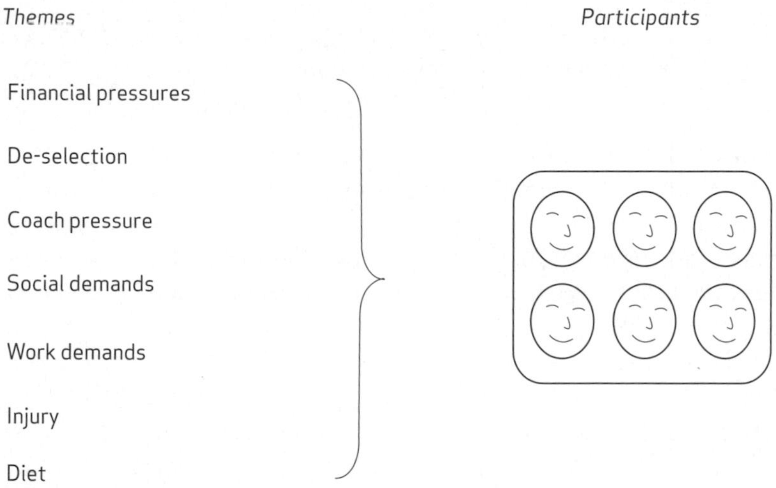

Financial pressures

De-selection

Coach pressure

Social demands

Work demands

Injury

Themes   Participants   **Figure 3.4**

Financial pressures

De-selection

Coach pressure

Social demands

Work demands

Injury

Diet

already identified. You may now have reached theoretical saturation. You interview participant eight to check this and, again, no new themes emerge. This means that you are only adding to the sample size and not adding any new themes. So you can conclude that with your eight participants you have reached theoretical saturation and you decide to stop interviewing.

Consideration two: sample selection

Interpretative researchers also need to consider how they will choose their sample. There may be 2000 athletes in the university population, so you need to consider how you will select the ten that you have chosen as your sample size. Think about how you might do this.

You might have answered that you would use a sample based on probability as suggested in the positivist paradigm. This is needed when we want to obtain a representative sample to generalise from our findings. However, unlike positivism, interpretative research does not aim to construct general laws that explain social behaviour. Instead, an interpretative approach will look to understand subjective meanings so we do not always need to use a representative sample.

You could choose a homogenous sample for your research (as in the above example of the university netball team). This would involve only taking a specific part of the available population. Alternatively, you may sample based on certain criteria, which is known as *purposive sampling*. An example of this could be that participants must have choked under pressure in an important competition.

The study by Rees et al. (2003) in Chapter 2 provides an example of selecting participants based on specific criteria. Participants were selected using the following criteria: (1) they had a spinal cord injury, and (2) this had occurred through playing sport.

See Study Skills Activity 3.2 in the internet chapter for an additional activity.

Further reading (sampling)

Neutens, JJ and Rubinson, L (2002) *Research techniques for the health sciences*, 3rd edition, pp. 139–146. San Francisco: Benjamin Cummings.
A clear summary of sampling that introduces some other forms of probability sampling.

Flick, U (1998) *An introduction to qualitative research*, pp. 122–133. London: Sage.
Discusses the role and importance of sampling in qualitative research.

Once we've identified our study rationale, hypothesis or question and sample, it would be tempting to begin collecting data; however, a final step is invaluable in planning research: the pilot study.

Conducting a pilot study

A pilot study is not a study of people who fly planes (bad joke) but is a trial run of your research. A good question to ask here is: Why not just get on with the exciting part of research . . . doing it? I'm sure you can identify a number of reasons why a trial run is a good idea, so list a few before you read on.

This is really a mixture of good science and commonsense, so I'll just highlight some key things a pilot study helps you to work out:

- the logistics of carrying out your research (e.g. how long things take and where to place your equipment);
- if the measures are suitable for your study (e.g. if studying children, can they understand the questionnaires you're using?);
- how to use any technical equipment;
- if your study will address your research question (e.g. if you're measuring the right variables at the right times or asking the right questions in an interview).

Once you've worked out the answers to questions like these, you're ready to start your research.

We've seen that planning research is a detailed and time-consuming process. We often produce a *research proposal* that outlines how and why the study will be conducted. For more discussion on proposals consult the Further Reading.

Further reading (research proposals)

Baumgartner, TA, Strong, CH and Hensley, LD (2002) *Conducting and reading research in health and human performance*, 3rd edition, pp. 42–76. Maidenhead: McGraw-Hill. Provides more details than we have been able to discuss here.

Review

We first identified that a literature review provides a background to and a rationale for your study, highlighting how the study will contribute to and build on existing knowledge, leading logically to the research question and/or hypothesis (LO 1). We then examined research questions and hypotheses. In positivist research, hypotheses are used and we report the research hypothesis that proposes a relationship or effect involving at least two variables. Interpretative research doesn't use hypotheses but uses research questions that focus on 'how' or 'what' (LO 2). We then considered sampling. In positivist research we use probability sampling, where each potential study participant has an equal chance of being selected; this is usually done by randomly selecting participants from the available population. In interpretative research we don't need to generalise our findings, so we don't randomly select participants and instead select them purposively. A criterion for inclusion in a study is often a shared experience between participants; therefore, sample sizes are usually small and samples are homogenous (LO 3). We concluded by discussing the pilot study, which provides a trial run of the research to make sure your study is appropriately designed to test your hypothesis or examine your research question (LO 4).

Now work through the review questions in Study Skills Activity 3.2 in the internet chapter for an additional activity.

Table 3.5: Completed null and research hypotheses

Null hypothesis	Research hypothesis
Imagery use will have no effect on self-confidence.	Imagery use will result in higher levels of self-confidence.
Pre-exercise stretching will have no effect on flexibility.	Pre-exercise stretching will result in greater levels of flexibility.
Strength training will not be related to higher muscular power output.	Strength training will result in higher levels of muscular power output.
Goal setting will not be related to higher levels of motivation.	Goal setting will be related to higher levels of motivation.

Chapter 4

Positivist research

Joanne Thatcher

Chapter focus

In this chapter we look at how to conduct research using the positivist paradigm, examining the following key issues:

- different types of research design (experimental, quasi-experimental and non-experimental);
- reliability and validity.

Learning outcomes

This chapter is designed to help you be able to:
1 Explain the difference between experimental, quasi-experimental and non-experimental research;
2 Explain what we mean by randomisation, control and manipulation, and identify why these are important;
3 Define reliability and validity';
4 Understand what we mean by threats to reliability and validity in research.

Doing research

In this first section, we look at different approaches to research, or *designs* that are used to conduct research using the positivist paradigm:

- experimental;
- quasi-experimental;
- non-experimental.

In doing so, we revisit the ideas of control and randomisation that we looked at in Chapters 2 and 3. We also encounter some new concepts:

- different kinds of variable (independent, dependent, confounding, extraneous);
- reliability and validity.

So, we are looking at the *how* of research, known as a *research method*. Look back to Chapter 2 to see where this aspect of research fits into the research cycle. Just as there are different paradigms for conducting research, these different paradigms tend to use different methods for doing research (Burton and Bartlett, 2005). The two broad groups of methods that we will introduce you to are *quantitative* and *qualitative methods* [Key Point 4.1]. *Qualitative methods*, which you'll look at in Chapter 5, are most often used by researchers who adopt the *interpretative paradigm* whereas *quantitative methods* are most often used in research that adopts the *positivist paradigm* (ibid.).

Critical thinking activity 4.1

Read through the following summaries of three different types of research conducted in sport and exercise science. Note down the similarities and differences between them.

Research focus one

In 2005, Stagno et al. conducted a study to examine:

1 Changes in fitness levels in male hockey players throughout a season;
2 Heart rate during competition to see if recent rule changes (artificial pitches, 'roll-on, roll-off' substitutes, ball boys, removal of the offside rule) meant that players had to work harder during competition.

Study participants were nine male elite hockey players from the same team with at least three years' experience at this level.

Participants' fitness levels were assessed in the laboratory three times: pre-season, at the start of, and midway through the competitive season. Forty-eight hours prior to each fitness test, they did no exercise. Players' heart rates (HR) were measured throughout each match during the season. The study's design is summarised in Figure 4.1.

Results showed that the recent rule changes did not demand a higher work rate from players, compared with those reported by previous research conducted before the rule changes were introduced.

Pre-season training, aimed at increasing fitness, corresponded with an increase in players' fitness but the increased focus on tactical and technical training during the competitive phase was not related to a decrease in fitness. This is probably because the players were staying 'match fit' and maintaining their fitness by meeting the demands of competition.

However, players did not reach their optimal levels of fitness before the start of the competitive phase of the season. This may mean reconsidering pre-season preparation if we want players to be optimally fit at the start of this phase.

Figure 4.1

PRE-SEASON	START OF THE SEASON	MID-COMPETITIVE SEASON
Fitness test	Fitness test	Fitness test
	HR measured in matches	

Research focus two

Barker and Jones (2006) conducted a case study to see if an intervention including hypnosis, technique refinement and self-modelling could be used to increase a cricket bowler's self-confidence. The study involved a male semi-professional cricket bowler who approached one of the researchers for help with his match preparation and self-confidence.

The study involved three phases: baseline phase (lasting eight games); intervention phase (lasting eight weeks); and post-intervention phase (lasting 16 games). During the baseline and post-intervention phases, the cricketer completed questionnaires to measure: (1) his confidence as a cricketer in general, and (2) his confidence in performing well in each upcoming match. His bowling performance was recorded during each match he played in these two phases.

During the intervention phase, the cricketer received three different interventions: (1) hypnosis sessions; (2) technical coaching sessions; and (3) self-modelling (reviewing videos of himself training or performing well). The cricketer's confidence and performance levels were compared before and after the psychological interventions. The study's design is summarised in Figure 4.2.

Figure 4.2

BASELINE		INTERVENTION		POST-INTERVENTION
8 games	→	8 weeks	→	16 games
Performance and		Hypnosis, coaching,		Performance and
confidence measured		self-modelling		confidence measured

Results showed increases in match-specific self-confidence between baseline and post-intervention phases and similar increases in bowling performance.

These are useful findings for helping athletes who experience similar self-confidence problems. However, as the authors point out, it's impossible to know which of the three aspects of the intervention package (hypnosis, technique refinement, self-modelling) had the greatest, if any, effect on the athlete's self-confidence. As this study was conducted in a real-life setting, we also can't rule out the effects of any real-life experiences on his confidence, such as winning matches or a new, inspiring team coach.

Research focus three

Kalasountas et al. (2007) were interested in finding out if people who are given a placebo performance-enhancing drug would raise their expectations of how well they would perform on a strength exercise and so improve their performance.

Forty-two non-athletes were randomly divided into three groups: placebo/placebo (PP) group; placebo/no placebo (PN) group; and, a control group (CON). All participants completed three baseline tests, where, on separate days, in the laboratory, they completed bench and leg press exercise tests.

> A placebo is a dummy pill that has no physiological effects.
>
> (Elliott, 2001, p. 565)

Following these baseline tests, participants attended trial one. Ten minutes before they completed the tests, participants in the PP and PN groups were given milk-sugar tablets to take and told that they had immediate effects on strength performance. The CON group did not receive any tablets and simply performed the strength tests.

In trial two, the PP and CON groups did exactly what they had done in the previous trial. However, the intervention was changed for the PN group – they were told that a prominent coach had not seen any performance improvements with his athletes, was not satisfied with the drug and so participants were asked to perform the strength tests without taking the placebo drug. After completing trial two, the researchers conducted a *manipulation check* to see if participants did believe that the placebo pill would work and how they felt about taking it. This check confirmed that taking the placebo drug made participants feel, and expect to perform, better (and worse in the PN group when its effects were questioned in trial two). See Figure 4.3.

Figure 4.3

BASELINE TESTING	TRIAL ONE	TRIAL TWO
Three separate strength tests for all three groups →	CON – strength tests only PP/PN – placebo and strength tests →	CON – strength tests only PP – placebo and strength tets PN – negative feedback and strength tests

The researchers hypothesised that in trial one, after receiving the placebo drug, the PP and PN groups would show greater strength increases, compared with baseline performance, than the control group. Their second hypothesis was that, in trial two, the PN group's performance would decrease to match that of the control group.

There were no differences between the three groups at baseline, confirming that they were equally matched. At trial one, the PP and PN groups performed better than the control group, supporting hypothesis one. At trial two, whilst the PP group continued to improve and performed better than the control group, the PN group no longer outperformed the control group, supporting hypothesis two.

The authors suggest that their results can be used to deter athletes from using performance-enhancing drugs as it can be shown that some of the effect of these drugs is psychological (we feel and perform better because we expect to). So, using psychological interventions to achieve positive performance expectancies may be a safer way of improving performance than performance-enhancing drugs.

Each of these studies represents a different type of quantitative research, broadly classified as: *experimental*, *quasi-experimental* and *non-experimental*.

Experimental research

The final study by Kalasountas et al. (2007) is known as experimental research as it includes the three key characteristics of this type of research: *randomisation*, *control* and *manipulation* (Williams and Wragg, 2004). Table 4.1 explains each of these, the

Table 4.1: Randomisation, manipulation and control

What is it?	Why is it important?	Where in our example?
Randomisation Randomisation refers to the process we use to either select our sample or allocate participants to different groups or treatments in our study. As we saw previously, we can use probability sampling to choose a random sample. To randomly allocate participants to different groups, we could use the following method: give each participant a number and then use a random number table to select the first participant to go into group one (the first participant number we find in the random number table), the second into group two (depending on the second participant number in the random number table), the first participant into group three (the first participant number in the random number table). Then we start again, placing participants into groups one, two and three depending on when their numbers occur in the random number table, until we have allocated all our participants into our groups (Thomas and Nelson, 2001). Figure 4.4 shows how the first six participants in a sample of 30 would be allocated using a random number table.	1 A randomly selected sample ensures that our sample is not biased and is representative of the population it's taken from. So, we are able to *generalise* our results back to this population. In other words, we can suggest that the effects we saw in our sample would be seen in other members of this population. 2 Randomly allocating participants to groups ensures that if we see any treatment effects we can say that this is not due to our groups being biased (e.g. placing all the males in one group).	Kalasountas and colleagues (2007) randomly allocated participants into the three groups: PP, PN and, CON. The authors describe this group allocation as 'pseudo-random' (or 'resembling random') because they allocated the participants to groups in the order in which they were recruited to the study. So, the first person recruited was placed in group one (PP), the second in group two (PN), the third in group three (CON), the fourth in group one (PP), and so on. You can see how this is not *truly* random but I suspect this was done to ensure equal group sizes, once no more participants could be recruited to the study. However, the fact that there were no differences in the group's performances in the baseline testing (also known as a *pre-test*) suggests that this strategy did produce equivalent, unbiased groups.

Manipulation
Manipulation only occurs with experimental groups and involves the researcher changing, or manipulating, something about the participant's experience. Examples of manipulation (also known as an intervention or treatment) include giving participants a nutritional supplement before endurance exercise or providing social support during an exercise class. The thing that is manipulated is known as the *independent variable* (Baumgartner et al., 2002). Of course, the manipulation needs to be standardised; for example, if the manipulation involves giving participants a carbohydrate drink they all need to get the same type and quantity of drink at the same time.

To conduct a true experiment we need to change something about the participant's experience, to administer a treatment or implement an intervention; we can't simply observe what normally happens. We need to make a change, or 'experiment' with something to see what the effects of this experiment are on the *dependent variable* (Baumgartner et al., 2002), the name given to the variable(s) that we *measure* and that we expect will be affected by our treatment or independent variable (e.g. endurance training – *independent variable* – will improve endurance performance – *dependent variable*).

Kalasountas and colleagues (2007) manipulated whether or not participants received a placebo drug and whether or not they received it before both trials. The experimental groups (PP and PN) received the manipulation but only one received it prior to both trials (PP) and the control group received no manipulation. Participants in the experimental groups received the same amount of the placebo at the same time and with the same information about its effects in trial one. In trial two, the drug was administered in the same amount at the same time to PP group participants and, although the experimental groups received different information, members within each group received the same information. *Placebo drug* was the *independent variable* and *strength test performance* was the *dependent variable*.

Control
Control refers to being in control of potential errors, so that we can examine the effects of our manipulation, or independent variable (Neutens and Rubinson, 2002). In a true experiment, we always have a *control group* (a group that does not receive the manipulation, treatment or intervention; Williams and Wragg, 2004). We also attempt to achieve control by ruling out the effects of any variables that may affect our results

If we don't have control, we don't have a true experiment (Neutens and Rubinson, 2002), as we cannot say that any changes in the variable we're interested in, the dependent variable, are caused by our treatment (our independent variable). If, however, when we test our participants before and after they have received the treatment (or at *pre-test* and *post-test*; critical aspects of an experimental design), there's a change in the experimental

Kalasountas et al. (2007) included a control group that received no placebo drug manipulation, participants were randomly allocated to groups to control for any initial strength differences between the groups and were all non-athletes. They received the same amount of the placebo drug at the same time, with the same instructions, completed the same number of baseline tests and performed the same strength tests at pre- and post-test (trials one and two).

Table 4.1: Continued

What is it?	Why is it important?	Where in our example?
instead of our independent variable, called *extraneous variables* (Kerlinger, 1973). For example, in the laboratory, we calibrate (or reset) equipment each time we use it so we rule out measurement error as an extraneous variable, or to control for the effects of current exercise level, we may only select inactive people in a study using psychological interventions to increase exercise adherence. In this second example, we achieve control by *excluding people* from the study. However, we could use an alternative approach by *including people* in our study. For example, we may include people with differing exercise levels and compare the effects of the intervention between people who exercise at different levels.	group(s) but not in the control group, we can say that the change is most likely due to our manipulation (Hyllegard et al., 1996). Similarly, by controlling extraneous variables we can be more certain that the dependent variable changed because of our manipulation and not because, for example, the testing equipment wasn't calibrated or the instructions given to participants weren't standardised. There's one last point I'd like to make about control groups. So far we have discussed a study design where the control and experimental groups contain *different* people; this is known as a *between-subjects* design. However, we could instead use what's known as a *within-subjects* design, where our participants undergo both the control and experimental conditions (Hyllegard et al., 1996). If so, we need to account for *order effects*, where completing one condition may influence how we respond to the next one. To deal with this, we *counterbalance* the order in which participants complete the conditions (Hyllegard et al., 1996); some do the control condition first, followed by the experimental condition and vice versa.	Some other control measures were put in place too, which you can read about in the paper, but those listed here should give you an idea of some ways to achieve experimental control.

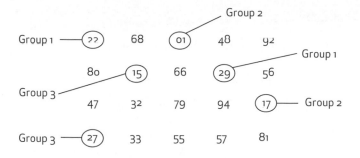

Figure 4.4: Using a hypothetical random number table to allocate participants to groups

reason why they are important in experimental research and identifies how they were achieved in our examples. Also see Figure 4.4.

Quasi-experimental research

Now we've identified the key elements of experimental research, we can use this knowledge to develop an understanding of quasi-experimental research. This is almost the next level down from experimental research, as it doesn't include all of the three key elements of experimental research: randomisation, control and manipulation. For some researchers, experimental designs are the only 'true' form of positivist research; however, particularly in areas like sport and exercise science where we're interested in finding out about real-life situations, involving real people and changing circumstances, it's not always possible to conduct a true experiment that includes randomisation, control and manipulation.

Critical thinking activity 4.2

Let's look at our example study by Barker and Jones (2006) to see what we mean by quasi-experimental research by evaluating this study against the three key elements of experimental research. Have a go at this yourself using Table 4.2. Decide if your answer is 'yes' or 'no' to each question, then write your justification for your answer in the appropriate box.

Table 4.2: Critical evaluation of Barker and Jones (2006)

	Yes, because . . .	No, because . . .
Is randomisation included in Barker and Jones' (2006) study?		
Is manipulation included in Barker and Jones' study?		
Is control included in Barker and Jones' study?		

Now check your answers with those in the completed table (Table 4.3).

Table 4.3: Critical evaluation of Barker and Jones (2006): some answers

	Yes, because . . .	No, because . . .
Is randomisation included in Barker and Jones' (2006) study?		. . . the study only involves one participant, who was not randomly selected for the study; he selected himself by approaching the researchers for help with his confidence and match preparation.
Is manipulation included in Barker and Jones' study?	. . . the study involved an intervention phase where the cricketer received three different types of intervention: hypnosis, technique coaching and self-modelling.	
*Is control included in Barker and Jones' study?**	. . . the study did involve some control by including baseline (pre-test) and post-intervention (post-test) measures of the dependent variables (confidence and performance).	. . . with only one participant, the study clearly does not include a control group.

* You may have answered 'yes' or 'no' or 'yes and no' here!

So, what does this tell us about quasi-experimental studies and the conclusions we can draw from them? The answers to these questions are shown in Figure 4.5 (Hyllegard et al., 1996).

Non-experimental research

Now let's take a look at our remaining research paper, by Stagno et al. (2005). This is an example of non-experimental research and to help us to see why, have a go at completing Table 4.4 first.

Now check your answers with those in the completed table (Table 4.5).

So, what does this tell us about non-experimental research studies, and the conclusions we can draw from them (Baumgartner et al., 2002)?

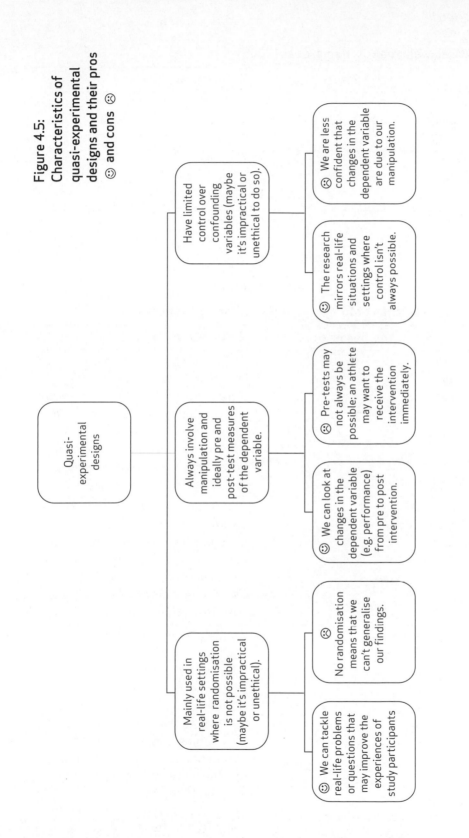

Figure 4.5:
Characteristics of
quasi-experimental
designs and their pros
☺ and cons ☹

Table 4.4: Critical evaluation of Stagno et al. (2005)

	Yes, because . . .	No, because . . .
Is randomisation included in Stagno et al.'s (2005) study?		
Is manipulation included in Stagno et al.'s study?		
Is control included in Stagno et al.'s study?		

Table 4.5: Critical evaluation of Stagno et al. (2005): some answers

	Yes, because . . .	No, because . . .
Is randomisation included in Stagno et al.'s (2005) study?		. . . participants were what's known as an *intact sample*; they weren't randomly selected but were selected because they were all in the same team. Most likely this is a *convenience sample* – convenient because the researchers had access to the team.
Is manipulation included in Stagno et al.'s study?		. . . the authors did not implement an intervention or change anything about the players' normal environment; they simply observed the players' usual experiences: changes in their fitness levels and their HR during matches.
Is control included in Stagno et al.'s study?		. . . the authors did not attempt to control any variables that may influence their dependent variables (HR and fitness level), such as training completed by players in addition to the prescribed programme, the standard of the opposition or the weather during matches. They did control those variables they were able to, for instance all players completed the same fitness tests at the same time of the season.

1   Non-experimental research does not aim to establish cause and effect (i.e. one variable causes another variable (or variables) to change systematically, for instance drinking a carbohydrate drink causes improvements in endurance performance). Instead, the aim is to observe and describe people's usual responses or experiences. Another example of a non-experimental research study is one that uses questionnaires to measure exercisers' body image concerns and the amount of exercise they do. The aim here would be to see if there is a relationship between body image concern and exercise participation.

> The aim of non-experimental research is to describe natural phenomena or to identify relationships between different variables (like body image concern and amount of exercise).

2   As non-experimental research does not aim to show cause and effect between variables, manipulation, randomisation and control are not required. The researcher observes (or measures) the variables as they would occur or be reported by participants normally, without any intervention or manipulation from the researcher. This means that, as in our example, the researcher has no control over some variables, such as weather conditions or a change in coaching staff. These are known as *confounding variables*, as they may influence the results. However, researchers do ensure control where they are able to, as we saw in our example, by using standardised fitness tests and testing times. Of course, we could have a random sample in a non-experimental study but it is not a requirement. If we did, we would then be able to say that it is more likely that our results could be generalised to other similar groups of people.

See Study Skills Activity 4.1 in the internet chapter for an additional activity.

Further reading (research designs)

Thomas, JR and Nelson, JK (2001) *Research methods in physical activity*, 4th edition, Chapter 17. Leeds: Human Kinetics.
Discusses experimental designs and presents some additional information that I haven't had space to cover here.

Williams, C and Wragg, C (2004) *Data analysis and research for sport and exercise science*, pp. 37–46. London: Routledge.
Overviews different designs, including non-experimental and quasi-experimental designs (these authors refer to group-based quasi-experimental designs but our example of a single participant study is another example of a quasi-experimental design).

Reliability and validity

In the final section of this chapter, we're going to look at two of the most important concepts in quantitative research and, in fact, they really underpin what we might term high quality or good quantitative research. These concepts are reliability and validity.

Personal reflection 4.1

Before we look at the formal definitions of these concepts, take a moment to think about and jot down examples of how we use the terms reliable and valid in everyday life.

What did you come up with? Below are some of my own examples.

Reliable

I need a car that is reliable and starts every morning so that I can get to work on time.

I need a reliable stopwatch that counts 60 seconds in each minute, with each second of equal length to make sure that when I go running I don't miscalculate my times and think I'm improving when I'm not!

Valid

When a student asks me for an extension on their essay, I can only say yes if they have a valid reason for being unable to meet the deadline. So, their reason must convince me that it's a suitable explanation for them falling behind.

As I don't want to carry around lots of credit cards, I want to have a credit card that is valid in lots of different shops when I go shopping (sorry if that sounds like a credit card advert). So I need to know that my card is valid for use in lots of different shops and not just specific ones.

Thinking about reliability and validity in this way will hopefully be useful as they are quite difficult concepts to get your head round and I have found that students sometimes struggle with them. So, let's consider how we define reliability and validity within quantitative research and then return to these everyday ideas to help understand these concepts.

Reliability within quantitative research

Reliability: the consistency of measurements and observations.
(Williams and Wragg, 2004)

Reliability means that when we measure something in quantitative research, unless we are expecting to see a change, we should end up with the same result each time. The three main forms of reliability you're most likely to encounter are summarised in Figure 4.6.

Figure 4.6: Different kinds of reliability

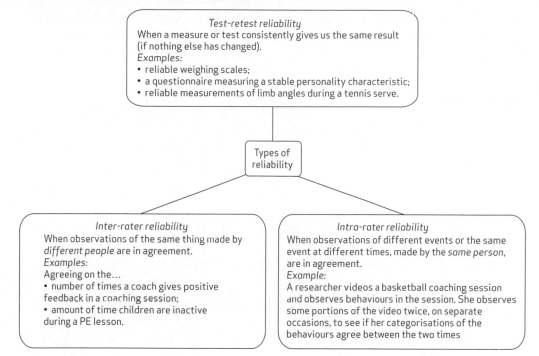

Returning to our research examples, we can see how the researchers all ensured that the studies had high levels of reliability. Some of the points in Table 4.6 aren't included in the study descriptions above as there's not enough space but trust me (I'm reliable) you can find them if you read the papers.

Table 4.6: Reliability in published research examples

Stagno et al. (2005)	Barker and Jones (2006)	Kalasountas et al. (2007)
• All players completed the same fitness tests at each of the three time points. • Tests were carried out in the same laboratories using the same equipment. • The same HR equipment was used for each match. • All equipment was calibrated before use. • Subjects did not exercise, consume alcohol, tobacco or caffeine 48 hours before testing.	• The participant completed the same confidence measures and performance was measured in the same way during the baseline and post-intervention phases. • The researchers used questionnaires that were already published and have been shown by previous researchers to provide a reliable measure of self-confidence.	• The same strength tests were used at baseline, trial one and trial two. • The tests were conducted in the same location using the same equipment and instructions at all data collection points. • The same placebo was given to the participants at the same time.

Validity within quantitative research

There are two types of validity that we're interested in: *internal* and *external validity*.

Internal validity refers to how certain we can be that any changes we've observed in our dependent variable are due to our independent variable (our manipulation or intervention) and not to any confounding, uncontrolled or extraneous variables.

> Internal validity: changes in the dependent variable are due to the independent variable (intervention/manipulation).
>
> (Hyllegard et al., 1996)

External validity is also known as *ecological validity* and refers to whether or not we can apply our findings from an unnatural setting (e.g. administering a placebo in a laboratory setting) to real-life settings, such as an exercise class or hockey match. External validity also refers to whether or not we can apply the findings obtained from our sample to other samples (other groups/types of people).

> External validity: we can apply, or generalise, our findings to other samples or contexts.
>
> (Hyllegard et al., 1996)

We can use our research examples to look at how they achieve different levels of validity. See Table 4.7.

It's clear from our research examples that, in any individual study, it's difficult to achieve high levels of internal *and* external validity. So, when choosing our research design (non-experimental, quasi-experimental or experimental) we have to decide if, for example, we use an experimental design, whether we are happy to sacrifice ecological validity for internal validity; or, if we use a quasi-experimental design, whether we are happy to sacrifice internal validity for ecological validity. The decision is yours.

Going back to our everyday concepts of reliability and validity, we can see similarities between their use in everyday meaning and in research. Reliability is all about consistency and dependability, whereas validity is concerned with whether or not something is plausible (a plausible explanation for an outcome or result, or a plausible application to other people or contexts).

Threats to validity

Once we've made our decision about which type of validity we feel is more important to achieve in our study, we need to design the study to reduce the number of threats to experimental validity. Just as we have different kinds of validity, the threats to internal and external validity are different. The example below of a fictitious and poorly-designed study aims to illustrate each of these threats. Warning: don't try this study at home as you'll be wasting your time. See Table 4.8.

Table 4.7: Validity in published research examples

Stagno et al. (2005)	Barker and Jones (2006)	Kalasountas et al. (2007)
• *Internal validity:* this study does not have a high level of internal validity but this isn't really a problem, as the authors didn't aim to manipulate anything or intervene. So, we can't say with certainty that the players' fitness levels were due to their training and competition schedules as there were too many uncontrolled variables that may have affected fitness. However, it's likely that they were responsible for the observed fitness levels as all the players completed the same training and competition schedules. • *External validity:* the sample wasn't randomly selected and was specific (elite male hockey players) so it's unlikely that results will generalise to other samples. However, the study has a high level of ecological validity as it was conducted in a real-life setting with no changes made to the players' usual experiences.	• *Internal validity:* the study has quite good internal validity as the researchers took pre- and post-test measures to examine the effects of their intervention. Although the participant acted as his own control, without a control group and control over extraneous variables, the researchers still can't be certain that confidence and performance didn't just change naturally. • *External validity:* with only one participant who wasn't selected randomly, there is very limited generalisability of the results to other samples. However, the study used an intervention that is widely used and was conducted in a real-life setting and so it has high ecological validity.	• *Internal validity:* as the study includes a control group, took pre- and post-test measures using the same equipment in the same location, it has a high level of internal validity. • *External validity:* the study was conducted in a gym, increasing its ecological validity, but the setting and the manipulation were still controlled, which then reduce it. However, the random allocation of subjects to groups and the high degree of control mean that it's likely that the results could be generalised to other samples.

Table 4.8: Example of a study with poor validity

Professor Nohope wants to examine the effects of a sports promotion intervention on children's participation in and enjoyment of sport, and their fitness levels. He collects together a group of *his friends' children (threat one)* and splits them into an experimental and a control group (good start) by *letting them choose which group they want to be in (oh dear . . . threat two).*

He conducts *pre-tests (threat three)* with both groups (good move) to measure the children's levels of fitness, participation in and enjoyment of sport. He then introduces his intervention to the experimental group: *free sports coaching and inspirational talks from famous athletes (threat four).*

He conducts his study during the London Olympics in 2012 when *the whole country is gripped with Olympic fever (threat five).* Unbeknown to Professor Nohope, the control group has heard about the free coaching and talks from famous athletes that the experimental group has been offered. They feel very left out and unhappy about this. So, they *don't put any effort into the post-test fitness test or into completing the participation and enjoyment measures (threat six).*

After the intervention he conducts *post-tests* to see if the children's fitness, participation in and enjoyment of sport have changed *(threat seven)*. His usual laboratory and equipment (the one where he did the pre-tests) aren't available so he uses *different equipment and a different laboratory to conduct the post-tests (threat eight).*

Threat one: Participant effect. This sample is biased as he knows the children so it's likely that the intervention may not work with a different group of participants.

Threat two: Selection. Participants weren't randomly allocated to the groups so they may not be equal and results may not be due to the intervention but to the type of participants who were in the experimental group.

Threat three: Pre-test sensitisation. Including a pre-test is important to look for changes but in the real world we wouldn't include a pre-test before somebody exercises, for example. So it may be that the intervention only works when a participant is given a pre-test as it highlights to the participant what variables the researcher is expecting to change.

Threat four: Multiple treatment interaction. These seem like worthwhile interventions but by using two interventions he won't know if either one will be effective on its own; they may only be effective if used together, which may not be possible in a real-life setting.

Threat five: History. As the Olympics are talking place in London at the same time as the study, this may influence the children's sport participation and enjoyment, and not the intervention.

Table 4.8: Continued

Threat six: Resentful demoralisation. The control group gives up on the post-test as they feel resentful and demoralised because they are not receiving the intervention; so they no longer offer a realistic comparison with the experimental group.

Threat seven: Post-test sensitisation. The participants become aware of what the intervention is aimed at and so their responses may differ in comparison with what they might be in real-life when a post-test isn't included.

Threat eight: Instrumentation. Using different testing conditions in the pre- and post-tests means that he can't be sure if any changes he sees are due to his intervention or to the difference in equipment and testing conditions.

Clearly, Professor Nohope is unlikely to get any worthwhile results from his study and has lots to learn about positivist research (maybe he should read this chapter). There are some other threats to validity that didn't feature in Professor Nohope's study and these are included in the summary table (Table 4.9). You may find them with different labels in different texts and you may find some more too, but this is enough to start with and to illustrate the main threats we might encounter.

See Study Skills Activity 4.2 in the internet chapter for an additional activity.

Further reading (reliability and validity)

Thomas, JR and Nelson, JK (2001) *Research methods in physical activity*, 4th edition, Chapter 17. Leeds: Human Kinetics.
Discusses internal and external validity (reliability) and explains some of the threats listed above in more detail.

Review

In this chapter we have discussed three types of quantitative research: experimental, quasi-experimental and non-experimental. Experimental research aims to establish cause and effect and includes manipulation, control and randomisation. Quasi-experimental research always involves manipulation but may not include control or randomisation as it may be unethical and/or impractical to do so. Non-experimental research does not necessarily include any of these three elements and its aim is to describe relationships and events (LO 1).

We defined randomisation as either randomly selecting study participants or allocating them to groups; it is important to ensure we don't have a biased sample or groups. Control refers to controlling extraneous variables; it is important to ensure we

Table 4.9: Threats to reliability and validity (Hyllegard et al., 1996; Jonas et al., 2001; Neutens and Rubinson, 2002; Thomas and Nelson, 2001)

Threat	To	Description
History	Internal validity	Events that happen alongside your study that may affect your results instead of your intervention.
Maturation	Internal validity	Natural changes in participants that may produce your results instead of your intervention (e.g. getting older/tired).
Testing	Internal validity	Repeated testing may familiarise participants with tests/encourage learning that may produce your results, not your intervention.
Instrumentation	Internal validity	Instrumentation may not be accurately calibrated, causing changes in results instead of your intervention.
Selection	Internal validity	If the sample is not randomly selected or allocated to groups, this may create selection bias, which may cause your results instead of your intervention.
Imitation of treatments	Internal validity	Control group participants seek out and follow the experimental treatment, unbeknown to the researcher.
Compensatory rivalry	Internal validity	Control group participants discover they are in the control group and so try harder to outperform the experimental group in post-tests.
Resentful demoralisation	Internal validity	Control group participants discover they are in the control group, feel left out and so give up trying in the post-tests.
Participant effect	External validity	The treatment/intervention only works with this group and can't be generalised to other groups of people.
Experimental setting effect	External validity	The treatment/intervention only works in this setting (e.g. an exercise class) and so can't be applied to other settings (e.g. individual training).
Multiple treatment interaction	External validity	The treatment/intervention only works in combination with others, so results can't be applied to settings where only one treatment/intervention is used.
Pre-test sensitisation	External validity	The treatment/intervention only works when a pre-test is given as it sensitises participants to the study's aim, so results may not apply to real-life settings without a pre-test.
Post-test sensitisation	External validity	The post-test helps participants make sense of the treatment and so they perceive that it 'works' when possibly it wasn't so effective. This may not generalise to real-life settings without a post-test.

can attribute any changes in our dependent variables to our independent variable. Manipulation refers to something the researcher implements, like an intervention, and is important to examine cause and effect (LO 2).

We then defined reliability as the consistency of our measurements or observations. Internal validity refers to how sure we can be that any effects on our dependent variable(s) were due to our independent variable (the thing we manipulated). External validity refers to whether or not we can generalise our results to samples and situations other than those used in our study (LO 3).

We finished by discussing threats to internal validity that reduce the confidence with which we can say that any effects we've observed are due to our manipulation; for instance, if natural changes occur in the participants or we don't randomly allocate participants to groups. Threats to external validity limit how much we can apply our findings to other situations and samples; for instance, conducting research in the laboratory may mean that the results are not applicable in real-life situations (LO 4).

Work through the review questions in Study Skills Activity 4.3 in the internet chapter for an additional activity.

Chapter 5

Interpretative research

Melissa Day

Chapter focus

This chapter focuses on how to conduct research using the interpretative paradigm. We start by examining two methods of collecting data that may be used in sport and exercise science research (interviews and observation). Following this, we examine the use of case studies in interpretative research. In any interpretative research project it is important to consider the quality of the study, so we will discuss the criteria that may be used to judge the quality of interpretative research and how to enhance this quality. This means that there are two key issues in this chapter:

- types of research in the interpretative paradigm;
- enhancing quality in the research process.

Learning outcomes

This chapter is designed to help you:

1   Explain the three types of interviews and the differences between them;
2   Understand the skills of a good interviewer and why these are important;
3   Explain the advantages and disadvantages of covert and overt observation.
4   Understand the advantages of using a case study;
5   Explain what we mean by quality in interpretative research and how this can be enhanced.

Let's start this chapter with one of the most popular methods of collecting interpretative data: the research interview.

Interviewing

At some point, you may have already had experience of taking part in an interview. This could have been when you applied for a place at college or university, or an interview for a job. You can probably think of many examples throughout your life when you have been or could be asked to take part in an interview. There are a number of parallels that may be drawn between interviews such as these and interviews that are used in research. You can use your previous experiences to help you understand how to conduct a research interview.

Think about the last time that you took part in an interview. Ask yourself *why* you were invited to take part in this interview; what was the reason that an interview was chosen? If this was an interview for a job or university or college place, then you may already have sent in your CV and qualifications. Why do you think you may also be invited to interview? Try to come up with at least three reasons that explain why you were also asked to take part in an interview.

Reason 1: ....

....

Reason 2: ....

....

Reason 3: ....

....

Your answers may reflect the fact that interviews are useful for finding out about things that we can't observe directly. You may have written that you were interviewed to assess your personality, your enthusiasm or your interpersonal skills. These are all qualities that an employer or university would not be able to gauge from an application form. This means that they are not directly observable.

Other aspects of yourself that are not directly observable are your thoughts and feelings. A research project on stress and coping may use observation to examine how athletes behave when they are under high levels of stress. However, this data collection technique would only tell you the observable behaviours of that athlete. Let's use an example to explain this. You may choose to observe a tennis match in which the player throws his racquet across the court after losing an important point. Using observation, you would be able to record this behaviour; it is something that is directly observable. However, you would not be able to understand *why* the player did this, what he was thinking as he did this, or how he was feeling at the time. Using an interview would allow you to ask questions to understand his thoughts and feelings. You may be thinking that you could understand or guess at why he threw his racquet across the court. It may be likely that he felt frustrated and unable to cope with the stress. However, this would be your own interpretation of the event and not that of your research participant. Consequently, the purpose of an interview is to gain information on someone else's perspective and allow them to give information from their point of view. This is why interviews are such a key part of the interpretative approach – because they allow us to understand the world through someone else's eyes.

Interview structure

You may have decided that using an interview is going to be the method of data collection that best suits your research project. The next step that you need to think about is how you are going to structure your interview. There are three types of interview that you may consider: *structured*, *semi-structured* and *unstructured*. To decide when each of these may be appropriate, we will look at each and assess some of their benefits and limitations.

The structured interview

If you choose to conduct a structured interview, this would first involve compiling a list of questions that you are going to ask your participants. There are advantages and disadvantages of using this method of interviewing. The main advantage is that you can be more certain of ensuring that you ask appropriate questions, since you will have prepared these beforehand. However, to your participant the structured interview may come across as a barrage of questions and you may miss key areas that are important to him/her because you have not formulated a question on these. This means that, although you may cover all the questions that *you* think are important, you may also get less depth of information from a structured interview as you may miss some things that are important to the participant. Dale (1996) highlights this point by stressing that what might be a relevant question for one person might not be at all relevant for another.

The semi-structured interview

Alternatively, you may choose to use a semi-structured interview. Using this approach, you would need to decide on broad areas that you want to focus on rather than specific questions. This would be in the form of an interview guide rather than set interview questions. You may find this more difficult when you start to research, as you will need to formulate specific questions during the interview, based on your research topic and the responses of your participant. This method of interviewing does ensure that you have some guidance as an interviewer in the questions that you ask and the areas that you cover. However, in comparison to the structured interview, it allows the participant to talk more freely about the issues that concern her and so topics that are important to her are likely to emerge. As an interviewer your job is to guide the interview and ask questions as they occur, rather than using a set structure.

The unstructured interview

The unstructured interview does not use pre-determined questions or interview guides. Instead, the researcher is aware of the topic that he or she wishes to research but does not plan the direction of the interviews or the questions that they will ask. This type of interviewing is reliant on what the participant discusses. Questions are formed during the interview based on the topics that are of importance to the participant. This may be the most difficult type of interview for a novice researcher, as you will need to be able to formulate questions as the interview is happening. The advantage of this method is that it focuses on what is important to the participant. However, the difficulty with this approach may be that what is important to your participant is not the topic that you were hoping to research.

It is important to remember that *focus groups* also use interviews. A focus group interview is an interview with a small group of people. Often this group is made up of five to ten people who all share a similar experience. For example, you may invite a group of sedentary people to discuss their reasons for not participating in exercise. Since this group of people have a shared characteristic, they may have shared experiences that they can discuss during a focus group. The advantage of using a focus group is that you can gather information from a large number of people at one time. This means that, rather than conducting five individual interviews, you can conduct one focus group instead. Also, these participants may trigger conversation or topics for each other, demonstrating either a shared view or a number of different views.

There are also limitations to this method. It may be that some people do not feel comfortable sharing their opinions in a focus group and therefore feel unable to speak out. Also, there may be some individuals within the focus group who influence the opinions of others, meaning that some people within the group feel obliged to follow the group opinion even if this does not reflect their own views.

Interview skills

Think back again to the last time that you attended an interview; was it a positive or a negative experience for you? If it was a positive experience, this may be partly because of the skills of the interviewer. Take a couple of minutes now to jot down, following the layout of Table 5.1, the differences between the skills of someone who is a good interviewer and someone who is poor at interviewing. Use your own experiences and examples of interviews to help you to do this.

You may have included that a good interviewer listens to what you are saying, does not interrupt, looks attentive, makes you feel comfortable, or is welcoming, and asks relevant questions. These are some of the common skills of someone who is good at interviewing. During the research interview it is important to establish good *rapport* with the person you are interviewing. Rapport means that the relationship between yourself and the participant is built on mutual trust and respect. This is important in an interview setting because it will allow your participant to feel more at ease during the interview and is likely to lead to fuller and more honest responses to your questions. According to Patton (2002), rapport is built on the ability to convey empathy and understanding without judgement. You may have also included in your list of good interview skills that the interviewer would be non-judgemental. Andersen (2005) suggests that the richness and meaningfulness of the information that you collect will be dependent on the quality of the relationship between researcher and participant. This means that the more rapport you can establish prior to the interview, the better data you'll collect.

Table 5.1 Interviewing skills

A good interviewer. . .	A poor interviewer. . .

> ## Critical thinking activity 5.1
>
> Before you embark on a research project using interviews, you may want to practise how to establish rapport with your interviewee. Try to find someone who is willing to take part in a mock interview with you. People such as friends and classmates may be a good choice for this exercise as they will be able to give you honest feedback. Choose any topic for your interview; for example, what stressors they experience during sports competition or why they don't exercise. Conduct either a structured or a semi-structured interview. The main aim of this activity is to receive feedback from your interviewee on your interview style. Below is a checklist of questions that you may ask your interviewee to reflect on following the interview. You may also wish to add your own questions:
>
> - Did you feel relaxed during the interview?
> - Were you able to respond honestly to my questions?
> - Did you feel that I was judgemental at any point?
> - Was there anything that you wanted to say but didn't?
> - Did you feel that I listened to your answers and responded accordingly?
>
> Use the answers to these questions to help develop your ability as an interviewer. What are the skills that you are good at? What are the skills that you need to improve?

To understand how to use interviews in a research project, it is helpful to look at published research that has used this technique. There are a number of papers within sport and exercise science that use interviews; Research focus one provides an overview of one such paper. As you read through this summary, try to complete Table 5.2 to identify any examples of good research practice in this paper; an example is included within it.

Table 5.2: Good practice in Giacobbi et al. (2004b)

Research focus one – Giacobbi et al. (2004b)	
Example of good practice	Why this is important
The authors used focus groups and individual interviews.	It allowed them to collect more information. Participants in focus groups may feel pressured to conform to group opinions. Some people may prefer group situations to one-to-one interviews.

Research focus one

Giacobbi et al. (2004b) conducted a study into stress and coping during the transition to university for first-year female athletes. The aims of this study were to examine the sources of stress that were experienced by these athletes, the responses that they used to cope with these stressors, and how they adjusted to university life.

The participants in this study were five first-year female university swimmers who agreed to take part in focus groups and interviews over a six-month period. The authors used focus groups to examine participants' thoughts, beliefs and meanings regarding their experiences as first-year athletes. They used focus groups to provide a great deal of data on the topics of interest and felt that these groups would help them to develop trust and rapport with the participants. During these focus groups an interview guide was used, although the direction of the conversations dictated the flow of the questions.

After two focus groups, an individual interview was also conducted with each participant. The purpose of this was to allow participants to discuss their sources of stress and coping strategies away from their team mates and to explore their personal feelings and attitudes about their transition into university sport. Giacobbi and colleagues also felt that using an individual interview would elicit more in-depth information.

In both the focus groups and individual interviews, *member checking* was used. To do this, participants were provided with a written summary of their sources of stress and coping strategies. They were then encouraged to elaborate on any discrepancies between this summary and their experiences, making additions or modifications so that the summary accurately reflected their experiences.

There were a number of ways in which the researchers established the quality of their data:

1   The raw data (participants' comments/quotes) were examined by a number of researchers;
2   Research group meetings were held to examine any discrepancies between the researchers' analysis of the data;
3   Member checks were used after focus groups and individual interviews;
4   Familiarity, trust and rapport were built between the interviewer and the participants.

The analysis of participants' comments from the focus groups and individual interviews resulted in five themes that described the stressors of these university swimmers: training intensity, high performance expectations, interpersonal relation-ships, being away from home, and academics. Strategies used to cope with these sources of stress were: social support, active cognitive efforts (focusing on the task, reinterpreting stressors, and gaining insight), emotional release and religion.

Now compare your examples of good practice with those provided in Table 5.3.
See Study Skills Activity 5.1 in the internet chapter for an additional activity.

Table 5.3: Good practice in Giacobbi et al. (2004b): some answers

Research focus one – Giacobbi et al. (2004b)	
Example of good practice	Why this is important
The authors used both focus groups and individual interviews.	It allowed them to collect more information. Participants in focus groups may feel pressured to conform to group opinions. Some people may prefer group situations to one-to-one interviews.
The authors used focus groups to establish trust and rapport with participants.	This may encourage some participants to be more open and honest and consequently mean that more in-depth responses are elicited.
An interview guide was used, although the direction of the conversations dictated the flow of the questions.	This shows that the interview process was not too rigid. Participants were given the opportunity to discuss topics that were important to them.
Member checking was used after focus groups and interviews.	This ensures that the researchers' interpretation of the data or interview transcript (a typed word-for-word account of the interview) does indeed match the experiences of the participant. This means that it will be a more accurate portrayal of the participant's perspective.
Data analysis used a number of researchers who met to discuss discrepancies between their coding.	Rather than the data analysis being based on one person's interpretation of the data, they were analysed by multiple researchers. Before themes were established all the researchers had to reach a consensus (agreement).

Further reading (interviews)

Kvale, S and Brinkman, S (2009) *Interviews: learning the craft of qualitative research interviewing.* London: Sage.
This provides a detailed commentary on how to prepare for and conduct research interviews.

Observation

So far we have looked at individual interviews and focus groups, both of which generate data through the spoken words of participants. This type of data can also be included in observational studies; however, verbal information from participants is just one part of the data that may be generated in this type of study.

Observational research refers to generating data through observing the environment, interactions, behaviours and actions of participants. To do this, the researcher must put themself into the research setting where the topic of interest occurs while they make these observations.

There are two main types of observation: *covert* and *overt*. During covert observation, the researcher does not inform the study participants that he is observing them. During overt participant observation, the participants are fully aware that they are being observed. A question that you might be asking is, 'How do I know which method of observation will be best for my study?' Let's look at an example to answer this question.

Imagine that you have been asked by your lecturers to conduct a study on aggressive behaviour in football. You decide that participant observation is the best method of doing this since you are interested in observable behaviours. However, you are faced with a dilemma, whether to use overt or covert observation. Using Table 5.4, try to think now about one possible benefit and limitation of using each method.

One of the key themes in your assessment of the benefits and limitations of each type of observation is that participants may change their behaviour when they know that they are being observed. Let's use the example of the football study. You approach the local football team and tell them the aims of your study. The manager agrees for you to come and observe a match and the players agree to take part in your study. However, over the 90 minutes of play you are not able to see any evidence of aggression on the pitch. Since the players are aware that you are watching them they have changed their behaviour and are being less aggressive. Based on your observation of this game, as a researcher, you make the conclusion that football is not an aggressive sport. This example demonstrates the limitation of overt research and the strength of covert research. If participants are not aware that they are being observed, they will not change their behaviour.

So, if by using overt observation techniques we are changing behaviour, then why not consistently use covert observation? You might find the answer to this question by asking yourself: do you feel it is ethical to observe other people for a research project without their permission? One of the key limitations of doing covert research is that many people feel it is not ethical to research other people without their consent. Imagine how you may feel as the manager of the football team if you were made aware that someone was researching the behaviour of your team without your permission.

Now read the summary of the article in Research focus two. This is based on a study that used overt participant observation, where the researcher not only observed the

Table 5.4: Covert and overt observation

	Benefit	Limitation
Covert observation		
Overt observation		

participants but also became part of the group. As you read through this article try to note down at least four key components that make this an observational study.

Research focus two

Holt and Sparkes (2001) conducted a study using participant observation to identify and examine the factors that contribute to team cohesion. The aim of the study was to better understand the dynamic nature of team cohesion and performance and the factors that may influence this relationship over time.

The participants in this study were players in a university football team who were competing in inter-university level matches. The first author of the study was also a member of this football team and coached at some of the team training sessions. The players were fully informed of the research project and knew that they were being observed. It was made clear that the first author would be keeping a research diary on his observations and may also ask players to take part in interviews throughout the year. The players were also assured that all information would be confidential. This meant that information discussed between a player and the researcher could not be told to any other player or the coach.

The researcher attended every training session, match, team meeting and social event over the season. This helped him to feel part of the team and build rapport with participants. While he did this, he was able to make observations of their behaviours, actions, interactions, events and crises. He was able to better understand these by actually being a part of the team. As well as this, Holt kept a reflective journal enabling him to be aware of his own assumptions and actions in the team setting. Throughout the research the second author of the study acted as a *critical friend* by questioning what had been written in the reflective journal and asking questions about the method used and the interpretations that had been made.

At the end of the data collection the researchers were able to identify themes that had emerged from the observations and the interviews. Member checks were used to ensure that the interpretations of the researchers represented the lived experiences of the participants. To do this, participants were contacted throughout the study to seek their views on the researchers' interpretations and on the accuracy of the data.

There were four key themes that influenced the cohesion of the team: clear and meaningful roles, selfishness/personal sacrifices, communication, and team goals. The study also indicated that task cohesion contributed to performance outcomes. The researchers highlight the value of using observation to study teams over the course of a season. This is because team cohesion is dynamic (changing) and so repeated observations may help to understand the complexity of team interactions.

Critical thinking activity 5.2

The key components that make this an observational study are:

-
-

Critical thinking activity 5.2 continued

-
-

Your list of some of the key components may have included:

- observations were conducted in participants' natural setting;
- participant role – needed to establish and maintain relationships with participants;
- observation included behaviours and verbalisations;
- the researcher immersed himself in the group (became an insider).

One of the key characteristics of Holt and Sparkes' research is that Holt became an insider in the group that he was studying. Mason (1998) states that, when planning to carry out an observational study, the researcher must ask: Do I intend to be a participant, an observer or a participant-observer? See Figure 5.1.

Figure 5.1: Observation continuum

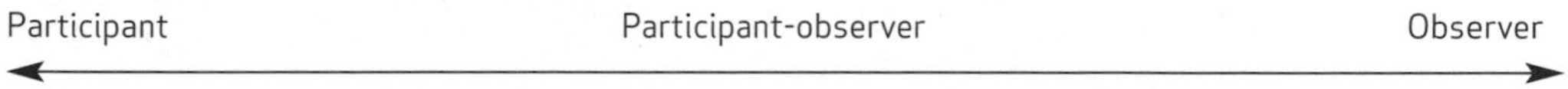

Participant	Participant-observer	Observer

As a participant, you would experience the environment of those whom you are researching. However, at the opposite end of the continuum, as a complete observer you would remain detached from this experience. In this study Holt was able to share some of the experiences of the participants by immersing himself in their environment. Therefore by becoming a participant observer he felt that he was able to develop rapport between himself and the study participants.

Critical thinking activity 5.3

Do you think Holt would have had the same results if he had taken the role of observer? If not, how do you think these would have been different?

Some researchers may feel that it is an advantage to be able to detach themselves from the data so that they can be more objective about their results and analysis of the data. Others would argue, however, that sharing in participant experiences enables the researcher to gain a better insight into the world of the participant and thus create a more accurate view of their experiences.

Now that we have reviewed both interviewing and participant observation, you may be asking yourself the question, *'Which method of data collection should I use?'* The section below lists some possible advantages and limitations of using observation and interviews.

Participant observation

Advantages

- This method allows you to study participants or groups as they change over time.
- This may help your understanding of participants' experiences, especially by becoming an insider.

Limitations

- Becoming an insider may be difficult. For example, you may not have the sporting talent to join the university football team, as Holt did in his study.
- You would also need to ensure that you had participants' permission to take part in the study. Some people may not want to take part in a research study where they know that they are being observed.

Interviews

Advantages
- Data can be collected on a specific topic of interest.
- Some people may feel more comfortable in an interview setting than knowing that they are being observed.

Limitations

- You are reliant on honest self-report from participants rather than experiencing or watching events as they happen.
- Data collected may not truly reflect participants' experiences and feelings when events were actually happening, as participants will have had time to reflect on events.

See Study Skills Activity 5.2 in the internet chapter for an additional activity.

Further reading (observation)

Sands, RR (2002) *Sport ethnography*, Chapter 3. Leeds: Human Kinetics.
Provides some useful examples of research that has used participant observation.

Case studies

Unlike interviewing and observing, a case study is not a method of data collection. Instead, interviewing and/or observation may be used to collect data, which could then be presented in a case study. A case study is an in-depth study of a single instance, event or phenomenon. Sport and exercise science researchers often use case studies of one particular team or one athlete. These case studies do not aim to produce findings that are generalisable but often present the case as an example of a particular situation. Research focus three outlines a case study; as you read through it try to answer the question in Critical thinking activity 5.4.

Critical thinking activity 5.4

What were the advantages of using a case study approach for this research? Think about the advantages of using a case study to examine motivation compared with another method such as interviewing multiple participants.

Research focus three

In 1997, Krane et al. published a case study that examined the motivation of an elite gymnast. They applied *goal perspective theory* (see Chapter 6) to interpret the experiences and behaviours of one gymnast.

The participant in this study was an American former elite level gymnast who had the goal of competing at the Olympic Games. However, throughout much of her career this gymnast had suffered from disordered eating and had experienced a number of quite serious injuries.

Krane and colleagues interviewed this participant on three occasions. These interviews were unstructured and focused on the gymnast's descriptions of her athletic career. During the first interview the gymnast was asked: 'Tell us about your gymnastics career and your experiences as a gymnast.' This formed the basis for most of the first interview, which mainly consisted of the gymnast discussing the progress of her career.

Following this first interview, the researchers familiarised themselves with the data and the key themes that had emerged. They then addressed these themes in subsequent interviews. The follow-up interview focused on the question: 'What drives an athlete to persist in sport under such extreme circumstances?'

Following each interview the researchers and the participant read a transcript of the interview. The participant was encouraged to read through the transcript and make any alterations, corrections or clarifications. The data from the three interviews were analysed using *open coding* (allowing patterns, categories and themes to emerge from the data) and *axial coding* (generating connections among the categories derived from open coding).

The coding of the data resulted in three themes: motivational climate, evidence of an ego orientation, and factors associated with ego involvement. In the results, each of these is explained and a number of participant quotes are used to illustrate them.

One of the main reasons for using a case study that you may have identified is the greater depth of information and understanding that this method provides in comparison with other methods. The interviewers used multiple interviews to gather a large amount of information from this gymnast that they could then interpret using theory. The reader is able to gain insight into the motivation of this gymnast through the participant quotes that are used throughout the results and discussion. During a case study the quantification of data is not a priority; instead, the research can focus on understanding the experiences of the athlete.

Another advantage is that, by using a case study, the researchers were able to research the experiences of an elite level athlete. It may be difficult to recruit a number of athletes that have achieved this level of accomplishment in their sport, so a case study approach may be most appropriate.

See Study Skills Activity 5.3 in the internet chapter for an additional activity.

Further reading (case studies)

Yin, RK (2003) *Case study research: design and methods*. London: Sage.
This provides a comprehensive guide for anyone considering case study research,
including chapters on design, implementation and analysis.

Enhancing quality in the research process

Over the course of your studies it is likely that you will read and make use of many
research articles. There may be a number of different criteria that you use to judge each
article as you read it. These might include: How much did I enjoy reading this? How
easy/straightforward was it to read? How useful was the information? Can I apply this
information to the project/essay that I am working on? For everything that we read or
use as part of our research we need to be able to assess its quality.

There are a number of methods that could be used to enhance the quality of
interpretative research. Some of these are suggested by Lincoln and Guba (1985),
although this is not meant as an exhaustive list that must be covered, but rather as
suggested ways to enhance the quality.

Recognising the role of the researcher

The interpretative paradigm recognises the role that the researcher plays in shaping
the research process. The researcher's own values and experiences may shape the
interactions and rapport which they have with participants. However, this influence of
the researcher is not inherently a positive or negative influence on the research and can
be viewed both as a help (e.g. in developing rapport) and a hindrance (e.g. influencing
interpretation of results) in the research process. Interpretative researchers must
acknowledge their biases and address these rationally and appropriately in their
research. This could be done through the use of a bracketing interview or a reflective
diary.

The bracketing interview

According to Creswell (1998), the researcher must bracket her own preconceived ideas
about the phenomenon in question to ensure an understanding of the true perspective
of the participant. This means that prior to (and possibly during) the research project
the researcher needs to gain an awareness of her biases and assumptions. Imagine
that you were about to do a research study into the sport that you play. Prior to
starting this study you will already have pre-conceived ideas about this research based
on your own experiences. Bracketing aims to help you identify what these pre-
conceived ideas are.

Since interpretative interviews involve the possible subjective influence of the
researcher, it becomes important to understand our biases as these may be influential
during an interview. This awareness of personal biases and assumptions will sensitise
the researcher and help them to ensure that their own biases are not imposed on their
interpretation of the participants' experiences.

Reflective diary

As recommended by researchers such as Lincoln and Guba, a reflective diary can help to enhance the quality of the research. Researchers may choose to write about biases that occur during the study or about difficulties with the research. To do this, you need to keep a diary throughout the study and write about your own assumptions, ideas about the data that you are collecting, and potential difficulties that you are experiencing. You could then use another researcher as a critical friend to question you about what you have written.

Secondary analysis

Often one researcher initially completes the analysis of interpretative data. Using a secondary analyst (often someone who is blind to the study aims and objectives) to analyse at least part of the data can enhance the quality of the study. Thus the analysis is not just one researcher's interpretation but represents a consensus from two researchers.

Member checking

This involves sending the participants in your study either their whole interview transcript or the data analysis that has been completed. Participants are then asked to make comments on these and return them to the researcher. Participants may add additional information to interview transcripts where they feel it is valid or they may make amendments to comments that they had made. The aim of member checking is for the interview transcript to best represent their actual experiences. Member checking of data analysis asks participants to verify the interpretations of their experiences that have been made. For example, your analysis may include a theme that is not seen as particularly important to the experiences of participants. By using member checking, a researcher can ensure that their interpretation closely represents the reality of the participant.

Engagement with the data

Previous chapters have demonstrated that interpretative research aims to understand the world from the participant's point of view. To do this the researcher must immerse themself in the research project. This may include building rapport and trust with interviewees, listening to interview tapes, and re-reading transcripts to gain familiarity with the data.

Critical thinking activity 5.5

Now that we have examined some of the methods of enhancing quality in research, it is important to be able to spot these within research that you read. Go back now to each of the three research focus articles in this chapter and, for each, explain whether it uses the methods discussed above to enhance quality. Use Table 5.5 to organise your response.

See Study Skills Activity 5.4 in the internet chapter for an additional activity.

Table 5.5: Quality in research examples

	Research focus one	Research focus two	Research focus three
Recognising role of researcher			
Bracketing			
Reflective diary			
Secondary analysis			
Member checking			
Engagement with data			

Further reading (quality in interpretative research)

Flick, U (2007) *Managing quality in qualitative research.* London: Sage.
This includes discussion on various measures that may be taken to enhance the quality of interpretative research.

Review

In this chapter we have discussed two methods of collecting data in interpretative research: interviewing and observation. We identified that interviews can be structured, semi-structured or unstructured (LO 1). In examining these, we also discussed the skills of a good interviewer and provided an exercise to help you reflect on and improve your interviewing skills (LO 2). The different types of participant observation were also discussed, along with the advantages and limitations of each (LO 3). We also examined the use of case studies in sport and exercise science research and presented an example of research that illustrates the advantages of using this approach (LO 4). Finally, this chapter looked at how to judge the quality of research. We included suggestions for enhancing quality that could help whether you are thinking of conducting a research project or looking to assess the research that you are reading (LO 5).

Work through the review questions in Study Skills Activity 5.5 in the internet chapter for an additional activity.

Chapter 6

Motivation in sport and exercise

Joanne Thatcher

Chapter focus

This chapter focuses on motivation in sport and exercise. Key definitions are:

> Motive – the drive, stimulus or *reason* why we do something;
> Motivation – the energy and direction that drive our behaviour;
> Direction refers to *what* we do (where we direct our energy);
> Energy refers to *how much* effort we put into what we do.
>
> (Roberts, 1992)

We first consider what we mean by a motive and what factors may influence motives for participating in sport and exercise. Next, we describe the main theories that are used to understand motivation, or lack of motivation, in sport and exercise. To illustrate how each theory can be practically applied to understand people's motivation in sport and exercise, we provide case studies or ask you to reflect on your experiences.

Learning outcomes

This chapter is designed to help you:
1 Understand what we mean by participation motives.
2 Critically interpret descriptive data you have collected.
3 Describe what each theory tells us about motivation in sport and exercise.
4 Use your experiences in sport and exercise to explain these theories of motivation.
5 Explain what a theory is and why theories are useful for increasing our understanding of sport and exercise psychology.

Sport and exercise motives

Consider the group of people in Figure 6.1. Each person is describing their *motive* to exercise or play sport; so, motives provide the drive, the reasons for doing what we do. Note any observations you can make about the motives described in Figure 6.1.

Figure 6.1: Sport and exercise motives

You may have noticed that: (1) people's motives vary greatly, even for the same activity (like sport/exercise); (2) people can have more than one motive for participating in an activity; and (3) whilst some of these motives come from the person (*intrinsic motives*), others come from outside the person (*extrinsic motives*). We'll return to these later.

Critical thinking activity 6.1

Find out the sport and exercise participation motives of people you know and produce a table like Table 6.1. Try to include a range of people (males, females, sportspeople, exercisers, old, young). Can you identify any patterns in their motives?

Table 6.1: Motives for sport/exercise participation

Name	Type of activity	Age	Male/ Female	Length of participation	Motive(s)

You may recognise this as *descriptive research*. Look back to Chapter 3 if this doesn't ring a bell.

You may have noticed:

• gender differences – females tend to have more social motives (like making friends) for participating in sport, whereas males are motivated more by competition (e.g. Biddle and Bailey, 1985);

- age differences – as we get older our motives change from making friends and having fun to becoming more health and competition focused (e.g. Kremer et al., 1997; Weiss and Petchlikoff, 1989);
- experience – the longer someone has participated in sport or exercise, the more likely they are to have intrinsic motives, partly because this is what keeps them going (e.g. Ryan et al., 1997).

You may have made some different observations, which is great; discuss them with your tutor and fellow students.

Understanding individuals' motives for sport and exercise participation is useful but a more scientific approach to studying and understanding motivation is to use a *theory* that provides a more general explanation for different people's behaviour. There are a number of reasons why theories are useful for sport and exercise psychologists but, before we examine these, let's look at some of the most well-established theories used to understand motivation in sport and exercise situations.

Need achievement theory

Consider a classic FA Cup clash between one of the Premiership giants like Chelsea and a lower-league club like Torquay United. The incentive for winning is high for both teams but whilst the non-league team may dream of success and playing at Wembley, in reality, the probability of success, for them, is normally pretty low. For the Premiership team, the probability of success is very high. So, when the clash is played out, it's not unreasonable for Torquay United to adopt a defensive style of play to minimise the chances of the Premiership side scoring. In other words, instead of going out to win the match, their goal is not to lose the match.

In this example of what might happen in team sports, we find some of the ideas that are proposed by McClelland (1961) and Atkinson (1974), in their Need Achievement Theory (see Figure 6.2).

Figure 6.2: Model of need achievement theory

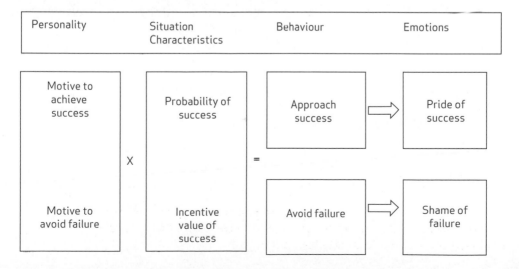

A central idea, here, is the distinction between being motivated to achieve success (the Premiership team in our example) and being motivated to avoid failure (the lower-league team in our example). McClelland and Atkinson see these as personality attributes (*personality*), so that some of us have a greater tendency to enter into a situation, like a sports competition, with the *motive to achieve success*. In contrast, other people have a greater tendency to enter into such situations with a *motive to avoid failure*. At a specific competition, whether we *approach success* or *avoid failure* (*behaviour*) is based on this motive and both the *probability and value of succeeding* (*situation characteristics*; Lavallee et al., 2004). The probability of succeeding refers to how likely it is that we'll achieve our goal and the value of succeeding refers to whether this is a worthwhile goal (e.g. beating a good opponent has more value than beating a weak opponent).

People with a high motive to achieve success are likely to be *high achievers*, whilst those with a high motive to avoid failure are likely to be *low achievers*. Clews and Gross (1995) discuss the three main implications for motivational behaviour that McClelland (1961) and Atkinson (1974) suggested are associated with these motivational tendencies, summarised in the box below.

> High achievers (high motive to succeed) will select challenging tasks, display a high level of effort, continue to try hard in difficult situations (like potential failure) and focus on the pride of success.
>
> Low achievers (high motive to avoid failure) avoid challenging activities, exert less effort and persistence when they do take part and focus on the shame of failure.

See Study Skills Activity 6.1 in the internet chapter for an additional activity.

Further reading (need achievement theory)

Clews, GJ and Gross, JB (1995) In Morris, T and Summer, J (eds), *Sport psychology: theories, applications and issues*, pp. 103–109). Brisbane: Wiley.
Discusses the achievement behaviours mentioned above and gives examples of applying this theory.

Moran, AP (2004) *Sport and exercise psychology: a critical introduction*, pp. 43–44. London: Routledge.
Provides a critical discussion of Need Achievement Theory.

Weinberg, RS and Gould, D (2003) *Foundations of sport and exercise psychology*, 3rd edition, pp. 61–63. Leeds: Human Kinetics.
Provides a clear summary of the theory.

Personal reflection 6.1

Think about a person you know who has a higher tendency to achieve success and one who has a higher motive to avoid failure in sport and exercise in general or in a specific sport/exercise activity. Describe how their behaviours differ as a result of their different motivational tendencies.

Attribution theory

Whenever we do something, for example lose a race, achieve a personal best distance in a javelin competition or gain a medal in dance, we often look for reasons for the outcome, particularly when it is unexpected. These reasons are called *attributions*, defined by Hanrahan (1995, p. 122) as, 'reasons that people use to explain cause and effect relationships.' As we saw with motives, it's possible to make a whole variety of attributions: *we worked really hard*; *the opposition wasn't very good*; *it's something I'm very good at*; or *we had a lucky break*. And again, whilst understanding individual attributions can be useful, a theory that pulls all this together to provide a more general picture would be even more useful. Attribution theory, proposed first by Heider (1958) and developed further by Weiner (1985), does just that.

Heider first suggested that attributions can be classified into four main groups: *ability*, *effort*, *task difficulty* and *luck*. We can see how the examples above can be classified using these groups:

- we worked really hard – effort;
- the opposition wasn't very good – task difficulty;
- it's something I'm very good at – ability;
- we had a lucky break – luck.

This way of grouping attributions is useful but are these really the only four attributions that athletes and exercisers are likely to make for their failures and successes? Well, personal experience will no doubt suggest not, and this is supported by research that has examined the attributions made by sport and exercise participants (see McAuley and Blissmer, 2002).

Dimension: a way of classifying types of attribution.

With this in mind, Weiner expanded Heider's model to provide a classification system that can be used for all possible attributions and not just the four Heider originally suggested.

The first group (or 'dimension' to use Weiner's term) is whether or not the attribution is *stable* or *unstable*. Ability is an attribution that may be classified as stable, as it is largely inherent and something that we can't really change. In comparison, an athlete's form can be quite changeable depending on the quality of their recent training, health and so on. Form is an attribution that can therefore be classified as unstable.

These examples might hint at the next dimension: *internal* or *external*. Ability is an example of an internal attribution, or one that is to do with the person (athlete or exerciser) who is making the attribution. It follows that an external attribution is one that is to do with factors that are outside of the person, such as poor weather conditions.

Again, this dimension gives us a clue to the final dimension: *controllable* or *uncontrollable*. Both of the examples above (ability and weather) are classified as uncontrollable since the athlete or exerciser is unable to control the level of their inherent ability or the weather (as much as they may like to). In contrast, though, they can control their level of preparation or how hard they work in training, so these are classified as controllable attributions.

You may have spotted a subtle difference in the examples used here to explain the controllability dimension: whether or not the attribution we make is controllable by us (*internally controllable* or *internally uncontrollable*) or is controllable by factors outside of us (*externally controllable* or *externally uncontrollable*). Ability is an uncontrollable attribution and effort is a controllable attribution but both are *internal*. In comparison, poor weather is uncontrollable, but an athlete might classify poor coaching as controllable – not by them, but by their coach, making these attributions *externally uncontrollable* (weather) and *externally controllable* (poor coaching).

You also may have realised that we don't just use one dimension to classify attributions; each attribution can be classified using all three dimensions. Let's return to Heider's four original attributions to see how this works (see Table 6.2). The table includes the formal label that Weiner gave to each of the dimensions for classifying attributions.

Table 6.2: Classification of example attributions using all three classification dimensions

Attribution	Stable/Unstable	Internal/External	Controllable/ Uncontrollable
	Stability	*Locus of causality*	*Locus of controllability*
Ability	Stable	Internal	Uncontrollable
Effort	Unstable	Internal	Controllable
Luck	Unstable	External	Uncontrollable
Task difficulty	Stable	External	Uncontrollable

Hopefully you now have some understanding of what we mean by an attribution and how different attributions can be classified using the dimensions identified by Weiner. You may still be wondering what this tells us about motivation. Well, the answer lies in the effects that our attributions have on us: on our *emotions*, *thoughts* and *behaviours* (McAuley and Blissmer, 2002). An example may help you to understand these relationships.

CASE STUDY EXAMPLE

Clare is a 400m runner who prepared well and trained hard for her last race. She won. She attributed this win to *hard work*.	Analysing Clare's attribution
She feels *pride* (emotional response).	'I won due to my hard work'
She *expects to succeed* in future races if she works hard (thoughts).	This is an internal, personally controllable, unstable attribution.
She *works hard* in training (behavioural response).	It was MY hard work (internal) . . . . . . this makes me feel proud
Her attributions, positive emotions, thoughts and behaviours mean that she is *motivated* to train and succeed in future races.	Success was under my control . . . . . . I can achieve in future Effort is not stable . . . . . . I need to keep working hard

Personal reflection 6.2

Produce your own example, like the one provided above, based on your own experiences to illustrate the relationships between attributions, emotions, thoughts and behaviours.

A key point here is that it's not really the attribution that influences our emotions, thoughts and behaviours, but the dimensions of the attribution (stability, locus of causality, locus of controllability) that influence these responses. So, two people may make the same attribution for success but classify this attribution differently. Therefore their emotions, behaviours and thoughts may differ. This is because attributions are based on our individual judgements or *perceptions*, so these are likely to change from person to person (McAuley and Blissmer, 2002).

See Study Skills Activity 6.2 in the internet chapter for an additional activity.

Further reading (attribution theory)

McAuley, E and Blissmer, B (2002) In Horn, T (ed.), *Advances in sport psychology*, 2nd edition. Leeds: Human Kinetics.
    Discusses the measurement of causal dimensions, provides more detail on attribution theory and reviews attribution theory-based research in sport and exercise.

Moran, AP (2004) *Sport and exercise psychology: a critical introduction*, pp. 48–55. London: Routledge.
    Provides a critical discussion of attribution theory and introduces the idea of attributional style.

Goal perspective theory

Before we look at our next theory, complete the scale in Table 6.3 and use the scoring instructions to work out your score.

Please read each of the statements listed in the table and indicate how much you personally agree with each statement by circling the appropriate response. Next, add up all your scores for questions 2, 5, 7, 8, 10, 12 and 13, and then divide by seven to calculate your average score. This is your *task mastery orientation score*. Add up all your scores for questions 1, 3, 4, 6, 9 and 11, and then divide by six to calculate your average score. This is your *ego orientation score*.

Table 6.3: TEOSQ (see Duda, 1989; Duda and Whitehead, 1998)

	Strongly disagree	Disagree	Neutral	Agree	Strongly agree
I feel most successful in sport when:					
1. I'm the only one who can do the play or skill.	1	2	3	4	5
2. I learn a new skill and it makes me want to practise more.	1	2	3	4	5
3. I can do better than my friends.	1	2	3	4	5
4. The others can't do as well as me.	1	2	3	4	5
5. I learn something that is fun to do.	1	2	3	4	5
6. Others mess up and I don't.	1	2	3	4	5
7. I learn a new skill by trying hard.	1	2	3	4	5
8. I work really hard.	1	2	3	4	5
9. I score the most points/goals/hits, etc.	1	2	3	4	5
10. Something I learn makes me want to go and practise more.	1	2	3	4	5
11. I'm the best.	1	2	3	4	5
12. A skill I learn really feels right.	1	2	3	4	5
13. I do my very best.	1	2	3	4	5

Table 6.3 is the Task and Ego Orientation in Sport Questionnaire (TEOSQ), developed by Duda and Nicholls to measure how much an athlete is task mastery or ego orientated (or, their *goal orientation*; see Duda, 1989; Duda and Whitehead, 1998). A goal orientation, or perspective, is a way of describing how we approach an activity like sport and exercise, what we see as important and what motivates us to take part in the activity. These are the key ideas in goal perspective theory, so we'll take a closer look at them.

Critical thinking activity 6.2

Go back to the TEOSQ and read through the questions in the task mastery orientation subscale. What do you notice about them? What do they all have in common? Using Table 6.4, write down a few ideas and then do the same for the ego orientation subscale.

Table 6.4: Goal orientations

Task mastery orientation subscale is about . . .	Ego orientation subscale is about . . .

You may have noted that, in the task mastery orientation subscale, the questions focus on:

* comparing yourself with your own previous standards;
* working hard;
* learning new skills.

You may have noted that, in the ego orientation subscale, the questions focus on:

* comparing yourself with others;
* being more skilled than others;
* beating others.

These characteristics provide us with the basic definitions of the two goal orientations or perspectives that were originally proposed by Maehr and Nicholls (1980) in their goal perspective theory (see Lavallee et al., 2004 and Table 6.5).

Table 6.5: Characteristics of task mastery and ego goal orientations

	Task mastery orientation	Ego orientation
Main goals of sport/ exercise participation	• to improve personal skills/performance • to master new skills	• to demonstrate superior ability to others • to beat others in competition
Method used to evaluate our ability	Comparisons are made with oneself (e.g. personal bests, previous level of skill)	Comparisons are made with others (e.g. winning a race or competition)

Critical thinking activity 6.3

Think about these different goal orientations and how they are likely to influence motivation. Jot some ideas down following the layout of Table 6.6.

Table 6.6: Motivation and goal orientations

	Task mastery orientation	Ego orientation
Effects on motivation		

Some of the motivational implications of these two goal orientations that you may have noted and which research in sport and physical activity settings has identified (see Chi, 2004) are listed in Table 6.7.

It may seem reasonable to think that task mastery orientation is the good cop and ego orientation is the bad cop. However, it's not quite as simple as this, as the two goal orientations are independent of each other. Just because you may have scored high on task mastery orientation does not *necessarily* mean you scored low on ego orientation, and vice versa. What research tells us (e.g. Wang and Biddle, 2001) is that it's the combination of these two goal orientations that's important. A high ego orientation is not a problem for motivation as long as it's paired with a high task mastery orientation. It's when ego orientation is high and task mastery orientation is low that motivational problems can occur. Look back at the key characteristics of these goal orientations and their motivational implications and it's easy to see why.

See Study Skills Activity 6.3 in the internet chapter for an additional activity.

Table 6.7: Motivational outcomes of different goal orientations

	Task mastery orientation	Ego orientation
Effects on motivation	• Chooses tasks that are challenging and success is uncertain • Believes that success is gained through hard work and cooperation • Inputs high effort and persists with an activity even when failing • Less likely to experience anxiety in competition	• Chooses less challenging tasks where success is certain • Believes that success is gained through ability, deception or cheating • Drops out or reduces effort when failing • More likely to experience anxiety in competition

Further reading (goal perspective theory)

Chi, L (2004) in Morris, T and Summers, J (eds), *Sport psychology: theory, applications and issues*, 2nd edition, Chapter 5. Brisbane: Wiley.
Discusses the development of goal orientations, research that has examined the motivational implications of goal orientations, the role of perceived competence in relation to goal orientation and motivation, and practical applications of goal perspective theory.

Competence motivation theory

A useful start to understanding Harter's competence motivation theory (1981) is your own experience. Take a few moments to complete the activity in Figure 6.3 on page 78.

Compare your responses with the examples below. I think it's likely that they'll include some of the following:

Very motivated
- I'm good at it
- It makes me feel satisfied
- I enjoy it
- I feel good about myself
- I just like doing it
- I keep improving at it

Very unmotivated
- I'm no good at it
- I find it boring
- It makes me feel useless and a failure
- I never seem to get any better

These may seem like quite obvious reasons for taking part in an activity, or not taking part, but they're also very powerful reasons and they form the basic ideas in competence motivation theory. The theory is best described using a somewhat simplified diagram (Figure 6.4) that explains how all the different elements relate to each other. Let's look at activities that we're motivated to do.

Figure 6.3: Personal reflections on sport/exercise involvement

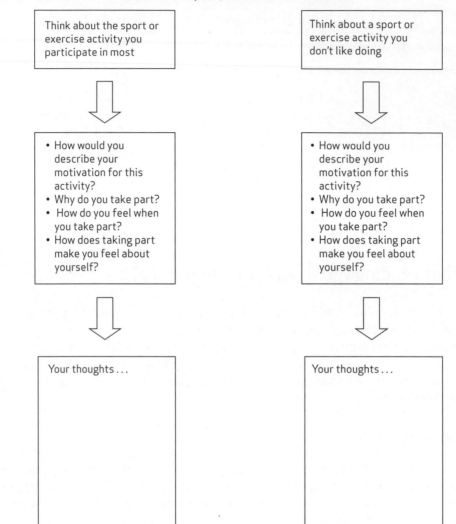

Follow Figure 6.4 round in number order to see how the elements link together to explain why we're motivated to take part in the activities that we do (Weiss and Ferrer-Caja, 2002).

When we try an activity, like playing basketball or running a 10K, our attempt can be either successful or unsuccessful – in this case, we're only considering successful attempts (we may define success in different ways, whether it's finishing the 10K or achieving a personal best). This has to be success on an optimally challenging activity, not something that is too easy or too difficult.

Experiencing success results in many positive outcomes; the key ones are:

- we think we are good at the activity – *high perceived competence*;
- we feel emotions like joy and happiness – *positive emotions*;
- we feel confident in our ability – *high self-efficacy*.

Figure 6.4: Example application of competence motivation theory

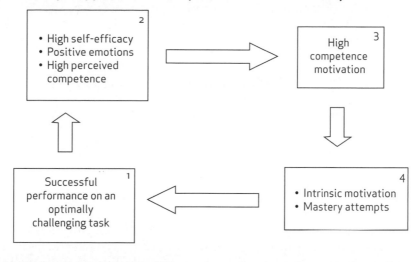

> Self-efficacy is another word for confidence at a specific task.

These positive outcomes lead us to *be motivated* to do this activity again, to develop and demonstrate competence and *feel competent*. This helps us to develop *intrinsic motivation* so we try the activity again (mastery attempts).

> Harter's main argument is that we are inherently motivated to feel and develop competence; so, when we're successful, we feel positive emotions and feel good about ourselves, which motivates us to repeat the activity to gain more competence and success and so it continues. . .

Critical thinking activity 6.4

Consider how the model in Figure 6.4 explains why we're not motivated to participate in certain activities (Weiss and Ferrer-Caja, 2002) and give an explanation of the model to a friend.

This seems like a suitable point to consider how psychologists define intrinsic motivation and how this differs from extrinsic motivation. We do a lot of things in life because we have to; many people only show up to work because they get paid and some exercisers only attend the gym because their doctor says they must. Clearly these people are motivated to work and to exercise, not because they want to, but because of some external reason, or *extrinsic motive* (Ryan and Deci, 2007). In contrast, though, when we do things because we want to and for no other reason than the pleasure and satisfaction we get from taking part, we are *intrinsically motivated* (ibid.). We are not forced by any external reasons or motives to go to the gym, walk up a mountain or go rollerblading. As we've seen in competence motivation theory, intrinsic motivation is highly desirable – it's associated with high perceived competence, positive emotions and a willingness to try out challenging activities.

See Study Skills Activity 6.4 in the internet chapter for an additional activity.

Further reading (competence motivation theory)

Horn, T (ed.) (2002) *Advances in sport psychology*, 2nd edition, pp. 101–124. Leeds: Human Kinetics.

Discusses the historical origins of Harter's theory.

Links the different concepts together, for instance illustrating the role of social support and significant others in the model.

Discusses research into sources of perceived competence, social support and motivation.

Just viewing motives as either intrinsic or extrinsic is a little too simple. Whilst some of the motives we looked at previously are clearly intrinsic (e.g. 'I go to aerobics because it's fun') and some are clearly extrinsic (e.g. 'I walk because my doctor says I have to reduce my blood pressure'), others are less clearly intrinsic or extrinsic. For instance, how would you classify the motive, 'I run to stay fit', or 'I exercise because I want to lose weight'? They are certainly more intrinsic than extrinsic but are they totally intrinsic, as the motives involve reasons other than exercising for the enjoyment and pleasure of taking part (i.e. staying fit or losing weight)? The answer is no, and to understand why, we need to look at our final theory that has been used to explain motivation in sport and exercise: self-determination theory.

Self-determination theory

The first important proposal Deci and Ryan (1985) make in self-determination theory is that distinguishing between only intrinsic and extrinsic motivation is too simple, which we saw in our original examples of motives. Instead, they suggest that there's a continuum of motivation or, a *continuum of self-determination*. First let's consider a simplified version of this continuum – see Figure 6.5.

A continuum has a continuous structure, where one thing flows into the next, instead of being made up of completely separate parts. It's a bit like when someone is cycling: there's a beginning – when we start pedalling – and an end – when we stop pedalling – but in between, the cyclist's action is continuous, making it difficult to distinguish between one movement and the next.

Deci and Ryan suggest that at one end of the continuum lies amotivation – a complete lack of desire to even take part in an activity. At the other end lies intrinsic motivation – participating in an activity for no other reason than the intrinsic enjoyment and pleasure it offers. In between are different levels of extrinsic motivation, and as we move along the continuum from amotivation to intrinsic motivation, motivation becomes less and less extrinsic and more self-determined. Ryan and Deci (2007) proposed specific types of motivation and these are included in Figure 6.6 to provide a

Figure 6.5: Motivation continuum

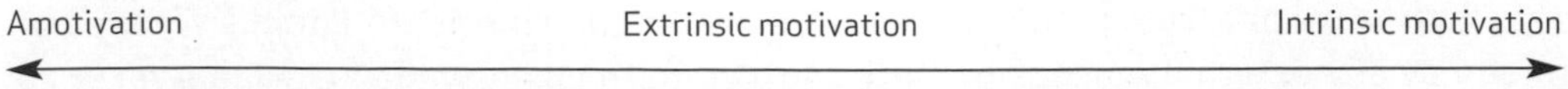

Amotivation	Extrinsic motivation	Intrinsic motivation

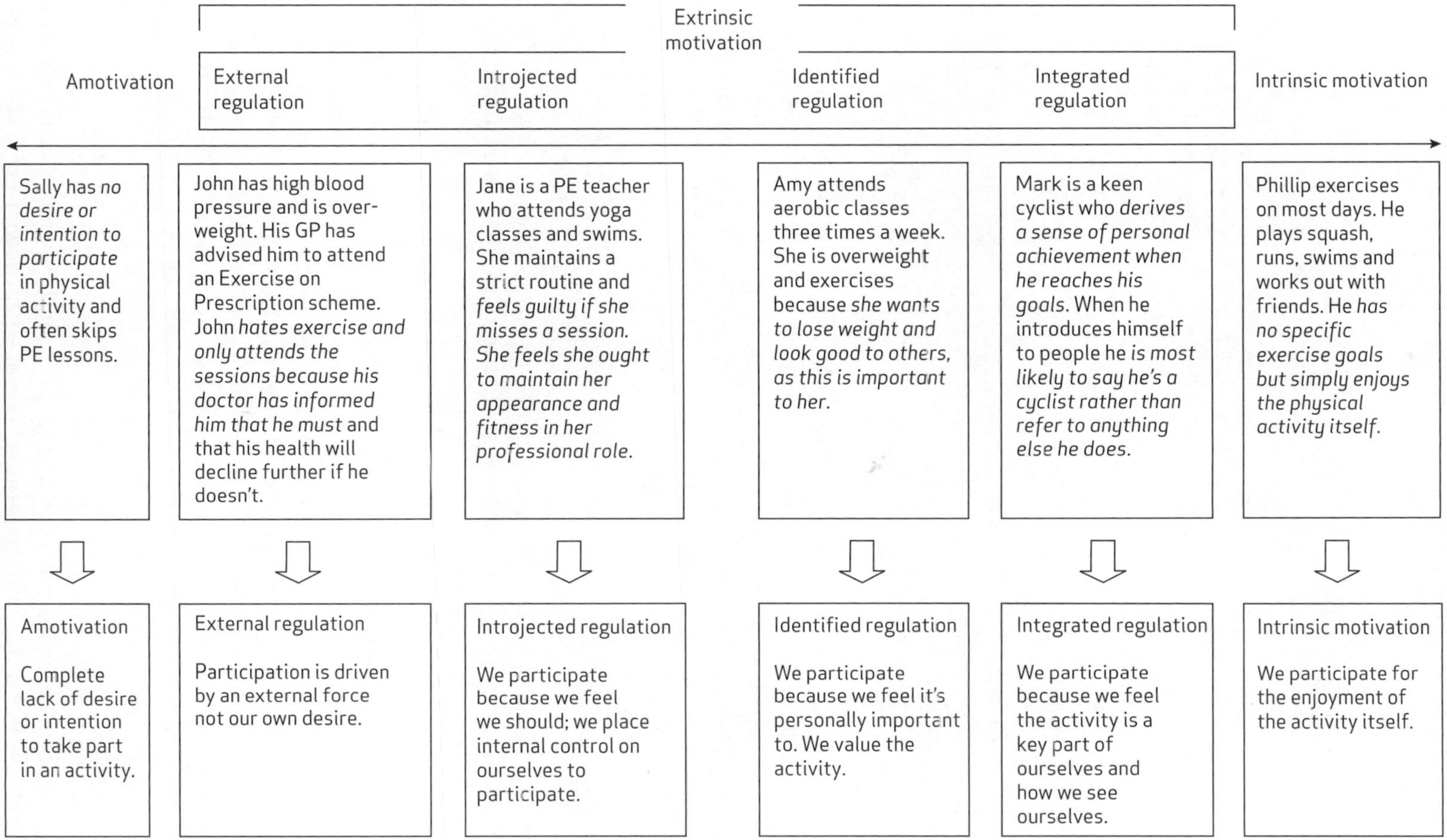

Amotivation	Extrinsic motivation				Intrinsic motivation
	External regulation	Introjected regulation	Identified regulation	Integrated regulation	
Sally has *no desire or intention to participate in physical activity and often skips PE lessons.*	John has high blood pressure and is over-weight. His GP has advised him to attend an Exercise on Prescription scheme. John *hates exercise and only attends the sessions because his doctor has informed him that he must and that his health will decline further if he doesn't.*	Jane is a PE teacher who attends yoga classes and swims. She maintains a strict routine and *feels guilty if she misses a session. She feels she ought to maintain her appearance and fitness in her professional role.*	Amy attends aerobic classes three times a week. She is overweight and exercises *because she wants to lose weight and look good to others, as this is important to her.*	Mark is a keen cyclist who derives *a sense of personal achievement when he reaches his goals.* When he introduces himself *to people he is most likely to say he's a cyclist rather than refer to anything else he does.*	Phillip exercises on most days. He plays squash, runs, swims and works out with friends. He has *no specific exercise goals but simply enjoys the physical activity itself.*
Amotivation	External regulation	Introjected regulation	Identified regulation	Integrated regulation	Intrinsic motivation
Complete lack of desire or intention to take part in an activity.	Participation is driven by an external force not our own desire.	We participate because we feel we should; we place internal control on ourselves to participate.	We participate because we feel it's personally important to. We value the activity.	We participate because we feel the activity is a key part of ourselves and how we see ourselves.	We participate for the enjoyment of the activity itself.

Figure 6.6: Motivational orientations within self-determination theory

complete illustration of the continuum. The key factors that distinguish between each of the different types of motivation on the continuum are underlined in each example.

The second important proposal in Self-Determination Theory is that we all have three basic psychological needs.

Three basic psychological needs		
Autonomy	**Competence**	**Relatedness**
• We all have a need to feel autonomous – to make our own decisions about what to do and to be in control of ourselves and our behaviours • e.g. going to the gym because you want to, not because someone says you should	• We all have a need to feel competent and able to accomplish things • e.g. mastering a new move in ice skating or completing a workout	• We all have a need to feel related to others, to belong and feel accepted • e.g. being part of a football team

We have many opportunities to fulfil these needs for autonomy, competence and relatedness in all areas of our life, including sport and exercise. For instance, the head coach gives one of his junior coaches responsibility for running the team's fitness training, helping her to meet her need for autonomy. A swimmer sets targets to reach in training and fulfils his need to feel competent by meeting them. Runners in a running club have their need for relatedness met by feeling a sense of belonging to the group.

Personal reflection 6.3

How does your sport and exercise involvement help you to meet your own needs for autonomy, competence and relatedness? Discuss your ideas with a partner and ask them to do the same.

The fact that your sport or exercise involvement helps to fulfil these needs doesn't happen by chance. In fact, Deci and Ryan (1985) suggested that we are motivated in a particular situation because we can meet some or all of our needs for autonomy, competence or relatedness in that situation. So, the more an activity fulfils these needs, the more motivated we are to take part. In fact, these authors suggest that competence, autonomy and relatedness satisfaction are essential for developing and maintaining self-determined motivation.

Research focus

Spray et al. (2006) combined the ideas of goal perspective and self-determination theories in a study that involved 80 boys and 67 girls aged between 11 and 16 years. In the study they were required to putt a golf ball from one metre away from the hole. Before doing so, the children were randomly split into four groups.

- *Group one – task involving/autonomous*. This group was encouraged to adopt a task orientation to the golf-putting task, focusing on learning and mastering the technique, and, to increase autonomy, were given an explanation for their participation in the task and the choice of whether or not they wanted to participate.
- *Group two – task involving/controlling*. Task orientation was encouraged but this group was *not* encouraged to feel autonomous – they were not given an explanation for their involvement or the choice to withdraw from the task.
- *Group three – ego involving/autonomous*. Feelings of autonomy were encouraged as above but this group was encouraged to adopt an ego orientation, trying to obtain a score that would place them in the top rankings.
- *Group four – ego involving/controlling*. This group received both the ego involving and controlling manipulations described above.

Following these manipulations, each participant performed ten practice and ten measured golf putts, after which they had a free-choice period where they could spend more time golf putting or read magazines. More time spent on the golf task was used to indicate that the participant was intrinsically motivated to perform the task when given free choice. Amongst other measures, they rated how much they enjoyed performing the task.

Results showed that autonomy was associated with more enjoyment and intrinsic motivation, and autonomy and task involvement resulted in better performance scores.

These results suggest that teachers should encourage feelings of autonomy and task orientation to increase children's intrinsic motivation, performance and enjoyment in physical activity.

Research Methods Recap

Experimental study design
- Random allocation to groups
- Manipulation of goal involvement and autonomy
- Controlled experimental conditions

Independent variable
- Motivational orientation

Dependent variables
- Performance
- Enjoyment
- Intrinsic motivation

Critical thinking activity 6.5

1   Note down three key proposals of self-determination theory.
2   Develop some examples of your own to illustrate each kind of motivation included in Deci and Ryan's self-determination continuum. Use people you know to stimulate your ideas.

Further reading (self-determination theory)

Horn, T (ed.) (2002) *Advances in sport psychology*, 2nd edition, pp. 126–137. Leeds: Human Kinetics.
Discusses the relationship between perceived competence, competition, rewards and intrinsic motivation.

What is a theory?

As we have examined a number of theories in this chapter a suitable way to end is by looking at what we mean by a theory. Let's draw on and combine a couple of definitions here (both paraphrased), from Deutsch and Krauss (1965) and Oskamp and Schultz (1998):

Theories are intellectual tools for organising data so that we can make suggestions about and transfer logic from one set of data to another; in other words, we can generalise from one set of data to another using theories. Theories also provide an integrated set of ideas that guides our investigations, observations, discoveries, predictions and explanations for what we observe happening around us.

Why are theories useful?

At the start of the chapter we suggested that theories play an important role in sport and exercise psychology. Now you are familiar with a number of theories of motivation, hopefully you have some ideas of your own about why this is so.

Critical thinking activity 6.6

With a partner, identify up to five reasons why theories are useful for sport and exercise psychologists. Compare your answers with the reasons described below.

Theories help us to organise our ideas about something; they:
 • provide us with precisely defined and measurable constructs;
 • tell us about the relationships between different constructs;
 • highlight the important constructs that we need to concentrate on.

Theories help us to make predictions about what will happen in different situations and with different people; they provide us with:

- hypotheses to test in research;
- suggestions for application in real-life settings;
- a general framework that can be applied to everyone rather than trying to understand each individual separately;
- a way of comparing findings between studies that have used the same theoretical approach.

Review

We began by examining motives for participation in sport and exercise, defining these as descriptive reasons for people's participation (LO 1). You collected some descriptive data about people's sport and exercise motives, and we highlighted differences in relation to factors like age and gender (LO 2). We then examined different theories of motivation, considering the main proposals within each theory and how they might help us to understand people's motivational behaviours, emotions and thoughts within sport and exercise (LO 3). Throughout the chapter we asked you to use your own experiences to understand and apply these theories (LO 4). We finished by explaining the definition of a theory as a set of integrated ideas that we can use to predict, guide and explain what we observe, and highlighted the reasons why theories are important to sport and exercise psychologists (LO 5).

Work through the review questions in Study Skills Activity 6.5 in the internet chapter for an additional activity.

Chapter 7

Stress, anxiety and emotions

Melissa Day

Chapter focus

The purpose of this chapter is to introduce you to the theories that explain what happens to athletes in sporting situations that provoke a high level of stress. We start by considering how we define something as stressful. To do this we look at how research has tried to describe and categorise stressful events in sport. Once we can categorise an event as stressful, the next step is to examine how an athlete may react to this stress, e.g. with elevated levels of arousal. We look at the emotions that may occur in a stressful situation and how athletes cope with stressors. One possible emotional reaction to stress is anxiety. This is a popular area in sport psychology research and so we examine a number of theories that describe the link between anxiety/arousal in sport.

For each theory, we provide case studies or practical examples, as it is always important to test your understanding by applying theory to real-life situations. So the chapter discusses the whole stress process, from the initial stressor through to the coping response of the athlete.

The theories that will be covered in this chapter are as follows:

- Lazarus and Folkman's (1984) theory of stress, appraisal and coping;
- drive theory (Spence and Spence, 1966);
- the inverted U hypothesis (Yerkes and Dodson, 1908);
- the individual zone of optimal functioning theory (Hanin, 1980).

Learning outcomes

This chapter is designed to help you be able to:
1. Explain what is meant by the term 'stress';
2. Identify and explain the three different perspectives on the study of stress;
3. Describe Lazarus and Folkman's (1984) theory of stress, appraisal and coping and relate this to your own experiences in sport;
4. Understand how coping strategies are categorised;
5. Identify the main ideas behind each theory of anxiety/arousal discussed in this chapter;

Understanding stress

Before we can start to identify the events that may be stressful in sport, it is important to first think about how we define stress. Think back over the past few days and consider how many times you may have felt 'stressed'. Often we use the word stress in our everyday lives to describe a negative feeling. We may tell others that we are feeling stressed about work, or about an assignment that we are writing. Try to think about how you felt when you were stressed; what kind of words would you use to describe this feeling? See if you can write down five words that describe how being 'stressed' may have felt to you.

You may have come up with a variety of different words to describe the feelings associated with stress. This shows how important it is to have a universal definition to make sure that when we discuss stress the meaning is always the same.

The definition of stress that is most frequently used in sport is provided by Lazarus and Folkman, and states that stress will occur when:

> A situation is appraised as taxing or exceeding an individual's resources and endangering their well-being.
>
> (1984, p. 105)

This definition means that to identify something as stressful there are two main factors that we need to consider:

1   Does the situation tax/exceed the individual's resources?
2   Does the situation endanger well-being?

Let us consider the case of Mark. Mark is a long distance runner who competes for his local club but recently says that he has been feeling stressed. See Figure 7.1. To know whether Mark is being affected by stress we can use Lazarus and Folkman's definition:

1   Does the situation tax/exceed resources?
    To answer this question, we need to examine if Mark has the resources to cope with his current situation. Mark has said that he does not have the time to fit in both training and school exams. This means that he does not have the resources (in this case, the time available) to be able to do anything about his situation; therefore the situation that he is in is taxing his resources. This means that, for Mark, the answer to this question is yes.

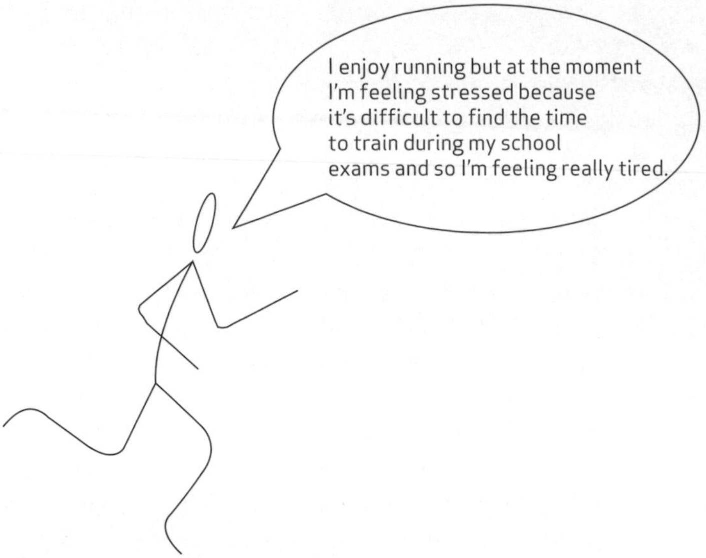

Figure 7.1:
Stressed athlete

2   Does the situation endanger well-being?
    Well-being can be physical (e.g. illness, injury) or psychological (e.g. anxiety, depression). Mark reports that he is feeling tired because of the situation. This tiredness could include both physical (e.g. muscular fatigue) and psychological (e.g. difficulty concentrating) well-being. Thus the answer to our second question is also yes.

Since Mark's situation fulfils both of these criteria, we can agree that the experience that he has described fits well with Lazarus and Folkman's definition of stress. Consequently, we may say that Mark is an athlete who is currently experiencing stress.

Personal reflection 7.1

Now think of a time when you have felt stressed in a sporting context, either in a competitive situation or in training. Try to compare how you felt to Lazarus and Folkman's definition of stress. Can you describe how your stress fits the two criteria needed for an event to be defined as stressful:

1   What resources were being taxed?
    Hint: resources could include time, money, energy . . .

2   What were the effects on your well-being?
    Hint: well-being can be physiological, psychological and emotional.

Your answers to these questions should show you that there are a number of resources that may be taxed in any sporting situation. You may also have noted a number of effects on your well-being when you felt stressed. Physiological effects may include factors such as tiredness, or physical symptoms such as headaches or muscle tightness. Psychological and emotional effects may include poor concentration, low confidence, sadness, anxiety, or similar negative emotions.

Research has shown us that stress can have a number of negative effects. These may include burnout and dropout (Taylor et al., 1990), injury (Smith et al., 1992) and performance decreases (Lazarus, 2000). Due to these negative effects of stress, it is important for sport psychology researchers to examine the situations in which stress may occur.

Now think back to the sporting situation that you defined as stressful. Think about *why* this was stressful for you. It might be that this was an important competition for you, or that there was a large audience watching. It may help you to identify these factors by comparing this stressful situation with one that you did not find stressful at all. What were the differences between the two situations?

Try to come up with as many *reasons* as you can for the stress that you were feeling and note them down.

The stimulus approach

You may have noticed that many of the stressors that you have written down are *environmental factors*. The environment can have a considerable impact on stress and sport performance and a substantial amount of research has been directed towards identifying these environmental stressors. Research that aims to identify the environmental stressors is based on a *stimulus* approach to stress. This means that this approach focuses on understanding and identifying the specific environmental causes of stress, often referred to as *sources of stress*.

Research focus one

In 2007, Thelwell et al. examined the sources of stress and coping responses in professional cricket batsmen. In this study, they aimed to identify what the commonly experienced stressors were for these athletes.

To do this, Thelwell and colleagues interviewed nine professional cricket batsmen about their sources of stress. Their participants were asked questions that would help to define and examine the most important sources of stress related to batting.

When the interviews were completed, Thelwell et al. used *inductive content analysis* to analyse their results. This meant that they grouped together similar themes in the data from all the cricketers to identify common sources of stress. Results from this study showed eight *main themes* for the sources of stress that had been experienced by the batsmen. For each of these main themes, there were also a number of *sub-themes*. These sub-themes show the more specific stressors that were discussed by the batsmen. Similar sub-themes are grouped together to form the main themes. Table 7.1 shows the results from this study.

Personal reflection 7.2

Now compare the sources of stress that Thelwell et al. (2007) found to those that you noted above from your own experience. Ask yourself the following questions:

- *Are there any similar themes/sources of stress?*
- *If your sources of stress are different to these, are there any reasons for this?*

Table 7.1: Sources of stress identified by Thelwell et al. (2007)

Main theme	Sub-themes
Perceptions of self	Self-induced pressure, emotional instability, insecurity
Match specific issues	Game situation worries, importance of game, conditions of play, umpires and team mates' performance
Current playing status	Current form, selection issues
Relationships with important others	Communication issues, perceived negative influence of relationships, expectations from others causing tension
External influences	Reputation of club, contractual issues, personal life, financial pressures, demands of the game
Views of others	Public, press, selectors
Opponents	Standard of opposition, knowledge of opposition, behaviour of opposition
Technique	Batting technique

The sources of stress that you have experienced could be quite specific to the sport that you play, or the level that you play at could also influence them. Thelwell and colleagues looked specifically at professional cricket batsmen and so this could be one reason for differences between this study's results and the sources of stress that you may have experienced. Because different sports may include different sources of stress, this has meant that research has needed to examine sources of stress in a number of different sports and situations in order to get a clear understanding of these. Some examples of this include figure skating (Scanlan et al., 1991), Australian football (Noblet and Gifford, 2002) and golf (Giacobbi et al., 2004a).

Critical thinking activity 7.1

In Table 7.2, try to identify the sources of stress in rugby and gymnastics. Once you have written at least five sources of stress, try to compare the two columns. Are there any key differences? Are there any similarities between the two sports?

Table 7.2: Sources of stress in rugby and gymnastics

Sources of stress in rugby	Sources of stress in gymnastics

The response approach

As we've seen, there may be differences in the sources of stress experienced in different sporting contexts, and, as mentioned earlier, identifying these sources of stress is known as the stimulus approach. Another way of looking at stress in sport is to use the *response approach*. Research that uses this approach examines the reaction that an individual has to a stressful situation to define that situation as stressful. Think back again to when you felt stressed in your sport and consider how you responded to this stress. Maybe you were angry, upset or frustrated. According to the response approach, these responses can be used to categorise whether you have had a stressful experience or not. However, this approach is not commonly used in sport psychology research. This may be because researchers using this approach are only able to categorise an event as stressful after it has actually happened because it is reliant on the individual's reaction.

Think back to the situation that you defined as stressful earlier on. If we put another person in the same situation, it is likely that they could react quite differently to you. Imagine one of your team mates or a friend in the same situation. On the one hand, they may find that situation overwhelmingly stressful and be unable to cope or, on the other hand, they may not find that situation stressful at all. The stimulus and response models do not explain why these individual differences may occur. However the *relational* approach is focused on explaining these differences.

The relational approach

This approach states that stress does not stem from either the environment or the individual's response to that environment but from the *relationship* between the two. This means that stress can be explained by looking at the individual's reaction to a stressor in relation to their environment. This approach is often associated with Lazarus and Folkman's (1984) theory of stress, appraisal and coping, as shown in Figure 7.2. Let's take a look at this model in more detail.

Environmental factors

According to Lazarus and Folkman's theory, it is the relationship between the person and the environment that causes stress. Environmental factors are based on how the

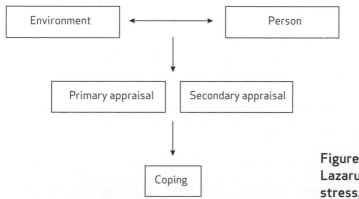

Figure 7.2:
Lazarus and Folkman's theory of stress, appraisal and coping

individual perceives their environment. Lazarus and Folkman proposed that there are eight environmental factors that may lead an individual to experience stress – as shown in Table 7.3.

In 2008, Thatcher and Day demonstrated that these environmental properties did indeed underlie the stress appraisals of athletes. They also found that two further properties were particularly relevant to the sporting environment – as shown in Table 7.4.

Table 7.3: Environmental factors that induce stress

Property	Description	Example
Novelty	Situations that the person has not previously experienced. Previous experience may include both experiencing a similar situation and gaining information that can be read, heard or inferred about the situation.	First injury of athletic career
Predictability	When the expectations we have are no longer met, the situation becomes unpredictable.	A change in competition structure compared to usual
Event uncertainty	The likelihood or probability of an event's occurrence. These can be subjective or objective probabilities, although subjective estimates do not necessarily match objective ones.	An 80 per cent chance of rain cancelling play
Imminence	The period of anticipation before an event occurs.	Anticipation while travelling to the competition
Duration	The length of an event. Events of a long duration will be deemed more stressful than shorter events.	A two-day competition
Temporal uncertainty	The individual knows that an event will definitely happen but is unsure of the precise timing.	Waiting to be called from a substitutes' bench
Ambiguity	When the information needed for appraisal is unclear or insufficient, resulting in a lack of clarity.	An unknown referee umpiring the game
Timing of events in relation to the life cycle	Events occurring at the same time as other stressful events in the individual's life cycle may be appraised in relation to these other events.	Competing during university exams

Table 7.4: Additional environmental sources of stress in sport

Property	Description	Example
Inadequate preparation	A lack of physical or mental preparation for sport.	Being asked to take a penalty without having practised penalty taking in training
Self and other comparisons	Comparing any physiological, psychological or social aspect of performance with another individual or with one's own earlier performances.	Comparing own performance to opposition while warming up

Person factors

The factors that constitute the person variable include the athlete's:

- goals for a specific event (e.g. beating a personal best);
- beliefs and expectations (e.g. I expect to win this match);
- personal resources (e.g. my family are all supporting me).

An athlete will not find an event stressful if he does not have any goals associated with the event, if he has no prior expectations, and if he has the resources (e.g. time, money, social support) to cope with the situation. However, once something in the environment threatens an athlete's goals, expectations or resources, then he will find the situation stressful.

Personal reflection 7.3

From your personal experience, try to identify one example for each of these three person factors.

A goal that I had set was:
-

My beliefs and expectations were:
-

The resources available to me were:
-

Primary appraisal

Once an athlete has perceived that at least one environmental factor is present in a situation, she will appraise that situation. Primary and secondary appraisals occur simultaneously, even though their names suggest that they occur one after the other.

Primary appraisal is an assessment of what is at stake in an encounter. The athlete asks herself, 'Do I have a goal at stake or are any of my values or expectations threatened?' If the answer to this question is yes, then she may go on to ask herself, 'What might the outcome be?' Imagine a 100m race where you are expected to win first place based on your good results all season. Then, while you are warming up, you notice that your main rival is looking fitter and more focused than they have done all season. You may start to doubt your ability to win the race. This would be because both your goal and expectation of winning the race have been threatened. When thinking about the outcome of this threat you may start to imagine that this opponent could now win the race. You might have noticed from this example that primary appraisal is an assessment of whether or not, and how, what is happening relates to the person factors of the situation.

When answering these primary appraisal questions, the athlete may decide that, for her, the situation is:

- harmful;
- threatening;
- challenging, or;
- beneficial.

Harm and threat appraisals are based on negative perceptions of the situation. The athlete appraises that either something harmful has already happened or that something harmful could happen in the future (threat). On the other hand, challenge and benefit appraisals are based on positive perceptions of the situation. An athlete who makes a challenge appraisal assesses that there is some potential for gain in the future, while an athlete who makes a benefit appraisal already perceives that she has gained something from the situation.

These different types of appraisal can help us to understand why people react differently in the same situation. We can now see that some people may appraise what is happening in their environment as a cause of future harm (threat), whereas others may see this as the potential for gain (challenge). Let us continue to use the example of the 100m race. How would you appraise the situation? One option may be to appraise this as a threat. You may believe that, since your opponent is looking strong, you may now be unable to win the race and consequently the situation is appraised as threatening as there is the potential for future harm (e.g. you may lose out on sponsorship, your coach may be disappointed, or you will be angry with yourself for not winning). On the other hand, you may appraise the situation as a challenge. You may believe that, even though your opponent is looking strong, this will push you to go faster in the race and so you may even achieve a personal best. Consequently, you see the situation as challenging because you have assessed that there is the potential for future gain (e.g. achieving a faster time, experiencing positive emotions, receiving praise from your coach).

Anshel et al. (2001) examined how skilled athletes appraised stress during sport competition. Their results showed that the athlete's appraisal varied depending on the type of stressful event that was occurring. For example, some events, such as being reprimanded by a coach, produced very high levels of perceived threat and low levels of challenge. Other events, such as observing an opponent cheat, were associated with high levels of challenge, medium levels of harm and low levels of threat. They concluded that stressors differed to the extent that they were accompanied by each appraisal. Interestingly, Anshel and colleagues also found that females experienced more threat and fewer harm or challenge appraisals than males.

Secondary appraisal

Although secondary appraisal may sound like it should occur after primary appraisal, the two types of appraisal take place at the same time. Secondary appraisal is an evaluation of what can be done about the stressful person–environment relationship. The athlete may ask himself questions such as, 'Do I need to act?', 'When should I act?' and 'Am I capable of doing it?' The athlete is trying to decide what he can do about a situation and whether he can successfully apply the strategies he is considering. Thus the athlete assesses the coping strategies that he could use to overcome the situation.

Let's think about the secondary appraisals of the athlete warming up for the 100m race in our earlier example. In answer to the question, 'Do I need to act?', the athlete may decide that some kind of action is needed. This could include trying to become more focused or warming up well to ensure that he is ready for the race. The athlete may then decide that these actions need to take place straight away. Finally, the athlete needs to decide whether these actions can be carried out. This means that he will assess his ability to become more focused or to warm up well.

To briefly recap, the theory of stress, appraisal and coping can be explained as described in Figure 7.3.

See Study Skills Activity 7.1 in the internet chapter for an additional activity.

Figure 7.3: Lazarus and Folkman's theory of stress, appraisal and coping

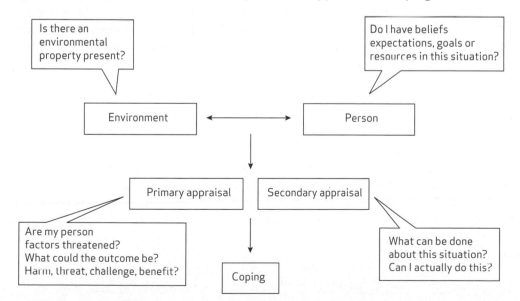

Coping

Once an event has been appraised as stressful, an athlete will need to be able to cope effectively with the situation. Coping strategies are the cognitive, affective and behavioural efforts that an athlete may use to manage the demands of the stressful environment (Crocker et al., 1998); in other words, the things we can think, how we can feel and what we can do to deal with the stressful situation. There are a number of ways in which an athlete may cope. Sport psychology research has categorised these into different types of coping strategies. There are two main methods of categorising coping, either *problem-focused* or *emotion-focused* coping, and *approach* or *avoidance* coping. Problem-focused coping is an effort to manage the specific problem, whereas emotion-focused coping is an effort to manage the emotional response caused by the stressor.

Case study

Kate is a gymnast who has a competition approaching in a few weeks' time. She has been working on a new dismount for her beam routine but has so far been unable to land this. Kate reports to her coach that she is feeling stressed because the dismount is not ready for the competition. Kate has a number of different coping options (see Table 7.5).

You may have noticed that not all of these coping strategies would be beneficial to Kate's performance. The example of avoidance coping means that Kate would not practise the skill or would drop out of training. These strategies are unlikely to help Kate to achieve the skill that she is finding difficult. However, even those strategies that are ineffective are still called coping strategies; therefore a coping strategy can be both effective and ineffective.

Table 7.5: Coping strategies

Coping strategy	Explanation	Practical example
Problem focused	Actions to remove the threatening event or lessen its impact by altering the environment itself.	Reducing the height of the beam, using more progressions to build up the skill
Emotion focused	Efforts to regulate the emotional response. This alters only what is in the athlete's mind.	Using imagery to visualise the dismount, shifting attentional focus
Approach	Confronting the source of stress by reducing its intensity or attempting to understand the situation.	Talking to the coach about the skill to get a better understanding of what is required
Avoidance	Behavioural and psychological efforts to disengage from the stressful situation.	Work on other skills instead, missing training

Coping effectiveness

Sport psychology research proposes that one of the most difficult issues facing coping research is measuring whether a strategy is effective or ineffective (Nicholls and Polman, 2007a) and it is important to examine both long-term and short-term effectiveness (Folkman and Moskowitz, 2004). Using the example above, the avoidance coping strategy of not attending training may be effective in the short term by lowering Kate's level of stress. However, in the long term this strategy will not be effective in helping Kate to achieve this skill. Thus the same coping strategy may have different short-term and long-term effectiveness.

Nicholls and Polman (2007b) examined the stressors, coping and coping effectiveness of adolescent rugby players who completed a daily diary for 31 days. The aim of this diary was to record the stressors that they experienced, how they coped with these stressors, and how effective their coping strategies were. To assess the effectiveness of coping strategies, players were asked to rate how effective these strategies had been on a five-point scale, with 1 being not effective and 5 being very effective. When the diaries had been completed, Nicholls and Polman examined the number of times each coping strategy had been used to cope with each stressor. For each strategy, they then calculated a mean coping effectiveness score. Their results showed that the most frequently cited coping strategies were not rated as being the most effective. Thus, even if an athlete consistently uses the same coping strategy this will not mean that it is necessarily any more effective than those strategies that are not used as often.

Personal reflection 7.4

Now that we have covered the key aspects of stress, see if you can apply Lazarus and Folkman's theory to your own experiences using Figure 7.4.

See Study Skills Activity 7.2 in the internet chapter for an additional activity.

Emotions

Lazarus (1990) stated that no other concept is more revealing of the way that an individual relates to the environment than emotion. Whereas only a few types of stress (harm, threat and challenge) have been distinguished, 15 or more emotions can be identified which allow for an understanding of how the athlete reacts to a particular stressor.

Lazarus (2000) proposed that an emotion is:

. . .a phenomenon that is an organized psychophysiological reaction to ongoing relationships with the environment.

(p. 230)

Figure 7.4: Personal reflections on stress, appraisal and coping

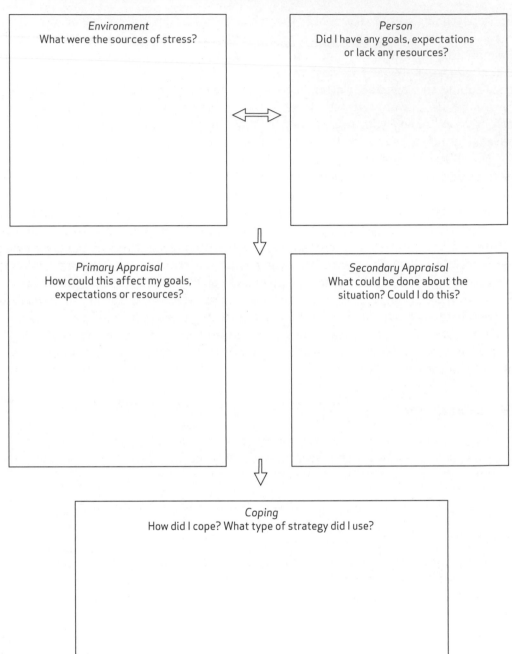

This means that emotions are based on our reactions to the environment. Emotions can be positive or negative. Examples of positive emotions may include happiness, joy, pride, relief, hope, love, compassion and gratitude. Examples of negative emotions may include anger, anxiety, fright, guilt, shame, sadness, envy and jealousy.

Despite research such as Lazarus' (1999, 2000) that has demonstrated the importance of emotions in sport, Cerin and Barnett (2006) suggested that research on athletes' emotional responses to competition has been limited. Unlike research into anxiety, fewer attempts have been made to examine other emotions in sport; although recent trends demonstrate a gradual advancement of sports emotion research (e.g. Mellalieu, 2004; Uphill and Jones, 2004). This scarcity of emotion research in sport is surprising since authors such as Hanin (2000) have suggested that some emotions will be good predictors of performance in individual athletes.

Despite the lack of research into some emotions, anxiety has consistently been a well-researched emotion in sport psychology. The following sections will examine theories that explain the relationship between anxiety and performance in sport.

Competitive anxiety and arousal

To understand anxiety theory, let's start by examining a sporting situation that shows how anxiety may be experienced. As a sport psychologist, you are approached by a tennis player (Andrew) who reports that he feels extremely anxious before playing important matches. Andrew tells you that sometimes this anxiety means that he does not play as well as usual.

There are a number of questions that you may need to be able to answer before you can help this player, for instance:

- What is anxiety and what does it mean when someone says that they are anxious?
- What are the theories that underpin anxiety and can these explain what happens when someone is anxious?
- How does anxiety influence performance? Is this always negative?
- How can we reduce or limit the effects of anxiety?

These are the questions that we will address in this section on anxiety, using the answers to better understand how we can help Andrew.

Personal reflection 7.5

How would you define anxiety? Take two minutes and try to write your own definition of anxiety, based on your own experiences. You may wish to think about what it felt like when you last felt anxious.

You may have included in your definition that anxiety is a negative emotional state that may include feelings of worry and nervousness about an upcoming event or situation. There are many symptoms of anxiety and you may have included some of these in your own definition of anxiety. We can separate these symptoms into what are termed *cognitive anxiety* and *somatic anxiety*. Cognitive anxiety is the thought component of anxiety. The symptoms of cognitive anxiety are characterised by thoughts of worry and apprehension. An athlete with a high level of cognitive anxiety may report:

- negative self talk;
- an inability to concentrate;

- difficulty sleeping;
- concerns about performing poorly.

Somatic anxiety refers to the athlete's perceptions of the degree of physiological activation experienced by the athlete. Symptoms may include:

- increased muscle tension;
- having 'butterflies';
- feeling ill or sick;
- having a headache;
- having a racing heart.

So, when our tennis player, Andrew, experiences anxiety he may experience cognitive anxiety, somatic anxiety or both types of anxiety symptoms. When an individual is in a situation where he has a high level of physiological and psychological activation, then we may say that he has a high level of *arousal*. Arousal levels vary on a continuum from coma to frenzy, although arousal is not automatically positive or negative. Anxiety is often associated with high levels of arousal in an individual. Indeed, Andrew's explanation of his poor performance seems to indicate high levels of arousal.

To assess whether an individual is experiencing physiological arousal, there are a number of measures that can be used. These may include heart rate, respiratory rate and galvanic skin response. Both somatic and cognitive anxiety can be measured using self-report questionnaires. The most frequently used questionnaire to measure anxiety in sport psychology research is the Competitive State Anxiety Inventory-2 (CSAI-2; Martens et al., 1990a).

This questionnaire contains 27 statements that athletes may use to describe their feelings prior to competition. It includes statements such as, 'I am concerned about losing' and 'My heart is racing'. When filling in this questionnaire, participants are asked to rate each statement in accordance with how they feel at that moment. The questionnaire measures three factors: cognitive anxiety, somatic anxiety and self-confidence. Self-confidence is included in this questionnaire since it has been shown to be a component related to anxiety. Self-confidence scores should be the opposite to anxiety scores; thus when anxiety is high, self-confidence scores should be low.

Despite being widely used, there remain some limitations to using questionnaires to measure anxiety. One main limitation is timing. It may not be reasonable to expect an athlete to complete a questionnaire immediately prior to performance; however, research has shown that different patterns of anxiety will occur depending on the closeness of the competition. Consequently, it may be difficult to obtain an accurate measure of competitive anxiety immediately prior to competition.

Now that we understand the meaning of anxiety and arousal and how they can be measured, the next step is to examine theory that could help us to understand the relationship between anxiety and sporting performance. Our tennis player, Andrew, reported that in situations where he felt particularly anxious his performance was worse. Let's look at this statement in relation to anxiety/arousal performance theories.

Arousal, anxiety and performance

Drive theory

One theory that has been used to examine the relationship between performance and arousal is drive theory (Spence and Spence, 1966). According to this theory, as arousal increases, the performance of the athlete will also increase. So, Andrew would play best when he has high levels of arousal. When he has low levels of arousal his performance would deteriorate. Figure 7.5a shows this relationship between arousal and performance.

However, many researchers have argued that this theory is too simplistic to accurately describe the relationship between arousal and performance. It does not

Figure 7.5: Theories of arousal and performance

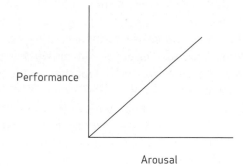

Performance

Arousal

(a) Drive Theory

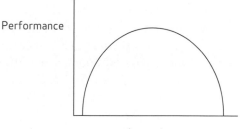

Performance

Arousal

(b) Inverted U Hypothesis

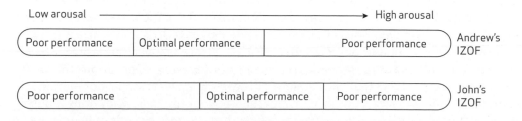

Low arousal ⟶ High arousal

| Poor performance | Optimal performance | Poor performance | Andrew's IZOF |

| Poor performance | Optimal performance | Poor performance | John's IZOF |

(b) Individual Zone of Optimal Functioning Theory

consider the complex tasks that may need to be performed by the athlete, and many athletes (such as Andrew) report the opposite effect of arousal on performance. So this theory can be criticised as it does not take into account that some levels of arousal may be detrimental for performance. Instead, it proposes that any increase in arousal will be beneficial to performance. Given these criticisms, it will come as no surprise that there is a lack of research support for this theory (Martens et al., 1990b).

The inverted U hypothesis

The inverted U hypothesis is an alternative approach to examining the relationship between arousal and performance (Yerkes and Dodson, 1908). This hypothesis proposes that arousal will enhance performance up to a certain point; however, after arousal levels have reached this point, there will then be a negative effect on performance (see Figure 7.5b). Using this approach, we could propose that Andrew's arousal levels are high since he is experiencing a drop in performance. We could also propose that, if his arousal levels were lower, his performance would improve.

This means that the optimal arousal levels for performance will be moderate. One of the strengths of this theory is that it also proposes that optimal arousal levels will vary for different sports and skills. Thus unlike drive theory, the inverted U hypothesis takes into account that arousal can be both beneficial and detrimental for performance, and that the athlete may be required to perform tasks of different complexities. However, research has also demonstrated the limitations of the inverted U hypothesis. Fazey and Hardy (1988) argued that, once arousal increases beyond an optimal point, then performance will drop suddenly and not gradually, as the inverted U hypothesis suggests. When this has occurred, a slight decrease in the athlete's arousal levels will not result in a return to the optimal point of performance, as the inverted U hypothesis predicts. A final criticism of this approach is that it is not able to explain why some athletes are able to perform well while experiencing high levels of arousal.

Individual zone of optimal functioning theory

A third theory that expands on the notion that optimum arousal levels will vary for individual athletes is the individual zone of optimal functioning theory (IZOF). According to Hanin (1980), every athlete will have a zone in which they produce their optimal performance.

Figure 7.5c shows the zone of optimal functioning as described by Andrew, the tennis player. His performance is best when he experiences only a small amount of arousal. When he experiences too much arousal he recognises that this is detrimental to his performance.

Another player on Andrew's tennis team (John) may describe that he does not perform well unless he has a high level of arousal. When he feels no arousal, then he is unable to perform at his best. However, in highly pressured situations such as important matches he feels more arousal and his tennis improves. His IZOF is shown in Figure 7.5c.

The two IZOF profiles of Andrew and John demonstrate that each athlete may have their own optimal zone of functioning. This theory has important implications for sport psychologists, as it shows that each athlete will have their own personal optimum level of arousal for performance. Consequently, for John, but not for Andrew, lowering arousal level may actually cause a drop in performance. This means that optimum levels of arousal should be considered on an individual basis.

The IZOF introduces the notion that individuals may interpret arousal in different ways. This has also been shown to be the case with anxiety. An individual may interpret their anxiety as either positive or negative; this is termed the 'direction' of anxiety. An individual who interprets anxiety negatively will view the effects of anxiety as *debilitative* (e.g. a swimmer may interpret that the increased muscle tension caused by anxiety will cause them to swim slower). Alternatively, an individual who interprets anxiety positively will view its effects as *facilitative* (e.g. a football player about to take a penalty kick interprets their anxiety as a sign of readiness and links this to improved performance). Consequently, it may be proposed that it is not only the *level* of anxiety that is an important consideration but also the *direction*.

Research focus two

In 1999, Hanton and Jones examined how elite competitive swimmers acquired the cognitive skills and strategies necessary to interpret pre-race thoughts as facilitative. To do this, they recruited elite swimmers, all of whom had competed internationally. The authors needed to verify that these elite swimmers did indeed interpret their anxiety as facilitative, so they were asked to complete a modified version of the CSAI-2, which also included both level and direction scales. Ten of the 13 participants reported facilitative interpretations and were therefore included in the study. The remaining three participants were excluded from the study as they reported both facilitative and debilitative interpretations. The ten participants who met the study inclusion criterion then took part in an interview. The interview discussed themes including their initial experiences of swimming and how this developed, their current experiences and mental skills used, and advice and recommendations about how debilitating interpretations of anxiety were restructured.

Hanton and Jones used inductive content analysis to analyse the data from the interviews. Overall, there were four general dimensions: early unwanted negative experiences, learning at an early age that nerves can be positive, pre-competition routine, and pre-race routine. Hanton and Jones were able to conclude that performers did not initially interpret anxiety as facilitative when they started competing. However, as they continued to gain experience in competitive swimming, they learned that the anxiety symptoms that they were experiencing could be positive for their performance. They were able to learn to make this facilitative interpretation by listening to others such as coaches and team mates who were more experienced, and also by learning psychological strategies. As the swimmers gained more experience, they recognised the importance of the anxiety symptoms and also developed and refined pre-competition and pre-race routines as part of a mental preparation package. In summary, Hanton and Jones reported that the swimmers had learned how to 'make the butterflies fly in formation' (p. 19) and to use these positively in competitive situations.

This study shows us that, when examining anxiety, it is not only the level of anxiety but also the direction that is important. Andrew, our tennis player, viewed his anxiety as negative. Sport psychologists may use interventions such as relaxation training, centring or imagery to lower his anxiety levels. However, Hanton and Jones' study also shows that Andrew's performance may be improved by helping him to re-interpret his anxiety so that when he feels anxious he is able to view this as having a positive influence on his performance. Thus the sport psychologist can help the athlete to change both the level and the direction of anxiety.

See Study Skills Activity 7.3 in the internet chapter for an additional activity.

Further reading (anxiety and arousal)

Murphy, S (2005) *The sport psych handbook*. Leeds: Human Kinetics.
Will help you to understand how a sport psychologist may use psychological strategies to help athletes to manage their anxiety and arousal.

Review

This chapter presented a number of key ideas and theories about the study of stress, appraisal, coping and anxiety, so we can now understand the complete process of stress from how to define 'stress' (LO 1) to how an individual may be likely to respond in a stressful situation. You will hopefully have an understanding of the three approaches that can be used to study stress: the stimulus, response and relational approach, and how these differ (LO 2).

The chapter also examined Lazarus and Folkman's model of stress, appraisal and coping (LO 3). This model highlights the important role of appraisals in determining how each individual responds to stressful situations. Coping strategies were also discussed and an outline of each type of coping was provided (LO 4). Coping can be both effective and ineffective depending on the long-term and short-term outcomes of our coping attempts.

After discussing stress, appraisal and coping, we then considered some emotions that may occur following experience of a stressor. The most researched emotion that may occur in stressful situations is anxiety. Three main theories that examine anxiety and arousal were presented (LO 5). These were: drive theory, the inverted U hypothesis and the individualised zone of optimal functioning theory, each of which presents a different perspective on the relationship between arousal and performance (LO 7). You will now be able to compare these three approaches and critically comment on each approach (LO 6).

Finally, we examined research by Hanton and Jones (1999) that demonstrated the importance of anxiety direction. Thus, as sport psychologists, we need to be aware that it is not only how much anxiety the athlete experiences but also how she interprets her anxiety.

Work through the review questions in Study Skills Activity 7.4 in the internet chapter for an additional activity.

Chapter 8

Group dynamics

Melissa Day

Chapter focus

The aim of this chapter is to introduce you to group dynamics. We start the chapter by examining what we mean by a group and how this differs from a team. We look at key features that are shared between groups and teams and the differences between them. We then consider how a group may become a team through a four-stage process of development. For any team to be successful it needs a high level of productivity. Thus Carron et al.'s (1998) model of productivity is discussed in detail. Using this model we examine how team roles and norms are formed and how a team can become a cohesive unit. The activities throughout this chapter should prompt you to reflect on your own experiences within a group or team and relate these to the theories we discuss.

Learning outcomes

This chapter is designed to help you:

1 Identify the similarities and differences between groups and teams;
2 Explain Tuckman's (1965) four stages of team developmen;
3 Describe Carron et al.'s (1998) model of group productivity;
4 Understand Steiner's (1972) model of group productivity;
5 Explain what is meant by team norms and team roles;
6 Define team cohesion and understand how this may be related to performance.

Personal reflection 8.1

Being part of a team is often one of the main reasons that people enjoy taking part in sport. You may have experience of playing in a team yourself, whether this was a school team or as part of a sports club. Before we look at theories that explain the dynamics of teams, take a few minutes to think about the advantages of being part of a team. What was is that made you enjoy participating in this team sport? Try to jot down at least five reasons.

You may have said that you enjoyed the camaraderie of being part of a team, that you had good friends on your team, or that you liked working together. Your team members may have also provided social support or increased your motivation to go to training. There are a number of different reasons why people take part in team sports. Often these reasons are linked to the dynamics of the team; in other words, we enjoy being part of a collective group of like-minded people.

Defining groups and teams

Although we have begun by discussing the advantages of being part of a team, you may have noticed that this chapter is titled 'Group dynamics'. So you may be asking yourself, 'What is the difference between a group and a team?' It's easy to think that they both describe the same thing; after all, they are quite similar and are often used interchangeably. However, although they share similarities, there are key differences between a group and a team. To clarify these terms, read the two scenarios below; in one of the scenarios you would be part of a team, in the other you would be part of a group. Can you identify which is which?

Scenario one
It is pouring with rain and you are standing at a train station waiting for the train to take you home. It is a busy Saturday afternoon and there are a number of other people at the station, also waiting to board the train. An announcement is made that the train has been delayed by 20 minutes. As this announcement is made, some people at the station sigh and start to grumble about the wait.

Scenario two
On a Saturday morning you play hockey for your local club. You have been warming up for the past 20 minutes when your coach informs you that the opposition is delayed and so the match will start 20 minutes late. Your other team members look annoyed and start to complain. The captain tells everyone to take a drink break and to be back on the pitch in ten minutes.

Critical thinking activity 8.1

Scenario ___ portrays a group situation.
Scenario ___ portrays a team situation.

Now note down one reason to explain your answers. What characteristics of these scenarios led you to identify one as a group and the other as a team?

In both of these scenarios you may have had goals in common with people around you. In scenario one, your common goal with the people waiting on the platform was to travel somewhere on the train. In scenario two, your common goal with your team mates was to play in the upcoming match. Despite the fact that you have shared goals with those people around you in each scenario, your relationship with those individuals differs. The key difference is that in scenario one you don't know the people who are waiting at the station, whereas in scenario two you know the people playing in your team. Can you think of another difference between the two scenarios? Jot down your ideas.

You may have written that in scenario one the people waiting at the station do not interact with each other; even though they are in the same situation, their interaction is minimal. In scenario two, however, there is more interaction between people as the players are all told by the captain to take a break. This highlights a key difference between groups and teams: team members interact with each other when pursuing a goal whereas group members do not. In scenario one, the lack of interaction also highlights that the people at the station do not support each other while waiting for the train. In scenario two, however, the players are supported by the captain, who provides them with a coping strategy when the opposition team is delayed.

We can conclude from these two scenarios that the people in scenario one are a group. They all share a common goal of boarding the train. However, they do not interact with or support each other to achieve that goal. In scenario two, the hockey players also share a common goal, but to achieve this goal they interact with and support each other, for instance by sharing coping strategies.

Distinguishing factor between a group and a team

Although both teams and groups may share a common goal, team, but not group, members interact with and support each other to achieve this goal.

Developing from a group into a team

Now that we know the difference between a group and a team, we can ask the question, 'Can a group become a team?' According to Tuckman (1965), the answer to this question is yes. Tuckman proposes that there are four stages that will lead people from participating in an activity as a group to becoming a team. These stages are: forming, storming, norming and performing.

Imagine that you have just decided to form a new sports team. Let's look at how that team might evolve from a group to a team.

Forming

You have arranged your first training session with your new team. As players start to arrive, they introduce themselves to each other and start to chat. You notice that some of the players are already talking about the positions that they play and what they would like to achieve within the team. You start the practice with a brief skills drill and during this you notice that many of the players are looking around at the others in the team. Although they are performing well, they seem to be comparing themselves to the other players.

Over the next few training sessions you start to put players into match type situations. The first few times that you do this, you notice that the players seem to struggle. Even those who seem to have the highest skill level have difficulty working with and adjusting to others' styles of play. However, as you anticipate, the more times you put these players into this situation, the more their performance as a team improves. You observe that they seem to communicate better with each other and adjust to different styles of play, which helps them to perform better as a team.

You also begin to notice certain personalities within the group. Some of the players are much quieter, whereas others are happy to take the lead. On arrival at training, some players volunteer to take the warm up. When this happens the rest of the players are happy to follow the instructions that they are given.

Storming

After a while you start to notice that there is some conflict between the players. Although initially players were compliant when asked to follow a warm up led by a team mate, now they start to complain. One of the players talks to you after a session and tells you that he believes that it should be the coach's responsibility to lead the warm up. You notice that during this time a few of the players start to split off into a smaller groups and perform their own warm up.

This situation seems to worsen when you tell the players that you will be announcing the team selection next week for the team's first match. In the following few practices the players start to become more competitive with each other. When an own goal is scored during a practice match the team members become extremely hostile towards the player who made this mistake. You decide to take action to try to solve the problem by working with some of the players who are struggling. However, when you do, some of the players complain that you spend more time coaching some players than others.

Norming

Gradually the players manage to resolve the conflicts they experienced. After you announce the team selection, the players start to give each other more support in training and you notice that the players are beginning to communicate effectively again. The elected team captain helps the players to recognise each other's strengths and roles and the players realise that they will need to work as a team to win their first match. The individual specialisms of individual team members begin to complement each other and the team plays better because of this.

One week after training the team go out for a meal to celebrate the start of the competitive season, organised by the players. During this meal you notice that the players interact well with each other and appear to enjoy each other's company.

Performing

During the final stage of this process, the team seems to have stabilised. The players are performing well and respect each other's roles and contributions to the team. They applaud each other during moments of exceptional performance and show support for each other when they are losing. After each match the players nominate a man of the match to recognise each other's accomplishments. As a coach, you believe that your team is now a cohesive unit that is able to work together and support team members to achieve team goals.

The above case study example illustrates how a group may become a team. Initially, when the group starts, they are a collection of players who do not interact effectively with each other and who need to spend time understanding each other's styles of play. This is reflected in their initial difficulty playing together and the competition and conflicts that develop within the team. As the team develops, they become a more cohesive unit; they communicate well and show respect for each player's abilities and the contribution that each player makes to the team. Figure 8.1 summarises this process of team development so that you can clearly see the key characteristics of each stage.

Personal reflection 8.2

Now think about a time when you joined a sports team, either as a player or as a coach. In the flow chart in Figure 8.2 fill in your own experiences of each stage of team development that is described by Tuckman (1965).

See Study Skills Activity 8.1 in the internet chapter for an additional activity.

Group productivity

One of the main aims of any sports team is to perform to the best of its ability. Consequently, a coach wants the team that he or she is coaching to be as productive as possible. Carron and colleagues (1998) suggested a sport specific model of group productivity that explains the factors that contribute to both group and individual productivity, as shown in Figure 8.3.

Let's look in more detail at each element of this model. The model first suggests that both member attributes and group environment will influence the development of the group's overall structure. We cannot examine the dynamics or productivity of a team without considering the members of the team and the environment in which this team operates.

Imagine that you want to bake a cake. You need to start with the individual ingredients that you need to put into the cake, as well as the right environment in which to bake your cake. Without the right ingredients your cake may not bake or taste as it should. Further, an old oven that does not get very hot may not result in a properly baked cake. Similarly, we need to look at the member attributes (or ingredients) of the team to understand its composition and assess its effectiveness. The environment (or oven) in which the team plays will also impact on its overall performance.

Member attributes

The resources available to any team will always be dependent on the individual team members. Therefore a team will only be productive if the members within that team have the necessary resources. Each team member brings certain resources to the team in which they play, including ability, motivation, dependability and emotional stability.

Figure 8.1: Tuckman's (1965) stages of team development

Figure 8.2: Personal experience of the stages of team development

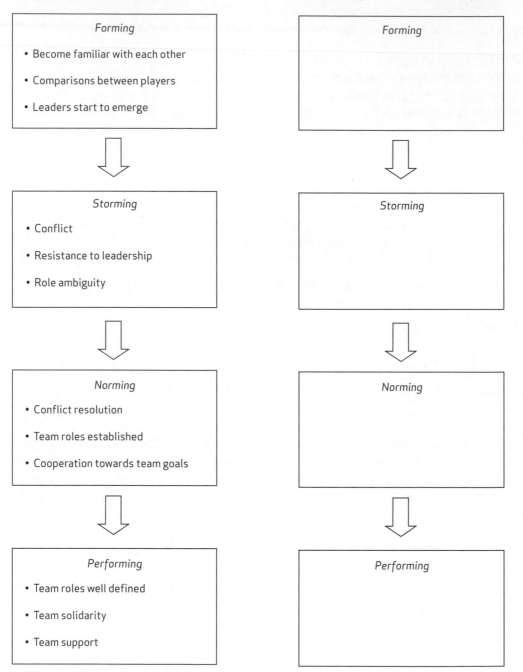

Figure 8.3: Carron et al.'s (1998) model of group productivity

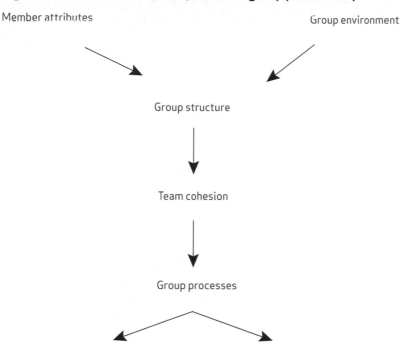

Member attributes

Group environment

Group structure

Team cohesion

Group processes

Individual productivity

Group productivity

Widmeyer and Loy (1981) suggest that we need to consider three factors when assessing team resources: the *amount* of resource possessed by the team, the *variability* in resources between team members, and the *compatibility* between team members. To understand these, let's look at a hypothetical question:

> If you were to take all the best ice hockey players in the world, would you have the best team possible?

This is a difficult question to answer because it is something that we cannot test. But, based on Widmeyer and Loy (1981), we could hypothesise that, if we select all of the top ranking players from around the world, this may not give us the best team possible. Although the amount of resources possessed by the team would be high (e.g. high amount of skill), the variability in resources and compatibility between team members may be quite low. By selecting the best players from around the world, the likelihood is that they may share the same strengths (e.g. be excellent goal scorers) yet lack in other skill areas. It is unlikely that we would end up with the ideal number of attacking and defending players and we may even end up with players who play in the same position. Consequently, our team members would not have compatible attributes. The best possible team would be one where the member attributes complement each other. So, within our ice hockey team we need both attacking and defending players who play in different positions and who have different strengths.

Group environment

In addition to member attributes, a second factor that contributes to the overall group structure is the environment in which the team trains and competes. Carron et al. (1998) propose that group environment includes two main factors:

1   The size of the team;
2   The physical territory that the team is in, such as the sports field or the gym.

Team size

In any team the number of players is important, although it is difficult to quantify the number of players that will make the best team. There are a number of anecdotal sayings that demonstrate the difficulty of achieving a productive group size: 'Two heads are better than one' and 'The more the merrier'. These sayings imply that more people will be more productive whereas others such as, 'Too many cooks spoil the broth' imply that more is not always better. These simple proverbs demonstrate the difficulty of quantifying an ideal group size. So, you may still be left asking the question: What is the optimum number of people for any sports team to be optimally productive?

One of the main theories to explain the link between quantity and productivity was proposed by Steiner (1972). According to Steiner, as the size of a group increases, so does the potential productivity of the group. However, once the group becomes too large, group productivity plateaus. If the group continues to grow in size, this undermines group coordination and productivity will decrease. To understand this more clearly, let's use a sporting example.

Mandy has started a cricket team to play in her local 7-a-side indoor league. After asking around her friends and family, seven people attended her first training session. These people began to tell their friends about the new cricket team, more people started to attend her training sessions and by the end of the season she had 13 players Mandy also noticed that, as more people became involved in her team, the standard of skill in the team increased. So, she believed that with more cricket players she had a better team. As a result, Mandy decided to recruit more players for her team.

To do so, she placed an advert in the local paper for people to join her team. Six new players joined and, although the team had initially shown improvements, this was no longer the case. Mandy thought that perhaps the team would start to improve again if she were to recruit a new set of players. So the players were encouraged to bring their friends and work colleagues to training sessions. However, contrary to Mandy's expectation, it soon became clear that the more people who joined the team, the worse the team's performance became.

Critical thinking activity 8.2

Try to plot the productivity of Mandy's team on the axes in Figure 8.4. You should have a graph that looks like Figure 8.5.

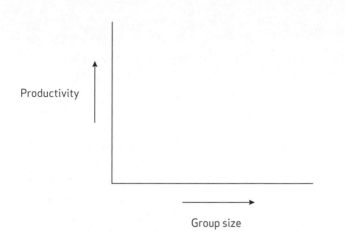

**Figure 8.4:
Group productivity
and group size**

The example of Mandy's cricket team illustrates the central proposal of Steiner's theory that all of the expertise necessary to play cricket was available within a certain number of players. As Mandy continued adding players to her team, no new resources were added. Then, as the team continued to expand team coordination was threatened and productivity (in this case, the team's performance) decreased.

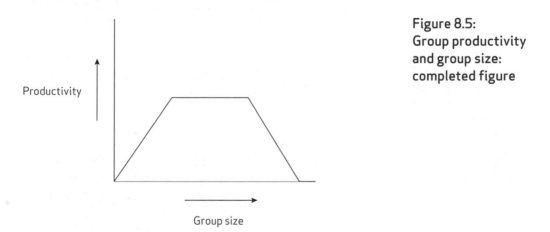

**Figure 8.5:
Group productivity
and group size:
completed figure**

Physical territory

As well as the number of players in a team, Carron et al. (1998) propose that the physical territory of the team is an important environmental factor that influences group structure. One of the key components of the environment is the location of competitive events. You may have heard of the term *home advantage*, which implies that teams will perform better when they play matches at home rather than away. There may be a number of reasons for this.

Critical thinking activity 8.3

Try to identify at least three reasons why you think a team may perform better at their home venue than at an away venue.

Critical thinking activity 8.3 continued

Your reasons may have included: at the team's home venue there are more supportive fans, the team is more familiar with the surroundings, and playing at home requires less travel and disruption to the team's usual routine.

So far we have seen that, according to Carron et al. (1998), there are two main factors that influence the structure of a group. Member attributes is the first factor that represents the different resources and skills possessed by the individual players that make up the team. A successful team has the right amount, variability and compatibility of these resources and skills. We also know that environmental factors influence team structure (e.g. where the team trains and competes). However, we now need to examine what we mean by group structure to fully understand how these two factors influence this construct.

Group structure

According to Carron et al. (1998), group structure includes both physical and psychological structures. The physical structure of a group refers to its hierarchical organisation. For example, a team may consist of a manager, three coaches, two sub-coaches, one physiotherapist and the players. This hierarchy within the team represents its physical structure. The psychological structure of the group includes the position of players within the group, their status, the group norms and roles. Let's look at the norms and roles that may occur in a group in more detail.

Group/team roles

During our discussion of the four stages involved in the development of a team we noted that, as the team evolves, some team members might begin to emerge as leaders. This is just one example of the different roles that will be adopted by individuals within a team.

A role is a pattern of expected behaviour and can be either formal or informal.

Formal roles might include the role of team captain or team kit manager. These roles are assigned to players, often by the coach, manager or other players, or the individuals themselves may volunteer.

Informal roles might include the team's motivator when the team is losing, the player who organises team social events, or the player whom others turn to for emotional support during times of difficulty. Informal roles are not assigned to players but often develop naturally as a result of different individuals' characteristics and strengths.

Think about a team that you are part of. If you do not play in a sports team, then you may want to think about your sport psychology seminar group, or any team or group that you belong to, such as a choir or a group of volunteers.

- What are the formal roles that exist in your group or team?
- Were these roles assigned by anyone?
- What are the informal roles that exist?
- How did these develop?

This activity should have helped you to reflect on the roles that exist in your group or team. Using the example of your sport psychology seminar group, the most obvious formal role is the role of teaching the seminar group, which has been assigned to your lecturer by your educational institution. If there are weeks when some class members are asked to present information to the rest of the class, then this peer-tutoring role is a second formal role that has been assigned in this situation. The students in the class also have a formal role, which involves listening and contributing to class discussions.

Let's consider the informal roles that might exist within your seminar group. For example, when a difficult question is asked the class may rely on one or two students to answer it. This informal role may have developed from their previous ability to answer questions and their confidence in doing so. There may be other roles, such as the class joker or the quiet student who does not answer any questions or makes few contributions to class discussions.

Think about your own informal role in your class; are you the quiet participant or the student who is relied on for all the answers? How did this role develop?

Two key features of team roles are *role clarity* and *role acceptance*. Team members must be clear about what their role entails, so the student who has the formal role of peer tutor on a specific week must be clear about the work she needs to do to fulfil this role, how to carry out this role in class and the consequences of her actions. This student must also accept her role as peer tutor in order for it to be effective. If she is unclear on what this role entails and unhappy that she has been assigned this role, she is unlikely to fulfil the role requirements. Thus she will fail to prepare for the seminar and the other students will gain little benefit from this.

Without role clarity, team members experience a high level of role ambiguity. This is defined as a lack of clear and consistent information on the expectations associated with an individual's role. Using the above example, if the student in the class accepts that her role is to do some research for the following seminar yet is unsure how much work she will need to do or how she will feed this back to the class, then her role is ambiguous.

Think about your own role in a team. How did your initial experiences or interpretations of your role within this team compare with your interpretations after six months? Initially, you may have been quite uncertain about your role in the team; however, as you gained experience and spent time within the team, your role may have become clearer. If so, this pattern reflects findings obtained by Eys et al. (2003), who examined role ambiguity in sports teams. They found that role ambiguity decreased from the start of the season to the end of the season, as, over time, athletes developed a clearer understanding of their role within the team (role clarity). Consistent with this, they also found that veteran athletes had lower levels of role ambiguity than first-year athletes.

Group norms

Within any team there will be certain norms that develop which represent standards of behaviour that are expected of team members. These norms enhance the identity of the team by drawing the team members together and providing information about what is expected of them. Norms can be:

- *Prescribed* – appropriate behaviour in the team situation;
- *Proscribed* – inappropriate behaviour in the team situation;
- *Permitted* – permitted but not required behaviour within the team;
- *Preferred* – preferred but not required behaviour within the team.

Critical thinking activity 8.5

Let's look at an example of how each of these norms functions in a team situation. As you read the following example try to identify the type of norm that John encounters.

John has recently joined a basketball team. It is important that he learns the team norms so that he is sure about the behaviour expected of him within this team. When he first arrives at practice, John is invited to join the team warm up. He notices that one team member has chosen to do his own warm up rather than joining the rest of the team members. He believes that joining the group warm up is a P_____ norm. The coach blows her whistle and all of the players jog in to meet her. This is a P_____ norm.

While they listen to the coach talk, John bounces the basketball that he is holding. The other players stop and look at him. Paying full attention to the coach is therefore a P_____ norm. The coach selects the first drill that the team will perform.

As the drill starts, John notices that a couple of players on the team are quite vocal and shout encouragement to the other team members. John is a little shy and does not want to do this but doesn't feel that he has to shout as there are a number of other team members who are also quite quiet. This is a P_____ norm.

Let's check through your responses. The first example is a *preferred norm*, as it is preferred that most team members join in the team warm up. All do, except for one, but this behaviour is still acceptable to the group. The second example is a *prescribed norm*; the coach does not instruct the players to come in to meet her but it is an appropriate behaviour within the group. The third example, where John bounces the ball while the coach is talking, is a *proscribed norm*. This is inappropriate behaviour for the situation and the team members make this clear to John through their non-verbal communication.

Finally, the fourth example, where John notices that some people are shouting encouragement, is a *permitted norm*. It is a behaviour that is accepted in the team but there is no requirement for all team members to conform to this norm.

Thus, within any team, there are specific norms of behaviour and specific roles that are played by individuals. These norms and roles are part of the group structure, which influences the next component of Carron et al.'s (1998) model: team cohesion. Before we examine this factor in more detail, take a moment to consider how, as the model suggests, member attributes and group environment might influence group structure.

You may have identified that group size influences the number and availability of team roles and the types of personalities in the team may influence the group norms that develop. If a team changes its environment, new roles and norms may develop; for example, when travelling to an international tournament, new norms for behavioural conduct may be developed by the team and new roles may be needed to meet the changed environmental demands.

Team cohesion

> Cohesion is the bond that accounts for the fact that many athletes with differing needs, personalities, motives, and goals can be formed together into one strong effective group.
>
> (Carron et al., 1998, p. 19)

A cohesive team sticks together in the pursuit of goals and objectives so that the needs of the team members are satisfied. It makes sense to assume that a more cohesive team will be more successful. However, Carron and Chelladurai (1981) proposed that cohesion will mainly be associated with enhanced team success in *interactive sports*. This means that team cohesion leads to performance improvement in sports such as football and netball because the nature of the sport requires interaction between players. In sports such as gymnastics, team cohesion will have a reduced, or little, effect on team success. Although an individual may be part of a gymnastics team, no interaction is required between the gymnasts on the team to perform well. Consequently, team cohesion is less likely to influence team performance. However, it is also important to recognise that team cohesion is not stable and consequently may change as the team develops and experiences changes in characteristics of the team such as member attributes and team environment.

Two forms of cohesion have been identified:

* *Task cohesion* – team members all strive to achieve the same goals, such as playing well and winning competitions.
* *Social cohesion* – team members like each other and enjoy spending time together.

Research focus

In 2002, Carron et al. examined the relationship between task cohesion and team success in 294 Canadian intercollegiate and club athletes from basketball and soccer teams. Participants completed the Group Environment Questionnaire (Carron et al., 1985) to assess team cohesion two weeks before the end of their competitive season. From their responses, Carron and colleagues calculated overall team cohesion scores for each team. They also measured the success level of each team by calculating each team's total winning percentage for the games that they played in their regular competitive schedule.

Results from the study provided evidence of a very strong relationship between task cohesion and success in sports teams. They also showed that perceptions of team cohesion were relatively consistent among members of the same team; in other words, all the players within a team shared the same views on how cohesive their team was. The authors suggest that coaches and sport psychologists working with interactive teams should develop effective team-building strategies in an attempt to improve task cohesion, as this is likely to be associated with greater team success.

Group processes

Once any team has been formed, it is important to recognise that it will continue to develop. To aid this development, Locke and Latham (1984) suggested that team goals are preferred over individual goals in sports that require a high level of team interaction. More recently, Senécal et al. (2008) also found that athletes who set team goals have higher perceptions of cohesion at the end of the season than athletes who do not set team goals.

As the team develops, there will be both cooperation and competition between players as they compete for places on the team, for certain positions, or even for the attention of the coach. Yet while they are playing they need to be able to cooperate with each other in order to be successful. For instance, the team will develop an accepted style of interpersonal communication that matches the personalities and goals of the team members.

As the team develops and evolves, it develops a sense of *collective efficacy*. This refers to team members' shared beliefs about the team's capabilities of achieving a desired outcome, such as winning a tournament or gaining promotion to a higher league. This collective efficacy will influence the performance of the team. Researchers such as Greenlees et al. (1999) have shown that, if individuals perceive a high level of collective efficacy within their team, they exert more effort into a subsequent task following failure. Consequently, teams with a high level of collective efficacy are likely to perform better, but, when they do fail, will continue to invest more effort than teams with a low level of collective efficacy.

The final outcome: individual and group productivity

Throughout this chapter we have discussed the factors that help to produce a highly productive team. For sports teams, this productivity could include winning most of the team's matches, showing improvement across the season, or even being a motivated team in which each player invests their maximum effort. Each of these outcomes requires both individual and group productivity. In fact, for the group to be productive as a whole, each individual must contribute to this productivity.

Critical thinking activity 8.6

Now that we have considered the whole of Carron et al's (1998) model, test your knowledge of the factors that we have discussed. The following paragraph is a summary of the model with some of the terms omitted. See if you can fill in the gaps without referring back to the earlier sections.

Carron's model of group P_____ allows us to understand how a team can perform to the best of its ability. There are two factors that lead to the development of a team structure. These are M_____, A_____ and group E_____ factors. These factors include the players' resources and the physical territory in which the team exists. Within this group structure there is a hierarchy of team members. These team members have their own expected patterns of behaviour, known as team N_____. They also have specific team roles, which can be F_____ or I_____.

To be successful, an interactive team needs a high level of task C_____, which refers to the bond between team members as they strive towards achieving team goals. However it is important to remember that the team dynamic is not stable. Instead it is a P_____, which can change and develop based on the team goals, levels of cooperation and communication within the team, and the team's C_____ E_____.

Check your answers against the earlier explanations of each part of Carron et al's (1998) model. If there were parts that you could not complete, you may wish to re-read this section.

See Study Skills Activity 8.2 in the internet chapter for an additional activity.

Further reading (group dynamics)

Carron, AV, Hausenblaus, HA and Eys, MA (1998) *Group dynamics in sport.* Morgantown, USA: Fitness Information Technology.
This book will help to consolidate your understanding of Carron et al's (1998) model of group productivity.

Carron, AV, Eys, MA and Burke, SM (2007) Team cohesion: nature, correlates, and development. In S Jowett and D Lavallee (eds), *Social psychology in sport*, pp. 91–101. Leeds: Human Kinetics.
This gives useful information on team cohesion and strategies to enhance cohesion in a sports team.

Review

We began this chapter by highlighting the similarities and differences between a team and a group (LO 1). We then examined how a group could become a team using a four-stage model of team development, which you then used to interpret your own experiences of team development (LO 2). Following this, we introduced Carron et al.' model of group productivity (LO 3). We used an example of a cricket club to explain Steiner's model of group productivity (LO 4). We also identified that within any team there will be certain team norms and roles that are adopted by team members (LO 5). Finally, we looked at how we define a cohesive team and how this may impact on performance (LO 6). We emphasised that team dynamics represent a continually evolving process in response to changes in collective efficacy, communication and competition within the team.

Work through the review questions in Study Skills Activity 8.3 in the internet chapter for an additional activity.

Chapter 9

Exercise psychology

Joanne Thatcher

Chapter focus

This chapter focuses on key topics within exercise psychology:

- exercise adherence and barriers;
- models of exercise behaviour;
- strategies to increase exercise behaviour;
- positive and negative outcomes of exercise.

We first consider common barriers that prevent people from beginning and sticking to exercise, then discuss some of the models of exercise behaviour that exercise psychologists use to understand why some people exercise regularly whilst others don't. Following this, we consider strategies that exercise psychologists might use to change or maintain exercise behaviour. Finally, we look at the psychological benefits (e.g. decreased anxiety) and potentially negative consequences (e.g. exercise dependence) of exercise.

Learning outcomes

This chapter is designed to help you:
1. Identify barriers to exercise and factors affecting exercise adherence;
2. Explain the proposals of the theory of planned behaviour (Ajzen, 1985) and the stages of change model (Prochaska and DiClemente, 1982);
3. Understand selected strategies for increasing exercise behaviour;
4. Describe the psychological effects of exercise and the reasons proposed to explain these effects;
5. Define primary and secondary exercise dependence;
6. Describe the link between exercise dependence and eating disorders.

Exercise participation and adherence

You may be surprised to learn how low physical activity levels are in the general population, with only 40 per cent of men and 28 per cent of women in the UK achieving the recommended levels of physical activity (30 minutes on at least five days each week; National Health Service Information Centre, 2008). This is a major concern as there are numerous physical health risks associated with inactivity, such as coronary heart disease and diabetes, and physical activity can help to maintain physical health and prevent psychological ill-health.

Clearly, with such a high percentage of sedentary adults in the UK, getting people to become active is not easy. However, starting an exercise programme is easier than sticking to one, as approximately 50 per cent of people who start an exercise programme drop out within six months. To try to understand why people are sedentary or don't adhere to exercise, let's start by considering why people don't exercise, or *barriers to exercise*.

Critical thinking activity 9.1

Talk to people you know who don't do any exercise or physical activity and ask them what stops them from exercising. Record their answers.

I'm sure that your list will include most of the barriers in Table 9.1, as these were the main barriers to activity in population surveys from Canada and the UK.

Let's imagine that we can overcome these barriers and get someone exercising (and we'll look at strategies for doing this later). What are the factors that will help them to stick/adhere to exercise?

Table 9.1: Most common barriers to physical activity (Canadian Fitness and Lifestyle Research Institute, 1996; Sports Council and Health Education Authority, 1992)

Lack of time	Physical factors
	    Overweight
	    Injured

Lack of energy	Emotional factors
	    Too embarrassed to exercise
	    Not seeing yourself as an 'exerciser'

Lack of motivation	Motivational factors
	    No energy
	    Don't enjoy exercise

	Time factors
	    Too many work commitments
	    Childcare

	External factors
	    No exercise facilities nearby
	    Can't afford exercise facilities

Compare your lists with those in Table 9.2. Here, I've subdivided the factors further and listed those that research has shown are associated with *higher levels of adherence*. *See Study Skills Activity 9.1 in the internet chapter for an additional activity.*

Table 9.2: Factors resulting in high levels of adherence to exercise

Personal factors	Environmental factors
Demographic variables	*Social variables*
• Younger people	• Social support from friends, family and exercise instructor
• Males	• Family influence and history of exercise
• White collar workers (e.g. office jobs)	• Attending a cohesive exercise group/socialising with group members
• More educated people	
• Higher socio-economic status	
Behavioural variables	*Physical environment*
• Previously participated in exercise/ an exercise programme	• Good weather
• Non-smokers	• Actual access to exercise facilities
	• Perceived access to exercise facilities
	• Less disruption to usual routine
Beliefs and attitudes	*Physical activity characteristics*
• Low perceived barriers	• Group-based rather than an individual exercise programme
• Enjoy exercise	• Good exercise leader
• Expect to gain benefits from exercise	• Exercising at moderate intensity
• Strong intentions to exercise	• Perception that exercise is not too much effort
• High levels of perceived health/fitness	
• Confident that can exercise	
• Self-motivated to exercise	
• More motivated for social aspects, enjoyment and feeling competent than motives like losing weight or toning up	

Further reading (barriers and adherence)

Biddle, SJH and Mutrie, N (2008) *Psychology of physical activity: determinants, well-being and interventions*, 2nd edition, pp. 39–53. London: Routledge.
Discusses research examining barriers to exercise, comparing dropouts and adherers to exercise, and discusses exercise motives that aren't considered in this chapter.

Models of exercise behaviour

Understanding barriers to exercise and factors affecting exercise adherence is useful but, as we highlighted in Chapter 6, this type of information only gives us a descriptive picture of people's exercise behaviour. We need to look at models or theories to fully understand and change exercise behaviour. Although there are others, those currently most widely used by exercise psychologists are self-determination theory (SDT), the theory of planned behaviour and the transtheoretical model. Return to Chapter 6 to recap on SDT.

The theory of planned behaviour (TPB)

The TPB was developed by Ajzen in 1985 and is shown in Figure 9.1. Ajzen's central proposal is that we form plans of what we aim to do (*intentions*) and these influence what we actually do (*behaviour*). The stronger our intentions, the more likely we are to carry out the behaviour. For instance, tomorrow, I intend to go for a run after work, so I take my running kit to work, and, though it may be raining when I finish work, because I've formed a strong intention to run, I'm more likely to do so.

Ajzen also suggests how we form our intentions, proposing that these are based on our feelings and opinions about the behaviour (*attitudes*) and whether or not others see the behaviour as something that is appropriate and acceptable for us to do (*subjective norms*). The model also suggests that our attitudes towards a behaviour are determined by what we feel we will gain from the behaviour in relation to what we might lose from doing it (*perceived consequences*). So, we weigh up the costs of the behaviour against the benefits we'll gain from it. Subjective norms are influenced by the opinions of family, friends and society (*significant others*) about whether or not this is an appropriate behaviour for us to do.

Figure 9.1: Theory of planned behaviour (Ajzen, 1985)

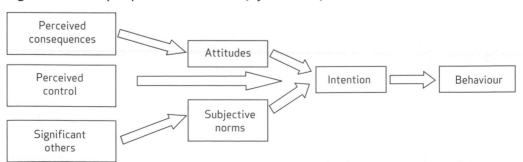

Returning to my example of going for a run after work, my attitude towards exercise and running is very positive; I enjoy running and, although it takes up some of my time, takes effort and on this occasion I will get wet, for me, the benefits (enjoyment, staying fit, etc.) outweigh such costs. I, and significant others around me, perceive that exercise is something I should do and they support my exercise.

Although I form strong intentions to exercise and this normally results in me exercising, sometimes I don't feel that I have control over whether or not I follow my intentions. Using my running example, we can see what this construct is. Let's imagine that, as I'm getting ready to go for my run, my boss presents me with some work that urgently needs completing. This is an unseen variable in my plans, and, probably muttering under my breath, I now consider that I can't run because something is stopping me. In other words, I no longer have *perceived control* over my behaviour. This construct was added to the original theory (the theory of reasoned action; Ajzen and Fishbein, 1980) to provide a fuller picture of the factors that predict intentions and behaviour.

It's important to note that Ajzen called this construct *perceived* control, as often we feel that we don't have control over our behaviour whereas, in fact, this does not reflect reality. For example, how often have you heard someone complain that they 'Just don't have time to exercise' and then notice that they spend five hours a day watching television or playing computer games? Perhaps here perceived and actual control do not match.

There's a lot of support for the use of the TPB for predicting exercise behaviour. Hagger et al. (2002) reviewed 72 studies published between 1975 and 2001, and intentions predicted whether or not people were physically active and attitudes were the most important predictor of these intentions. Therefore it seems that interventions that change people's attitudes towards physical activity are most likely to result in increased physical activity (ibid.). A study that provides you with an idea of how the TPB is tested in research and which shows the cross-cultural generalisability of the theory is presented below.

Research focus

Hagger et al. (2007) tested the TPB for predicting physical activity in teenagers from a number of countries: Britain, Estonia, Greece, Hungary and Singapore. They hypothesised that, whilst the TPB would predict behaviour in all these different cultures, there would be some cultural differences in the effects of attitudes and subjective norms on intentions to exercise.

They collected data at two time points: at time one, participants completed measures of their attitudes towards exercise, perceived subjective norms, perceived behavioural control over their exercise behaviour and intentions to exercise over the next five weeks. Five weeks later, at time two, participants reported their exercise over the past five weeks. The study's design is summarised below.

TIME ONE	TIME TWO
Measures:	Measures:
• Attitudes	• Exercise behaviour
• Subjective norms	
• Perceived control	(five weeks later)
• Intentions	

Results supported their first hypothesis, as the TPB variables did predict behaviour in all of the different samples and in the way in which the theory proposes, demonstrating its cross-cultural applicability.

Their second hypothesis also received some support: in the British and Estonian samples, attitude had a stronger influence on intentions. Subjective norm had a stronger influence on intentions in the Hungarian sample and no influence on intention in the remaining samples. Finally, in the Hungarian sample, perceived behavioural control was significantly lower than in the other samples.

These results provide strong support for TPB proposals, as the predicted relationships generalise across samples from different cultures. They also tell us that, although the overall predictions of the theory are upheld across cultures, there are some cultural differences in the strength of the relationships between the different TPB variables. For example, in the Hungarian sample, social factors (measured by subjective norms) were more important for forming these children's intentions to exercise, so interventions for increasing their exercise may be more effective if targeted at changing subjective norms rather than attitudes.

Critical thinking activity 9.3

Think about your own exercise behaviour and about someone you know who doesn't regularly exercise. Produce models to illustrate how the TPB explains your own regular exercise and the sedentary behaviour of someone who doesn't exercise.

The stages of change model

Critical thinking activity 9.4

Consider the case studies below and decide which category in Figure 9.2 best describes each person.

* Donna has decided to get in shape after having her first baby. She has bought an outfit for the gym and a pair of trainers, has been to one aerobics class and plans to go regularly in the future.
* Dafydd (Donna's husband) has decided to be a good role model for his son. He has been exercising for the past six months and intends to continue so he can play football with his son.

Critical thinking activity 9.4 continued

- John's main activities are watching TV and drinking. He never thinks about exercise and he has no plans to start exercising.
- Claire wants to lose weight and is thinking about taking up exercise to her help do so.
- Mark is a business executive who eats large business lunches and has a stressful, busy job. He is aware of the dangers of his lifestyle, so to keep healthy over the past year he has been going to the gym and playing squash.

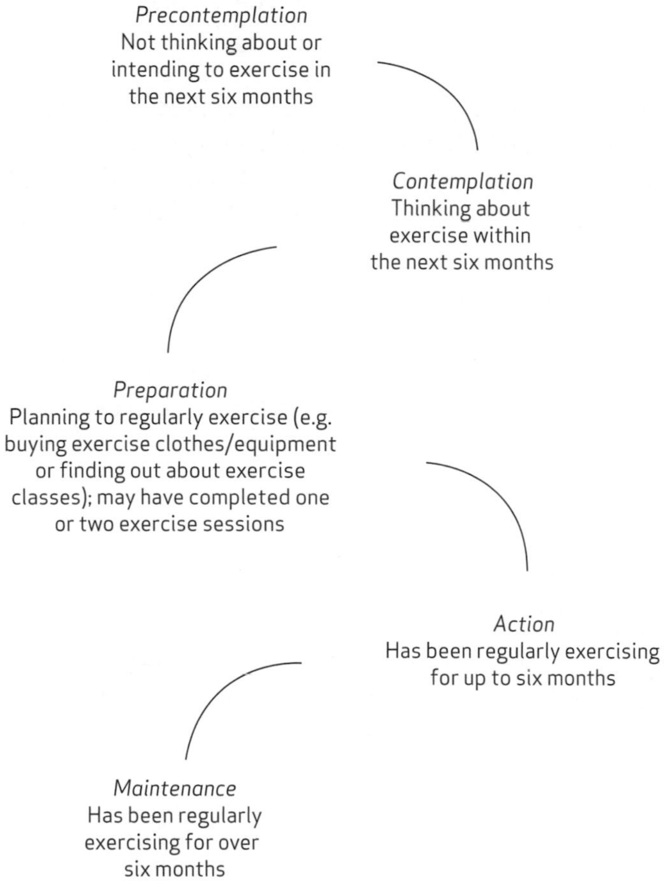

Precontemplation
Not thinking about or intending to exercise in the next six months

**Figure 9.2:
Stages of change model**

Contemplation
Thinking about exercise within the next six months

Preparation
Planning to regularly exercise (e.g. buying exercise clothes/equipment or finding out about exercise classes); may have completed one or two exercise sessions

Action
Has been regularly exercising for up to six months

Maintenance
Has been regularly exercising for over six months

Did you get them right?

- John – precontemplation
- Claire – contemplation
- Donna – preparation
- Dafydd –action
- Mark – maintenance

The categories in Figure 9.2 represent the different *stages of change* proposed by Prochaska and DiClemente (1982) in their transtheoretical model (TTM), which are used in research examining exercise behaviour. The stages of change model is a commonly used name for the TTM as it proposes that people move through different stages, from precontemplation to maintenance, when changing from being sedentary to a regular exerciser.

You may notice that there are no arrows connecting the different stages because, whilst we can move sequentially between the different stages, it's equally likely that we may miss out a stage, or move backwards between the stages if we experience a *relapse* in our behaviour. For example, you may decide to eat more healthily, things are going well and you move into the action stage, but then you go on holiday and forget about your healthy eating plan. After the holiday you return to the contemplation stage – considering whether or not you want to make the effort to start again in changing your eating behaviour.

So, changing our behaviour is not always a straightforward, linear process, and your personal experiences and those of people you know will likely reflect this. It's important to bear in mind that we have all reached different stages of change in relation to exercise when we consider strategies for changing different individuals' behaviour.

Personal reflection 9.1

Think of a health-related behaviour that you have changed (e.g. exercise, healthy eating). Identify the stages that you went through and any relapses you may have experienced. What might have triggered these relapses?

Characteristics of the stages of change

Researchers have identified characteristics of the different stages of change, factors that will influence what stage we currently experience and our movement between stages. Take a moment to reflect on the following questions, then check your responses with the information below (from a review by Marshall and Biddle, 2001).

As we move through the stages of change:

- How do you think physical activity levels change?
- How do you think self-efficacy to exercise changes?
- How do you think the perceived benefits and costs (pros and cons) of exercise change? What are some of these pros and cons?

Stages of change and physical activity

People at the later stages of change are more physically active than those at the earlier stages. The largest difference in physical activity levels between stages is between preparation and action. This makes sense, as people in the preparation stage are just beginning to be physically active and those in the action phase are regularly active.

Stages of change and self-efficacy

People in the later stages of change have higher levels of self-efficacy to exercise than those at the earlier stages. Also, increasing our self-efficacy can help us move towards the later stages.

Stages of change and pros and cons of exercise

Perceived benefits (pros) of exercise increase and costs (cons) decrease as we move through the stages of change. The biggest increase in perceived benefits and decrease in perceived costs occur between precontemplation and contemplation, which is not surprising as the individual has gone from not considering exercise to contemplating if they will start to exercise. Between the action and maintenance stages, perceived benefits increase least and perceived costs decrease least, which again makes sense as people are not changing their behaviour as they move between these stages but are maintaining a change they've already made. Examples of the perceived costs and benefits of exercise are provided below (Fahrenwald and Walker, 2003).

Pros/benefits of exercise	Cons/costs of exercise
• sense of personal accomplishment	• physical activity is tiring
• improved muscle strength and tone	• physical activity causes fatigue
• improved mental health	• physical activity is hard work

Stages of change and behaviour change strategies

Prochaska and DiClemente (1982) proposed two different groups of strategies for changing behaviour (which they called *processes of change*): *cognitive* and *behavioural*. They suggested that the cognitive processes are more effective at the early stages of change, as the goal is to encourage people to think differently about exercise and about themselves in relation to exercise: to change people's beliefs about and attitudes towards exercise. At the later stages, they propose that the behavioural processes are more effective, as these are aimed at helping people to modify their exercise behaviour and maintain this behaviour. Table 9.3 lists these strategies/processes, providing an example to illustrate each.

Whilst research has shown that all ten processes of change are used for increasing exercise behaviour, cognitive processes are not used more during the earlier stages of change and behavioural processes more at the later stages of change, as Prochaska and DiClemente (1982) suggested. The most processes were used to move from

Table 9.3: Processes of change (Prochaska and DiClemente, 1982)

Cognitive processes	Behavioural processes
Consciousness raising Providing information about different forms of exercise and its benefits, etc.	*Counter-conditioning* Substitute unhealthy behaviours with healthy alternatives
Dramatic relief Encouraging reflection on the health implications of not exercising	*Helping relationships* Social support from others (e.g. exercising with a friend)
Environmental re-evaluation Providing information about local opportunities for physical activity	*Reinforcement management* Receiving rewards for exercising
Self re-evaluation Encouraging re-evaluation of one's values and attitudes towards exercise	*Self-liberation* Developing a contract or an agreement to exercise
Social liberation Support from society and the community to exercise (e.g. community walking groups)	*Stimulus control* Using reminders to discourage sedentary behaviour and increase the likelihood of exercising

precontemplation to contemplation and the least from action to maintenance. So when we have developed a regular exercise habit, we don't need additional strategies to maintain it.

Further reading (models of exercise behaviour)

Biddle, SJH and Mutrie, N (2008) *Psychology of physical activity: determinants, well-being and interventions*, 2nd edition, Chapters 3 and 6. London: Routledge.
Provides detailed critical discussions of the models we've examined and introduces you to others that we haven't covered here.

See Study Skills Activity 9.2 in the internet chapter for an additional activity.

Changing exercise behaviour

We previously highlighted a range of barriers to exercise, which partially help to explain the high levels of inactivity in the UK. A major challenge for exercise psychologists is therefore to help people to overcome these barriers. In this section we will consider one cognitive and one behavioural strategy that could be used to increase exercise behaviour. We don't have space to look at all the strategies that could be used but you can read about others in the Further Reading.

Decision balance (cognitive strategy/process)

The aim of this strategy is to help people to think about their own perceived pros and cons of exercise, asking them to consider the benefits and costs of exercise for themselves and others who are significant to them. Lewis et al. (2002) suggested that, whilst some studies have found that decision balance-based interventions lead to increases in physical activity, this was not found consistently in all the studies they reviewed. They suggested that possibly people make changes in their decision balance concerning the benefits and costs of exercise before they begin an intervention, which may explain these inconsistent findings.

Critical thinking activity 9.5

Imagine that you are a 30-year-old married mother of three young children who doesn't exercise. Try to complete the decision balance sheet shown in Figure 9.3 in your imagined role.

Figure 9.3: Your example decision balance sheet

Benefits of exercise for me	Costs of exercise to me
Benefits of exercise for significant others	Costs of exercise to significant others

Figure 9.4 provides an example of what this young woman's decision balance sheet might look like; of course, yours may not look exactly the same. The sheet shows that, when she weighs up the pros and cons of exercise, our subject perceives more benefits

Figure 9.4: Completed example of a decision balance sheet

Benefits of exercise for me • Lose weight • Time to myself away from the family • Improved health	Costs of exercise to me • Already busy, may increase my stress trying to fit exercise in • Takes effort and will tire me out
Benefits of exercise for significant others • Fit enough to go on bike rides with husband • More energy to play with children • De-stressed when spending time with family	Costs of exercise to significant others • Paying for childcare and exercise facilities • Spend less time with children

than costs, which may encourage her to change her attitude towards exercise and start to become active.

Stimulus control (behavioural strategy/process)

This strategy involves manipulating cues to increase the likelihood that I'll do some exercise. For example, if I take my gym kit to work, I am more likely to go straight to the gym after work than if I have to come home for it, as other things may distract me. Another example is when a friend texts me an hour before our aerobics class to remind me to get ready in time for the class (this also includes social support). Blamey et al. (1995) used stimulus control by placing a poster in a public building that encouraged people to use the stairs instead of the lift. When the poster was displayed, more people used the stairs.

See Study Skills Activity 9.3 in the internet chapter for an additional activity.

Further reading (changing exercise behaviour)

Biddle, SJH and Mutrie, N (2008) *Psychology of physical activity: determinants, well-being and interventions*, 2nd edition, Chapter 11. London: Routledge.
A detailed review of interventions and the different contexts in which they can be used.

Psychological effects of exercise

How does exercising make you feel? Complete the measure of feeling states (the Exercise-Induced Feeling Inventory; Gauvin and Rejeski, 1993) in Table 9.4 before and after your next few exercise sessions. This questionnaire has four *subscales*, measuring: positive engagement, revitalisation, physical exhaustion and tranquillity. To calculate

Table 9.4: Exercise induced feeling inventory

	Do not feel	Feel slightly	Feel moderately	Feel strongly	Feel very strongly
1. Refreshed	0	1	2	3	4
2. Calm	0	1	2	3	4
3. Fatigued	0	1	2	3	4
4. Enthusiastic	0	1	2	3	4
5. Relaxed	0	1	2	3	4
6. Energetic	0	1	2	3	4
7. Happy	0	1	2	3	4
8. Tired	0	1	2	3	4
9. Revived	0	1	2	3	4
10. Peaceful	0	1	2	3	4
11. Worn out	0	1	2	3	4
12. Upbeat	0	1	2	3	4

your score on positive engagement, sum your ratings on questions 4, 7 and 12; for revitalisation: 1, 6 and 9; for physical exhaustion: 3, 8 and 11, and for tranquillity: 2, 5 and 10. Look at your pre- and post-exercise scores; do you notice any changes or patterns?

If you noticed that following exercise you reported higher levels of positive states (like feeling refreshed) and lower levels of negative states (like feeling anxious), then your responses match those in the general population. Exercise has been shown to result in more positive and less negative feelings (Biddle, 2000). These short-term changes are known as *acute effects* but exercise can also have more long-term psychological effects, or *chronic effects*.

Research has shown that, over the long-term, exercise can help people to increase their sense of well-being, perceive a higher quality of life, cope better with stress and decrease their chances of suffering from anxiety or depression (Biddle and Mutrie, 2008; Mutrie, 2000; Taylor, 2000). These results have been demonstrated in clinical (i.e. people suffering from a clinically diagnosed condition like cardiovascular disease or clinical depression) and non-clinical (i.e. people not suffering from clinical conditions) populations. So, exercise can play a *preventative role* in psychological health, for example preventing the likelihood that someone will develop a depressive disorder, and a *treatment role* by helping to treat people who suffer from clinical disorders. In clinical populations, exercise is used as an *adjunctive therapy*; not as a replacement for the patient's usual treatment, like medication or counselling, but in addition to these treatments.

Exercise can also benefit our self-perceptions, such as self-esteem, which represent our evaluations of ourselves. Spence et al. (2005) reviewed the findings from 113 studies, conducted between 1968 and 2003, to evaluate the effects of exercise on global self-esteem in adults. They focused on experimental studies that included a control group and an experimental group that received an exercise or physical activity intervention for over a week. Their results revealed that exercise produced small but significant improvements in global self-esteem and, if participants experienced greater increases in physical fitness levels, they experienced greater increases in global self-esteem. They also identified that exercise and lifestyle programmes produced increases in global self-esteem but programmes focused on skills training did not. As the authors note, these results suggest that participation in programmes designed to develop physical fitness, and not physical competence, seem more likely to increase global self-esteem in adults.

The Further Reading discusses some of the details of research findings concerning the relationship between exercise and psychological health, but why does exercise help to improve short- and long-term psychological health?

Critical thinking activity 9.6

Ask people you know who exercise regularly to complete the following sentence and note down their responses: *'Exercise makes me feel good because. . .'* Also jot down your own answers to this question.

Explanations for the psychological effects of exercise

Some possible responses to the sentence in Critical thinking activity 9.6 are included in Figure 9.5. So, people have a lot of reasons why they think exercise makes them feel good but which of these is the right answer? We can't say with any certainty at the moment but what we can say is that all these reasons contribute to the psychological benefits we can gain from exercise. These explanations are summarised below.

Figure 9.5: Possible reasons for the exercise 'feel good' effect

Mastery hypothesis ('I feel like I've achieved something when I do a good session') Exercise may offer a sense of *mastery*, like the sense of achievement you get when you've completed a hard session in the gym (e.g. Harter's competence motivation theory, 1981).	*Interaction hypothesis* ('I enjoy spending time with friends when I exercise') Exercise may offer opportunities for *social interaction*: making new friends, meeting old friends and feeling part of a social group (e.g. Fox, 1999).
Distraction hypothesis ('It's time out from my everyday worries and stresses') Exercise may offer distraction from everyday worries and stresses. So when you need a break from exam revision you may find it helps to go for a run or play badminton (e.g. Breus and O'Connor, 1998).	*Endorphin hypothesis* ('I get a buzz when I've worked hard') Exercise results in the release of endorphins ('feel good' hormones) into the bloodstream. This is certainly a possibility but is less easy to investigate than other explanations (e.g. Hoffman, 1997).

See Study Skills Activity 9.4 in the internet chapter for an additional activity.

Further reading (psychological effects of exercise)

Biddle, SJH and Mutrie, N (2008) *Psychology of physical activity: determinants, well-being and interventions*, 2nd edition, Chapter 8. London: Routledge.
An up-to-date review of our current knowledge in this area.

Negative aspects of exercise

I'm sure you've all heard the proverb: 'One man's meat is another man's poison.' In other words, what may be good for one person may not be for another, and exercise is no exception. Whilst the majority of people experience positive psychological outcomes from exercise, for some, there are negative implications. Two key negative outcomes are exercise dependence and eating disorders and we will take a look at these now.

CASE STUDY A

Michael is a keen bodybuilder. He attends the gym for an hour after work on three weekdays and for three hours every Saturday. Sunday is his rest day, when he hangs out with friends, and he spends a couple of evenings each week rehearsing with the band in which he plays guitar. He recently suffered a back injury so took two weeks off training and found that he enjoyed the extra time he had practising his guitar and socialising with friends. When his work as a graphic designer gets busy, Michael cuts down on his training to accommodate the extra hours he needs to spend at work.

CASE STUDY B

Kathy is a keen runner and runs every day for about two hours; she runs twice at weekends, in the morning and the evening. She runs the same routes so she can keep track of how far she's run each week and the number of calories she's burned. She's had a niggling calf injury for months but hasn't taken any time off running. She rarely socialises, as it would mean missing out on training sessions, and spends her holidays at training camps. If she's forced to miss a training session because of work commitments she feels grumpy, irritable, sluggish and overweight.

How do these exercisers compare? Exercise plays an important role in both their lives and they both follow a structured, regular exercise routine. However, there are some key differences between them.

For Michael, exercise is just a part of his life; he makes time for other interests and socialising with friends. However, Kathy's life revolves around her running and she is unwilling to compromise her training to make time for other interests or socialising.

If Michael becomes injured or is unusually busy at work, he doesn't train and experiences no negative psychological effects from doing so. In contrast, Kathy sticks rigidly to her training regime despite injuries, experiences negative emotions when she is prevented from training and plans her holidays around her training.

Although there are some similarities between Michael and Kathy, based on the differences between them we can describe Michael as a *committed exerciser* and Kathy as *exercise dependent*. Michael has a healthy approach to exercise, whilst Kathy's approach is unhealthy. Kathy's case study illustrates the key characteristics of exercise dependence and these are summarised below.

Characteristics of exercise dependence:

- A rigid, daily, abnormal* exercise schedule.
- Exercise is the main priority in life, above work, holidays, hobbies, etc.
- Severe withdrawal symptoms when you can't exercise which can only be relieved by exercise.
- Exercise interferes with your relationships with others, as it is prioritised above family and friends.
- Disturbed psychological functioning, such as extreme body image concerns, neuroticism or disordered eating (anorexia and bulimia nervosa; see below for definitions).

*'Abnormal' must be considered in the context of each person's lifestyle. For an elite athlete or exercise instructor, four to five hours of exercise per day is normal; whereas for the general population, with jobs and families, this is an abnormal level of exercise.

Anorexia Nervosa	*Bulimia Nervosa*
Intense fear of gaining weight	Bingeing and purging
Significant weight loss	Fear of being unable to stop eating
Menstruation stops	Self-evaluation defined by appearance
Disturbed body image	Aware of a problem
Unaware of a problem	
	(Thompson, 1987)

Let's take a closer look at the link between exercise dependence and disordered eating. Clearly, this is a particularly unhealthy outcome of exercise dependence and therefore this association has attracted the attention of exercise psychology researchers.

Exercise dependence and eating disorders

You may have noticed in Kathy's description that she monitors the number of calories she burns during exercise. Although results are not conclusive and do not apply to all athletic populations, reviews have revealed that athletes may be at more risk than the general population for developing eating disorders (Hausenblas and Carron, 1999; Smolak et al., 2000). It has also been suggested that people who are exercise dependent have an increased chance of suffering from an eating disorder, although there is less research evidence to support this relationship. As researchers observed that many individuals classed as exercise dependent also suffer from an eating disorder (Bamber et al., 2000), this led to the identification of two different forms of exercise dependence: *primary* and *secondary exercise dependence*.

Primary exercise dependence refers to a dependence on the exercise itself, and not on any secondary outcomes that can be gained from exercising, such as weight loss or increased muscle mass. Hausenblas and Giacobbi (2004, p. 1266) quite aptly refer to this as a 'craving for exercise'.

In comparison, secondary exercise dependence refers to a dependence on exercise as a form of weight control in people who suffer from an eating disorder. So, these individuals are not dependent on the *exercise* but on its use as a way of losing weight. There is some debate over whether or not primary exercise dependence actually exists or if exercise dependence only exists as part of an eating disorder (Bamber et al., 2000). The picture is not quite clear at the moment, but what we do know is that research investigating exercise dependence has revealed far more cases of secondary than primary exercise dependence. Nevertheless, some cases of primary exercise dependence have been noted (e.g. Blaydon et al., 2004), and it seems that, regardless of whether or not the individual shows signs of primary or secondary exercise dependence, both conditions have potentially damaging effects on psychological and physical health.

See Study Skills Activity 9.5 in the internet chapter for an additional activity.

Further reading (negative aspects of exercise)

Kerr, JH, Lindner, KJ and Blaydon, M (2007) *Exercise dependence*, pp. 113–135. London: Routledge
Presents an interesting discussion of studies in this area, with useful illustrative quotes from athletes. Some terms used from reversal theory may be unfamiliar to you but they won't stop you following the arguments.

Review

In this chapter we have considered the key topics in exercise psychology, beginning by examining barriers to exercise and exercise adherence, including both personal and environmental factors (LO 1). We developed this by considering two of the major theories that are used to understand why people do and don't exercise: the stages of change model and the theory of planned behaviour (LO 2). We saw that people move between stages when changing their behaviour, can relapse to earlier stages and show different characteristics (e.g. self-efficacy level) at different stages. The TPB explains how attitudes, perceived control and subjective norms predict intentions to exercise, which predict our exercise behaviour. We identified the processes of change proposed within the stages of change model and looked in detail at a cognitive (decision balance) and a behavioural (stimulus control) behaviour change strategy (LO 3).

We then considered the psychological benefits of exercise, such as decreased anxiety and increased self-esteem, noting both the preventative and treatment roles of exercise (LO 4). We also discussed possible explanations for the potential psychological benefits of exercise: mastery, distraction, social interaction and endorphin release (LO 4).

Finally, we focused on potential negative outcomes of exercise, defining primary and secondary exercise dependence as reliance on the exercise itself and reliance on the exercise as a form of weight control, respectively (LO 5), highlighting the link between secondary exercise dependence and eating disorders (LO 6).

Work through the review questions in Study Skills Activity 9.6 in the internet chapter for an additional activity.

Chapter 10

Nutrition

Rhys Thatcher

Chapter focus

This chapter introduces the components of food and examines how we can maintain health and influence sporting performance by controlling what we eat.

The food we eat not only provides the body with the energy we need to perform physical activity but also supplies the chemicals we need to extract that energy and the materials from which the body is made; indeed, you are what you eat. There is a great deal of interest in the role diet plays in a healthy lifestyle, with television programmes, the news and the daily papers all giving considerable coverage to the consequences of a poor diet. The most obvious of these consequences is the increasing number of people who are overweight and obese; we will examine some worrying statistics later in this chapter that indicate the scale of this problem.

For athletes diet is also a priority, as the energy to train and compete is contained in the food they eat. Furthermore, many athletes have to carefully monitor their weight, particularly those involved in weight-classified sports such as boxing and rowing. An important aspect of nutrition is how, after food has been consumed, its energy can be transferred into a form that muscles can use to perform physical work. In this chapter we examine the components of food, how energy is released from the food we eat and how we can manipulate what we eat to maintain health and maximise performance during sporting activities.

Learning outcomes

This chapter is designed to help you:
1. Identify the macro- and micronutrients contained in food;
2. Identify the roles of the macronutrients within the body;
3. Describe the metabolic pathways involved in energy provision;
4. Identify the components of a healthy diet;
5. Identify the components of energy expenditure;
6. Identify the classifications of overweight and obesity;
7. Explain the importance of water within the diet.

Macronutrients

The food we eat comprises three main components or macronutrients: carbohydrate, lipid and protein. It is these macronutrients that provide both the bulk to our food and the body's energy. They also provide the basic building blocks that are used to construct the body's tissues. We will now take a closer look at each in turn.

Carbohydrate

Carbohydrate in the diet comes in two major forms: simple sugars and complex carbohydrates. A third type, fibre, is important for transporting food through the digestive system but provides little in terms of nutritional value for the body. Simple sugars are abundant in processed foods but are also found in naturally occurring products such as honey and fruit. Complex carbohydrates can come from both plant and animal sources; plants provide starch and fibre, while the animal source is in the form of glycogen, which was stored by the animal in its own tissues.

There are three main sites in which carbohydrate is stored in the body: as glucose in the blood and as glycogen in skeletal muscle and the liver. Table 10.1 details the amount of carbohydrate that is found in a typical human body. The main role of carbohydrate in the body is to provide a source of energy and it is vital for several reasons. It is the only fuel that the central nervous system can use; it plays an important role in the break down of fat for energy; and it is the only fuel that the body can use anaerobically (without oxygen).

While carbohydrate is a very important form of energy, it is not the best way to store energy as it is not very energy dense, i.e. each gram of carbohydrate contains 4.1kcal (17.1kJ) of energy compared to 9.1kcal (38kJ) per gram of fat.

Key Point 10.1

The scientific standard unit for energy is the joule (J); however, you will be familiar with a different unit, the kilocalorie (kcal), which is used in food packaging. To convert from kcal to kJ, multiply by 4.18, so 1kcal = 4.18kJ. Since most food packaging uses the kcal, in this text we will provide you with values in both units – see Table 10.1.

Table 10.1: Energy stores in a typical 70kg male

Source	g	kcal	kJ
Carbohydrate			
Glycogen (muscle)	350	1 435	5 998
Glycogen (liver)	100	410	1 714
Glucose in blood	10	41	171
Total	460	1 886	7 883
Fat			
Subcutaneous	8 500	77 350	323 323
Intra-muscular	200	1 820	7 608
Total	8 700	79 170	330 931

Lipids

Lipids are found in several forms, including oils (liquid at room temperature) and fats (solid at room temperature). They have several important functions to play in the body. First, they are a very good source of energy as they are energy dense. In their storage form they also provide thermal insulation and protection for the internal organs; furthermore, they play an important role in controlling hunger.

As with carbohydrates, lipids can be classified into three groups: simple lipids, which are by far the most abundant and the type we will focus on in this section as they account for over 95 per cent of dietary intake; compound lipids; and derived lipids, which include cholesterol. The simple lipids can be split into saturated and unsaturated, terms you have probably read on food packaging.

Saturated fat intake increases the risk of heart disease and replacing saturated with unsaturated fat is more effective for reducing this risk than reducing total fat intake. As identified above, fat is very energy dense and, because of this, it is a very useful way in which to store energy (see Table 10.1). Fat is stored in two places within the body: inside muscle and under the skin, which is known as subcutaneous (sub-ku-ta ne-us; sub = under; cutis = to do with skin).

Protein

Protein differs from carbohydrate and lipid in that, while the main role of carbohydrate and fat is to provide energy, the main role of protein is to provide the building blocks from which the body is made. Protein can come from both animal and plant sources and is made up from amino acids, of which there are 20. Twelve of these can be made by the body (11 in children) and are called non-essential amino acids, while the remaining eight (nine in children) are called essential as it is essential that we get them from our diet.

When we eat protein it is broken down by the digestive system into these amino acids; the body then uses them to build whatever tissue it needs. This includes building new structures such as blood cells and repairing damaged structures such as injured muscle. Groups of less than 100 amino acids are called polypeptides, while groups of 100 or more are called proteins. There are over 50 000 different proteins in the body, all made from the same 20 amino acids but put together in different combinations.

Key Point 10.2

Think of amino acids as bricks and proteins as buildings; there are several different types of brick but many thousands of different types of building.

Protein can be used as a source of energy but it makes a minimal contribution to total energy used by the body when compared to carbohydrate and fat.

Micronutrients

While the bulk of our food is made up from macronutrients, food also provides us with vitamins and minerals that are known as micronutrients. While the macronutrients provide us with energy and the building blocks for the body, we would not be able to use them without the micronutrients. Vitamins and minerals enable the body to release the energy in food. They are also involved in the formation of hormones, bone, blood and teeth, and in vision and reproduction.

Vitamins

There are 13 vitamins, which are split into two groups: water-soluble and fat-soluble. Table 10.2 lists these vitamins and identifies their main functions within the body and the recommended daily allowance (RDA) for each. A healthy diet contains sufficient amounts of all the vitamins needed to achieve the RDA. Fat-soluble vitamins have the advantage of being stored within the body's tissues, therefore there is no need to consume them daily within the diet. Water-soluble vitamins, however, are found throughout the body's fluids and, while dietary deficiencies in fat-soluble vitamins may take years to become apparent, deficiencies in water-soluble vitamins can result in health complications within weeks.

Many people consume vitamin supplements believing they will improve either their health or their athletic performance; however, there is no scientific evidence to support any additional benefit of consuming amounts that exceed the RDA. Indeed, while water-soluble vitamins present few complications, if consumed in excess, fat-soluble vitamins can become toxic and result in headache, vomiting, weight loss and kidney damage.

Table 10.2: Vitamin function and recommended daily allowance (RDA)

Vitamin	Main functions	RDA (mg)
Water soluble		
Vitamin B1	Involved in the release of energy	1.4
Vitamin B2	Involved in the release of energy	1.6
Vitamin B6	Amino acid metabolism	2
Vitamin B12	Formation of red blood cells	0.001
Vitamin C	Formation of skin, cartilage, tendon and bone	60
Niacin	Nervous system function	18
Pantothenic acid	Involved in the release of energy	6
Folic acid	Liver function	0.2
Biotin	Synthesis of the non-essential amino acids	0.15
Fat soluble		
Vitamin A	Growth and repair of body tissues	0.8
Vitamin D	Growth of bone and teeth	0.005
Vitamin E	New blood vessels around damaged tissue	10
Vitamin K	Blood clotting	0.03

Minerals

In addition to macronutrients and vitamins, the body also needs minerals, which contribute approximately 4 per cent of total body mass. Minerals are classified as either major minerals, which are required in amounts greater than 100mg per day, or trace minerals, which are required in amounts of less than 100mg. All minerals are found in adequate amounts in a healthy diet and, as with vitamins, there is no need to take supplements to maintain health or improve athletic performance. There are three main functions that minerals play within the body:

1   Structure – they give teeth and bone their hardness;
2   Function – they aid nervous system function and maintain normal heart rhythm;
3   Regulation – they contribute to the structure of the enzymes and hormones that regulate cell activity.

Two minerals in particular receive a great deal of attention; calcium is by far the most abundant mineral found within the body and contributes to the structure of teeth and bone, and iron, a trace mineral, is vital in the formation of red blood cells. Inadequate intake of calcium can result in skeletal problems such as stunted growth and osteoporosis, while inadequate intake of iron can result in anaemia. However, while the negative consequences of excessive intake of calcium have not been reported, excessive iron can result in damage to the liver. Table 10.3 lists the major minerals and identifies the main functions and RDA for each.

Table 10.3: Major mineral functions and recommended daily allowance (RDA)

Mineral	Main functions	RDA (mg)
Calcium	Builds bones and teeth; muscle contraction	800–1200
Chlorine	Enables nutrients to pass into and out of the cell	700
Magnesium	Neuromuscular activity	300
Phosphorus	Builds bones and teeth; necessary in metabolism	800
Potassium	Nervous system function; heart rhythm	2000
Sodium	Body fluid volume; nervous system function	1100–3300
Sulphur	Protein metabolism	Not known

See Study Skills Activity 10.1 in the internet chapter for an additional activity.

Energy metabolism

We have seen that our energy comes from macronutrients and that micronutrients play an important role in the release of that energy. We will now examine the way that that energy is converted into a form that can be used by muscle to produce movement. The chemical and physical changes that occur in the cells of the body are known as metabolism. These changes include the break down of carbohydrate and fat to release their stored energy; as mentioned above, protein does contribute to energy metabolism but its contribution is negligible.

The energy in the macronutrients cannot be used directly by muscle so it has to be converted into a specific form, a compound called adenosine triphosphate (ah-den o-sen tri fos fate; ATP). ATP is used by the muscle to power muscular activity and, in the process, one of its three phosphates (tri = three) is removed, leaving adenosine diphosphate (ah-den o-sen di fos fate; di = two; ADP) and a phosphate ion. The energy stored within macronutrients is then used to re-form the ATP from the ADP and the phosphate ion so that the muscle can use the ATP again. During this process the macronutrients are broken down into smaller structures and it is the energy that is released during this process that is used to re-form the ATP. An overview of ATP production from the metabolism of macronutrients is shown in Figure 10.1.

Inside the muscle cell, carbohydrate is initially broken down into a substance called pyruvate (pi ru-vate) via a process called glycolysis (gli kol i-sis; glyco = to do with sugar; lysis = splitting). If a person is exercising at a low intensity, all of the pyruvate is then taken into a structure called the mitochondria, where it enters a process known as the citric acid cycle. It is in the citric acid cycle that carbohydrate is broken down completely to form water and carbon dioxide (which is taken by the blood to the lungs and expired; see Chapter 12).

The initial break down of carbohydrate to pyruvate is very fast and does not require the presence of oxygen, i.e. it is anaerobic, but it only re-forms two molecules of ATP. The processes within the citric acid cycle are known as aerobic as they do require the presence of oxygen (see Chapter 12). The complete break down of carbohydrate is a slower process but results in a total of 36 molecules of ATP, two from the break down of carbohydrate to pyruvate and 34 from the citric acid cycle. If a person is working at a high exercise intensity, the available oxygen will not be able to deal with all of the

Figure 10.1: An overview of ATP production from carbohydrate and fat

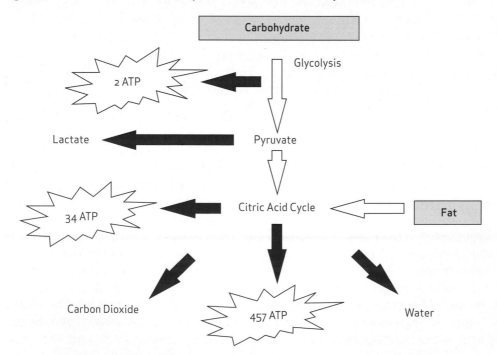

pyruvate that is being produced. Some of this pyruvate will be taken into the citric acid cycle but the remainder will be converted into lactic acid.

Think about a time when you have performed hard exercise; this could be uphill running or sit-ups. You would have experienced considerable discomfort, which could be described as a burning sensation within the muscle. This is due to lactic acid build-up. Fat cannot be broken down anaerobically and enters the citric acid cycle directly. Since fat metabolism is dependent on oxygen, the speed at which it can produce energy is limited. However, while one molecule of carbohydrate results in 36 molecules of re-formed ATP, one molecule of fat results in 457 molecules of ATP.

Therefore, through metabolic processes, the energy contained within the macro-nutrients is transferred into ATP and can be used by the muscle. However, the process is only approximately 25 per cent efficient. The remaining 75 per cent of the energy released during the metabolic process is lost as heat. It is through this heat production that mammals can keep their bodies warm, making them warm-blooded. This is something that you will be familiar with, as, when you increase your metabolic rate, during exercise for instance, the extra heat soon results in the body heating up. This heat has to be removed from the body and this is why we sweat during hot weather or when we perform physical work such as exercise.

Healthy eating

> ### Critical thinking activity 10.1
>
> Before we start this section, take a look at the following list of foodstuffs and put them in order of how much of each you think you should eat in a healthy diet, starting with the food you think you should eat most of:
>
> - meat products, sweets, pasta, fats such as butter and margarine, fruit, dairy products, breads, vegetables, oils, cereals, salt, and rice.

Figure 10.2 represents the different types of food and the proportions in which we should try to eat them for a healthy, balanced diet. The foods in the base of the pyramid are the complex carbohydrates in the form of breads, cereals, pasta and rice; every meal should contain portions from this group. Next we have fruit and vegetables; as well as providing more carbohydrate, this group also provides us with a range of micronutrients. Current guidelines recommend the consumption of five portions of fruit and vegetables per day. As we move up the pyramid, the quantity of the food reduces: dairy and meat products should be consumed less often, with two to three servings per day; and fat, oils, sweets and salt should only be consumed sparingly. Now compare your list from Critical thinking activity 10.1 with Figure 10.2.

A healthy, balanced diet provides all the macronutrients and micronutrients needed to maintain health and maximise athletic performance; however, many people in today's society in the UK, including athletes, do not have a healthy, balanced diet. This, in part, has led to the explosion in the number of overweight and obese individuals and, while the largest single factor to explain this increase is lack of physical activity, diet remains an important factor. A healthy, balanced diet should contain sufficient energy to meet

Figure 10.2: Healthy eating pyramid

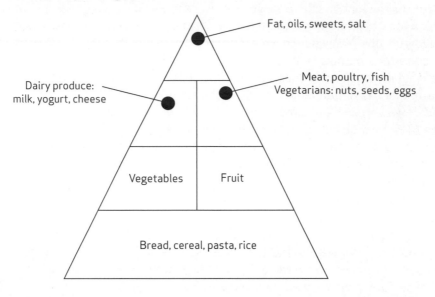

Fat, oils, sweets, salt

Meat, poultry, fish
Vegetarians: nuts, seeds, eggs

Dairy produce:
milk, yogurt, cheese

Vegetables

Fruit

Bread, cereal, pasta, rice

daily energy expenditure; any less and the body will have to use its fat reserves; any additional energy, regardless of whether it was provided by carbohydrate, fat or protein, will be converted to fat and stored. Similarly, it does not matter where the energy comes from (fat, carbohydrate or protein), but we need a varied diet to supply all the micronutrients for the body's requirements. Furthermore, over-consumption of high-fat foods, particularly foods high in saturated fat, will increase the risk of developing heart disease.

Many people are of course vegetarians and, although a vegetarian diet is generally a healthy option, there are some consequences which vegetarians must be aware of. All of the essential amino acids cannot be obtained from a single plant source; also, some of the micronutrients, particularly iron, are difficult to obtain from a vegetarian diet. So, vegetarians must ensure that they have a varied diet, which may involve taking supplements.

For a member of the non-athletic population, a balanced diet should provide most of the energy from carbohydrate, followed by fat and protein. Athletes should, however, increase their intake of carbohydrate above that of the general population – see Table 10.4. The other point to consider is the total amount of energy consumed; the

Table 10.4: Relative contribution of nutrients to energy intake

	Fat (%)	Protein (%)	Carbohydrate (%)
Recommended for general population	35	10 0.8g per kg body weight	55
Typical in general population	40–45	10–15	40–45
Recommended for athletes	15–20	12–15 1.2g per kg body weight	70

recommendation for a non-athletic male is 2500kcal (10450kJ), while for a non-athletic female the recommendation is 2000kcal (8360kJ). For an athlete, this can vary hugely depending on the training load; and in times of particularly heavy training or competition, consuming sufficient kcal can be difficult, e.g. during the Tour de France the average cyclist will burn 6000 kcal per day.

Critical thinking activity 10.2

Using Table 10.5, record everything you eat in a single day. Then using the packaging from the food you've eaten, work out the amount of each macronutrient you consumed and the amount of energy you got from each macronutrient. Once you have recorded all of this information, work out the percentage of your total energy intake that came from each macronutrient and compare your diet to Table 10.4.

Table 10.5: One-day dietary recording sheet

Food	Carbohydrate		Fat		Protein		Total kcal
	Weight (g)	No. of kcal	Weight (g)	No. of kcal	Weight (g)	No. of kcal	

See Study Skills Activity 10.2 in the internet chapter for an additional activity.

Energy balance and body composition

Obesity is a health issue in the UK. It is frequently in the news as the prevalence of obesity has recently exploded. In the UK today, 17 per cent of men and 21 per cent of women are classified as obese (twice as many as in the 1980s); a further 46 per cent of men and 32 per cent of women are classified as overweight. While the number of people who are either overweight or obese increases with age, this is not just a problem for adults. In the mid-1990s, 13 per cent of eight year olds and 17 per cent of 15 year olds were classified as obese and, since obese children are twice as likely to become overweight adults, this is a worrying statistic.

But why are we so interested in an individual's body mass? The answer is very simple: an individual's mass, or more precisely the amount of body fat they are carrying, is linked to the risk of developing diseases such as heart disease, cancer and diabetes. The method used to classify people according to their mass is the body mass index (BMI). However, care must be taken with this method as it does not take into account what the mass is made up of, i.e. muscle or fat. Can you think of an example when BMI would be misleading? It is far better, if the equipment and expertise are available, to use the individual's percentage body fat as a measure of overweight and obesity.

There are several methods available to measure body fat, some requiring large and expensive equipment; one method that is readily accessible, however, is the use of skin-folds. The skin-fold method is based on the fact that fat is stored under the skin; if you measure the thickness of that fat in several places around the body, you can predict the percentage of an individual's mass that is fat. A healthy value for men is around 15 per cent, while a healthy value for women is around 25 per cent.

Athletes can have very low values, particularly endurance athletes. Values for males can reach 3 per cent, while values of 11 per cent have been recorded in women. Values this low also come with health problems, and coaches, nutritionists and sport scientists have to take care to ensure that these athletes are receiving all the macro- and micronutrients they need in their diet.

Did you manage to think of an example of when BMI can be misleading? What about a body builder? They would have a high body mass, giving them a high BMI that would suggest they are overweight or obese, but they could have a very low body fat percentage.

Key Point 10.3

BMI is calculated by dividing the person's body mass in kg by their height in metres squared (kg/m²).

BMI = body mass (kg) ÷ [height (m) × height (m)]

The BMI classifications for overweight and obesity can be seen in Table 10.6.

Table 10.6: Classifications of overweight and obesity by BMI, and risk of developing associated diseases

Classification	BMI (kg/m²)	Risk of developing diseases associated with obesity
Underweight	Less than 18.5	Normal
Normal	18.5–24.9	Normal
Overweight	25.0–29.9	Increased
Obesity Class 1	30.0–34.9	High
Obesity Class 2	35.0–39.9	Very high
Obesity Class 3	Higher than 40.0	Extremely high

Whether you increase or decrease in mass is dependent on the amount of energy you consume compared to the energy you use. If you consume more than you use, you convert the extra energy to fat for storage and increase your mass; if you use more than you consume, you use the stored fat for energy and decrease your mass (Figure 10.3). There are three components of daily energy use: resting metabolic rate (RMR), physical activity and digesting food. Resting metabolic rate refers to the energy used to maintain the body's functions at rest and is the largest component of energy expenditure in the

Figure 10.3: Energy balance and body weight

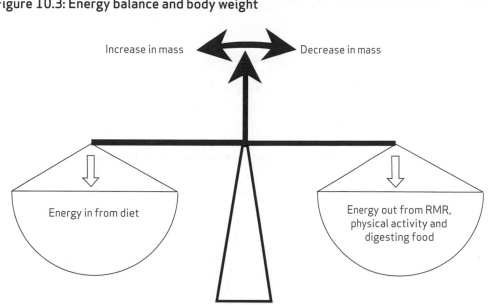

typical person, accounting for approximately 70 per cent of total energy use. The next component, physical activity, is extremely variable but, in the typical person, it accounts for approximately 20 per cent of daily energy use. Athletes, however, can use a huge amount of energy during heavy training and competition, sometimes reaching 400–600 per cent of the energy needed for RMR. The final component is the energy used to digest your food, which accounts for approximately 10 per cent of daily energy use.

See Study Skills Activity 10.3 in the internet chapter for an additional activity.

Fluid

Fifty to seventy per cent of body mass is water. The exact percentage depends on body composition, as 70 per cent of the mass of muscle is water, while only 10 per cent of fat mass is water; so the more muscular the individual, the higher the percentage of water in their body. While the human body can survive for weeks without food, death occurs within days if fluid is not consumed. Water is vital to the body for a number of reasons: in blood, it provides a medium through which substances can be transported around the body; the transfer of gases in the lungs must occur in a moist environment; and it serves as a lubricant in joints, the heart, lungs and eyes. See Table 10.7.

Table 10.7: Definition of terms related to hydration status

Term	Definition
Dehydration	The process of becoming hypohydrated
Rehydration	The process of becoming euhydrated or hyperhydrated
Hypohydrated	Low body water
Euhydrated	Body water in balance
Hyperhydrated	High body water

Figure 10.4: Water balance (* for definition of terms see Table 10.7)

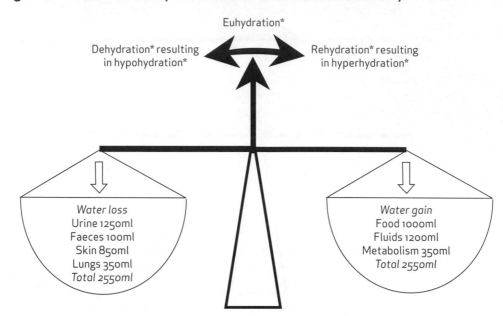

In addition to these functions, water is vital in maintaining body temperature, as it acts as a buffer for heat produced during metabolism and can evaporate on the surface of the skin in the form of sweat to lose heat to the environment. Figure 10.4 shows the water balance in the body during a typical day; if the weather is hot or you perform physical activity, the resulting heat will have to be removed from the body, which is done via sweating. An increase in sweat rate can increase water loss from the body dramatically, as the body can produce a litre of sweat each hour. However, this water must be replaced or the body will heat up, with potentially fatal consequences.

During a typical day an average person will gain 1000ml of water from food, 1200ml from fluid and 350ml is released from macronutrients when they are metabolised. Water is lost via urine (1250ml), faeces (100ml), via the skin as sweat (850ml) and from the lungs (350ml). It is lost from the lungs because as you breathe in, the air is warmed and moistened before it reaches the lungs and this moisture is then lost as you breathe the air back out. You can see this moisture on cold mornings when you breathe out: as the warm, moist air from the lungs reaches the cold air the water condenses out to form a cloud.

Nutritional ergogenic aids

The term ergogenic (er-go-jen ik; ergo = to do with work) refers to anything that improves an individual's capacity to work or perform exercise. Ergogenic aids therefore refer to physical practices such as training, mechanical aids such as specifically designed running shoes, psychological techniques intended to improve performance, and nutritional aids. Some of these nutritional ergogenic aids are legal and widely used by both recreational and professional athletes, while others, such as anabolic steroids, are illegal, and athletes can face lifetime bans from their sport if they are found using them. There are many nutritional techniques that can be used to improve performance and are therefore classed as ergogenic. We will focus on three techniques, two based on increasing carbohydrate intake and one that works by countering some of the negative effects of high intensity exercise.

As we have seen previously, carbohydrate is an important macronutrient and it has received a great deal of attention as an ergogenic aid. This is because during endurance activities one reason that an athlete may fatigue is low carbohydrate stores, especially at the end of a long event such as marathon running. A method used to increase carbohydrate stores is called carbohydrate loading. This involves the athlete consuming higher than normal amounts of carbohydrate in the three days before an endurance event. When originally using this method, prior to the three-day loading phase the athlete reduced the amount of carbohydrate in their diet; this resulted in low glycogen stores in the muscle. This was then followed by three days of increased carbohydrate intake – hence, carbohydrate loading.

The idea behind this approach was that the body would overcompensate for the low stores by storing as much of the available carbohydrate as possible and the athlete would compete with extremely high amounts of glycogen in the muscle. It has subsequently been found that the reduced intake phase is not needed and that the loading phase alone works just as well. The increased stores of carbohydrate are then available to supply energy during the athletic event. Another method of increasing available carbohydrate is to take it in liquid form during competition; this has led to numerous companies selling sports drinks aimed specifically at athletes. These drinks typically have 6 per cent carbohydrate in the form of glucose and have been shown in numerous scientific studies to improve exercise capacity.

The final nutritional ergogenic aid we will look at here works on a different principle and is used by athletes who compete in high intensity activities like sprinting. Can you remember what happens to pyruvate if oxygen is not available? It forms lactic acid, which makes the muscle acidic and can cause the athlete to fatigue. To counter the effects of this acidic environment in the muscle, an athlete can take a substance known as an alkali. A commonly used alkali is sodium bicarbonate, a key component in remedies for acid stomach. This substance makes the blood less acidic and has been shown to have beneficial effects on performance during high intensity exercise when a large amount of lactic acid is produced.

As we mentioned previously, there are many nutritional ergogenic aids on the market and, while some are based on sound scientific evidence, others are not and care must be taken when using them. Any sudden changes in diet can result in negative consequences such as upset stomach and diarrhoea, neither of which would help improve athletic performance; so when using these methods it is also wise to try them first several weeks or months before an important event.

Further reading (nutrition)

McArdle, WD, Katch, FI and Katch, VL (2006) *Exercise physiology: energy, nutrition, and human performance*, 6th edition, pp. 7–107 and pp. 109–253. Baltimore, Maryland: Lippincott Williams and Wilkins.
This textbook is written for undergraduate degree students and goes into some depth, but the quality of the figures can help with understanding some of the key issues.

The first section of this book (pp. 7–107) gives a lot more detail on the macro- and micronutrients, while the second section (pp. 109–253) provides information on energy transfer during exercise.

MacLaren, D (2007) *Nutrition in sport*. London: Churchill Livingstone Elsevier.
Jeukendrup, A and Gleeson, M (2004) *Sport nutrition: an introduction to energy production and performance*. Champaign, IL: Human Kinetics.
Used on undergraduate degree programmes, these are excellent texts that will provide you with a thorough overview of the key issues relating to the nutrition of athletes.

Review

Over the course of this chapter we have examined numerous issues. We started by examining the components of food: the macronutrients and the micronutrients (LO 1). This included an overview of the main roles of carbohydrate, lipid and protein (LO 2) and the metabolic pathways involved in the formation of adenosine triphosphate (ATP) from carbohydrate and fat (LO 3). We then started to examine some of the issues related to nutrition that affect today's society, i.e. the explosion in the incidence of overweight and obesity.

We first introduced key issues related to a healthy diet, considering both non-athletes and athletes (LO 4), before examining the components of energy expenditure (LO 5). We then related energy balance to weight gain and loss. Before we can say an individual is overweight or obese, we need a method to classify them according to their body mass; a commonly used, although limited, method is the body mass index (LO 6).

Next, we highlighted the importance of fluid in the body and the impact of physical exercise on the water balance (LO 7) before examining some of the nutritional ergogenic aids available to athletes.

Work through the review questions in Study Skills Activity 10.4 in the internet chapter for an additional activity.

Chapter 11

Skeletal muscle

Rhys Thatcher

Chapter focus

This chapter introduces the structure and function of skeletal muscle and examines how these influence force production and performance during sport and exercise activities.

When we think of muscle, the first thing that jumps to mind is usually the physique of body builders; indeed, skeletal muscle is the most abundant form of the three muscle types found in the human body. However, in addition to skeletal muscle we also have cardiac muscle, found in the heart, and smooth muscle, which is found in the walls of hollow organs like the stomach and blood vessels. Almost half of the human body is made up of muscle of one kind or another but we are only concerned, in this chapter, with skeletal muscle. As you will no doubt be aware, sporting performance is often based on the athlete's ability to produce force, which is used to move either himself or an object, like a javelin or a barbell in weight lifting.

Alternatively, the athlete may need to move his own body as quickly as possible in events such as running or swimming. Success in such events is dependent on the skeletal muscle's ability to produce force, which it does by converting chemical energy (stored in the body as fat, carbohydrate and protein) into mechanical energy. Thus, knowing the structure and function of skeletal muscle is important for understanding how they influence force production to determine sporting performance.

Learning outcomes

This chapter is designed to help you be able to:
1. Describe the functions and properties of skeletal muscle;
2. Describe the mechanisms of activation of skeletal muscle;
3. Describe the anatomy and basic micro-structure of skeletal muscle;
4. Understand the sliding filament model;
5. List key factors that influence muscle force production;
6. List the characteristics of the three types of muscle action: concentric, eccentric and isometric.

Functions of skeletal muscle

We have already highlighted the importance of skeletal muscle in the production of force to generate movement, but can you think of any other functions of skeletal muscle?

Critical thinking activity 11.1

- List all the functions of skeletal muscle you can think of and give a brief description, or example, of each.
- Now compare your list to the four functions of skeletal muscle identified in the following sections.

Movement

This is perhaps the most obvious of the functions of skeletal muscle, and we spend most of this chapter examining the production of movement. Examples of skeletal muscles producing movement range from moving your eyes to read the text on this page to moving your limbs to run on a netball court. In fact, all movement, both inside the body and outside of the body, is a direct result of muscle activity.

Maintaining posture

While you are sitting reading this chapter your skeletal muscle is working to maintain your posture. This occurs subconsciously so you are not aware of it and enables you to remain upright against the effect of gravity, which is always trying to push you to the ground. If you stand or sit in one position for a long time, you will notice that the muscles that are holding you in position will start to ache from the work that they are doing, and, to allow them to recover, you will have to change position.

Joint stability

Many of the body's skeletal muscles support the joints as they move through their range of motion; for example, the hamstring and quadriceps groups in the thigh support and protect the knee joint. The level of protection provided by the muscle is related to the level of muscle tone, which is the degree to which the muscle is being stimulated when it's at rest. If you exercise regularly, you increase muscle tone; this means that the muscle is 'switched on' to a greater extent thus providing a greater degree of protection to the joints.

Maintaining body heat

All mammals are warm-blooded animals; the heat needed to maintain their temperature is generated during normal metabolic processes (see Chapter 10) and, since a typical human body is 40 per cent skeletal muscle, a large portion of this heat comes from this tissue. This is most obvious when we exercise and increase the metabolic rate of muscle, which results in a huge increase in heat production.

Properties of skeletal muscle

Four properties allow skeletal muscle to perform the functions identified above, as described in the following sections.

Excitability

Excitability refers to the ability to respond to a stimulus. In the case of skeletal muscle, the stimulus is provided by a nerve impulse. For example, when you kick a football the brain figures out which muscles you need to activate and then sends a signal to them via the nervous system – this is the stimulus. The ability to co-ordinate the timing of different muscles contributes to some players being more skilful than others.

Extensibility

Extensibility refers to the ability to be lengthened. A muscle can be lengthened by the actions of other muscles within the body, such as the muscle antagonist (a muscle which works in opposition to the muscle concerned), or by an external force such as gravity. For example, in a standing position lift one foot off the floor so that your knee is level with your hip. To do this you have used your hip flexor muscles. If you then relax these muscles, your foot will return to the floor due to gravity pushing down, lengthening your hip flexor muscles.

Contractility

Contractility refers to the ability to become smaller or to shorten. When stimulated by a nerve impulse skeletal muscle can actively shorten, which results in movement around a joint. This property relates directly to the function of movement: for movement to occur the muscle contracts. This contraction produces tension and, because each end of the muscle is attached to two different bones, and the bones meet at a joint, the tension results in rotation around the joint.

Elasticity

Elasticity refers to the ability to return to normal shape after being stretched or squeezed. With skeletal muscle, we usually refer to muscle returning to its resting length after being stretched. As we shall see later, this property can be used to add to the force developed during explosive actions such as throwing and kicking.

As we progress through this chapter, note how each of these properties relates to force development and therefore how each property contributes to sporting performance.

Key Point 11.1

Some muscles are referred to as either flexors or extensors of a particular joint, for example the hip flexors or the elbow extensors, referring to the action of the muscle on the joint. When shortening, if the muscle reduces the angle at the joint it is referred to as a flexor and if it increases the angle at a joint it is referred to as an extensor, i.e. the biceps brachii is an elbow flexor while the triceps brachii is an elbow extensor.

See Study Skills Activity 11.1 in the internet chapter for an additional activity.

Structure of a muscle

To understand how muscle produces movement, let's examine the structure of a typical muscle. An individual muscle is considered to be an individual organ, such as the heart or the liver, which is made up of thousands of muscle cells or fibres (in relation to the muscle, the words cell and fibre are used interchangeably). Wrapped around each fibre is a layer of connective tissue called the endomysium (en do-mis e-um; endo = within; mys = muscle) and each fibre is bundled together with others to form a fascicle (fas i-kel; fasci = bundle). These fascicles are also surrounded by a layer of connective tissue called the perimysium (per-i-mis e-um; peri = around), which are again bundled together to form the muscle itself; this is finally surrounded by a layer called the epimysium (ep i-mis e-um; epi = on). Each of these layers runs the length of the muscle and is continuous with the tendon that inserts into the bone. It is the pull of the muscle through these connective tissues and tendons that results in rotation around a joint.

Micro-structure of a muscle fibre

The fibre is made up of myofibrils (mi o-fi bril), which run the full length of the fibre and appear striped under a microscope; this is why skeletal muscle is also called striated muscle (striated is another word for striped). The stripes are caused by the arrangement of two proteins or myofilaments called actin and myosin that lie parallel to each other (see Figure 11.1) and have a special role to play in movement, which we examine in the section below.

In addition to actin and myosin, there are three other proteins that we are interested in. The first is a stretchy protein called titin that runs along the length of the muscle fibre, connecting one myosin filament with the next and contributing greatly to the elastic property of muscle. The other two proteins, troponin (trop o-nin) and tropomyosin (tro po-mi o-sin) are not shown in Figure 11.1 as they are found on the actin myofilament; however, you can see them in detail in Figure 11.2, later in this chapter. The basic unit of the myofibril that contains all of the above myofilaments is called a sarcomere (sar ko-mer; muscle segment). The sarcomere are joined end to end at the 'Z Line' and run the full length of the myofibril (see Figure 11.1).

Now we have examined the basic structure of a typical muscle, we need to consider how muscles work. The myofilaments, actin and myosin, do not change length, so how

Figure 11.1(a): Longitudinal section through sarcomere

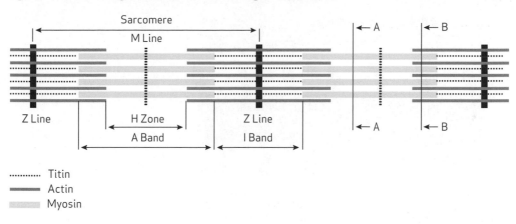

⋯⋯⋯	Titin
▬▬▬	Actin
▨▨▨	Myosin

Figure 11.1(b): Transverse section through sarcomere

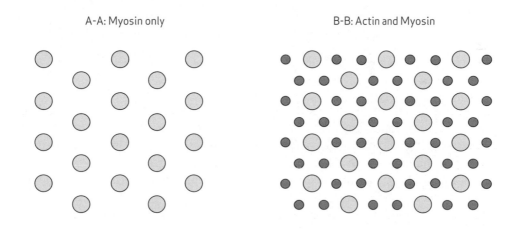

does a muscle generate tension to produce movement around a joint? The answer is addressed by the sliding filament model.

Sliding filament model

This is also known as Huxley's sliding filament model, as it was proposed by Hugh Huxley (Huxley and Hanson, 1954). He proposed that the myofilaments (actin and myosin) slide past each other and pull on the connective tissue surrounding the fibre, which in turn pulls on the bones to which the muscle is attached, resulting in rotation around the joint. To understand how this occurs, we need to have a closer look at actin and myosin.

Myosin is a relatively thick myofilament and is covered in 'myosin heads'. These heads are highly attracted to specific parts of the actin, called 'active sites', and they want to bind with the actin. However, these active sites are covered by tropomyosin therefore binding cannot occur (see Figure 11.2). When the fibre is stimulated by a nerve (see next section), the troponin moves the tropomyosin away from the active site, allowing the actin and myosin to bind and form a 'cross-bridge'. Once binding has taken place, the myosin head pivots and pulls itself along the actin myofilament and sliding

Figure 11.2: Detail of actin and myosin

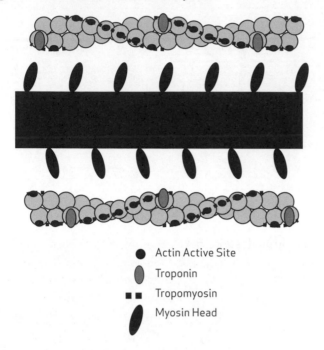

Actin (thin myofilament)

Myosin (thick myofilament)

Actin (thin myofilament)

- ● Actin Active Site
- ◖ Troponin
- ▪▪ Tropomyosin
- ❚ Myosin Head

occurs. At this point, the myosin head releases the active site and resumes its original position – this requires energy in the form of adenosine triphosphate (ATP; see Chapter 10). Now the head is in the original position and, if the nerve is still stimulating the fibre, it can bind to the next active site along the actin; this continues until the nerve signal stops. All of this happens thousands of times a second, so that from tiny individual movements throughout the fibre, the muscle fibre, and therefore the muscle, shortens.

You will see in Figure 11.1(a) that there are several bands and zones identified on the sarcomere: the H Zone and the A and I Bands. These zones and bands are caused by the overlap of the actin and myosin and during sliding they change in length. When the muscle receives the signal to shorten, the myosin head binds with the active site on the actin and sliding occurs. This moves the Z lines, which anchor the actin myofilaments, closer together and consequently the H Zone and I Band decrease in length as the actin and myosin slide past each other. The A Band remains the same length but now represents a much larger proportion of the sarcomere length, as the whole sarcomere has shortened.

Before we start to consider things on a larger (macro) scale, take some time to complete Table 11.1. Refer to the section above to check your answers.

Activation of skeletal muscle

Before a muscle can shorten it needs to be stimulated by a nerve signal. Let's use an example to illustrate this: you want to drink from a cup – your brain decides which muscles are needed to perform the action and then sends a signal to these muscles via the nervous system. The nerve is like an electric cable, which conducts a signal from the brain to the muscle. In addition to deciding which muscles to activate, the brain also

Table 11.1: Functions of skeletal muscle proteins

Protein	Main function
	Is a thin myofilament that has active sites to which myosin heads can bind.
Myosin	
	Contributes greatly to the elastic property of muscle.
	Is activated by calcium and once activated moves the tropomyosin from the active site.
Tropomyosin	

figures out how much force is needed and stimulates the muscles accordingly (see below). Once the signal reaches the muscle fibre a chemical, acetylcholine (as e-til-ko len), known as a neurotransmitter, is released from the nerve ending and is taken up by the muscle fibre. The presence of acetylcholine triggers several events, which result in the release of calcium from a structure within the fibre called the sarcoplasmic reticulum (sar ko-plaz mik re-tik u-lum; reticulum = network) into the inside of the fibre. This calcium binds with the troponin to move the tropomyosin away from the active site on the actin and the fibre shortens.

Motor units

No single fibre acts by itself but forms part of a group of fibres called a motor unit, which includes a single nerve that splits at the end so that it can contact all the fibres in the unit. When the nerve stimulates the muscle, all of the fibres it is in contact with shorten; so to control how much force you produce, you control the number of motor units you activate within the muscle.

For example, if you lift an empty cup you will activate a very small number of motor units; however, if the cup is full you need to activate more of the available motor units to pick up the additional weight. To lift a very heavy weight you have to activate a large number of the available motor units within the muscle. It is not possible to activate all of the motor units at the same time as this could result in damage to the muscle or the tendon that attaches it to the bone, so the body protects itself by limiting the number of units that can be activated at one time.

Determinants of muscular strength and performance

There are many factors that determine muscular strength and these are summarised in Figure 11.3. No action performed by a human is reliant on a single muscle; for example, while the biceps curl is used to train the biceps brachii, other muscles also contribute to the force produced, such as the brachialis and brachioradialis. Furthermore, since all muscle is under some degree of activation all of the time, known as muscle tone, the triceps brachii, which opposes the action of the biceps brachii, reduces the force which can be produced.

Figure 11.3: Determinants of muscular performance

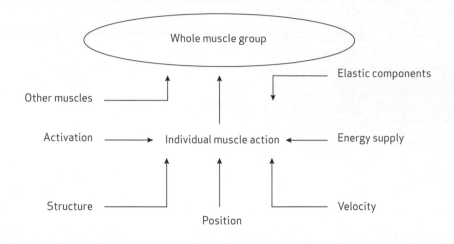

When you look at Figure 11.3 and think about the biceps curl, the 'whole muscle group' refers to all the muscles involved in bending the elbow and lifting a weight. 'Other muscles' refers to the brachialis and brachioradialis, which help the biceps brachii, known as the prime mover, and these helper muscles are known as synergists. 'Other muscles' also include the triceps brachii, which opposes the lift and is known as an antagonist. The synergists add to the force generated, while the antagonist reduces the force, as explained above.

See *Study Skills Activity 11.2 in the internet chapter for an additional activity.*
Let's consider each of the determinants of muscular performance identified in Figure 11.3. We have already discussed 'Activation' and 'Other muscles' and identified 'Individual muscle action' as the action of a specific muscle such as the biceps brachii. In the remainder of this chapter we examine the influence of muscle structure, speed (or velocity) of contraction, position and elastic components on force production and muscle performance. Energy supply is covered in Chapter 10.

Influence of structure on force production and muscle performance

There are several factors associated with the way a muscle is structured that directly influence the amount of force the muscle can produce: muscle cross-sectional area, or the size of the muscle; the orientation of the fibres in relation to the axis of the muscle, and, the fibre type. Let's look at each of these three factors.

Muscle cross-sectional area

The muscle cross-sectional area (CSA) is the area covered by the muscle if it were cut perpendicular to its axis at the widest point – the axis refers to an imaginary line drawn from top to bottom of the muscle (See Figure 11.4). It's no surprise that the larger the CSA, the greater the strength, as when we see strong athletes it is obvious that they have well-developed, large, muscles. This increase in size could come from one of two

Figure 11.4: Parallel (A) and pinnate (B) muscle fibres

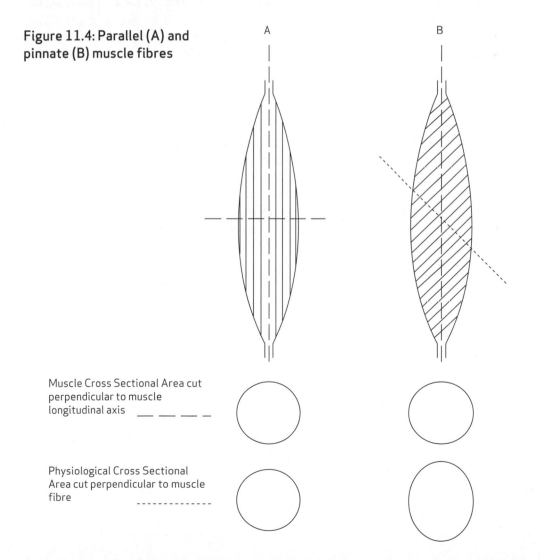

Muscle Cross Sectional Area cut perpendicular to muscle longitudinal axis

Physiological Cross Sectional Area cut perpendicular to muscle fibre

adaptations to the athlete's training; either the number of fibres within the muscle increases, known as hyperplasia (hi-per pla zhe-a; hyper = over; plas = grow), or the size of the individual fibres increases, known as hypertrophy (hi-per tro-fe; trophy = nourishment). In humans, under normal training conditions, hyperplasia doesn't occur – the number of muscle fibres remains constant, so any increase in size is due to hypertrophy.

The increased fibre size results from the synthesis of new proteins because of either a training stimulus or as part of the normal process of growing. These proteins are the ones we have already encountered, i.e. actin, myosin, titin, troponin and tropomyosin. The greater the number of these proteins within the fibre, the greater the number of cross-bridges that can be formed between the myosin head and the actin active site, therefore the greater the potential for force production.

Orientation of muscle fibres

Not all muscles have fibres that run parallel with the muscle axis; some have fibres that run at an angle to the muscle axis, known as pinnate (Figure 11.4). The muscle's characteristics and functional role will determine whether the fibres run parallel or pinnate to the muscle axis. The muscle's physiological cross-sectional area (PCSA) is the area covered by the muscle if it were cut perpendicular to the orientation of the fibres at the widest point.

As we see in Figure 11.4, which shows two muscles of similar CSA, the muscle in Figure 11.4(b) has a larger PCSA. This gives the muscle the advantage of greater force production but the limitation of low range of movement. This is because the fibres shorten by the same amount as those in muscle A, which has parallel fibres, but as the pinnate fibres lie at an angle to the muscle axis they don't shorten the full muscle to the same degree. The greater force production in the pinnate muscle is due to the greater number of cross-bridges. If you count the number of lines (representing the muscle fibres) cut by the line drawn perpendicular to the fibres, you will see the muscle with parallel fibres (A) has nine fibres (this would be thousands in a real muscle), while the muscle with pinnate fibres (B) has 11. The extra fibres relate directly to more cross-bridges and greater force production.

Muscles with a pinnate structure are found where large force production is necessary, such as the quadriceps and calf muscles that have to lift the full body weight when walking and climbing stairs, etc. Parallel fibres are found in muscles where a greater speed of contraction is needed, such as the hamstring group. Table 11.2 summarises the key characteristics of parallel and pinnate muscles.

Table 11.2: Characteristics of parallel and pinnate muscles

	Parallel	Pinnate
Example muscle	Hamstrings	Quadriceps
Fibre length	Long	Short
PCSA	Small	Large
Force production	Low	High
Amount of movement	High	Low
Speed of movement	Fast	Slow

Muscle fibre type

When we discussed the sliding filament model we stated that once the myosin head has attached to the active site on the actin it pivots. This pivot results in the sliding of myosin over actin and therefore muscle shortening. After this the myosin head releases the active site and regains its original position. This requires energy and while the micro-structure of individual fibres is very similar the way they provide this energy differs between fibre types. There are two main types of fibre with one intermediary, giving three fibre types known as types I, IIa and IIb; we will focus on types I and IIb which are the two main types here. The intermediary type, IIa, falls between these two main types and has characteristics of both.

Muscle fibre type I. Muscle fibre type I is also known as 'slow twitch' or 'red' for reasons that will become apparent. This type of fibre regenerates, or re-synthesises, its ATP for muscular work via aerobic means, i.e. it needs oxygen to break down carbohydrate and fat (see Chapter 10). Therefore this fibre type needs a large supply of blood, giving its red appearance. The 'slow twitch' label derives from the tension characteristics the fibre generates when stimulated by a nerve. When a fibre is removed from a muscle, placed within a force measuring device and given a single stimulus, it is known as a 'twitch'.

We can record the force generated and the time over which the force is generated and plot this on a graph (see Figure 11.5). The slow twitch fibre has a lower peak value and takes longer to generate its force when compared to the fast twitch fibre – hence, 'slow twitch'. Because of the preferred method of energy metabolism, i.e. aerobic, this fibre contains many aerobic enzymes and large mitochondria – the site of aerobic metabolism within the fibre. While this fibre type cannot produce as high a force as other types, it is very resistant to fatigue. If we combine these characteristics, we can see that type I fibres are good for prolonged activities where high power outputs are not needed.

Critical thinking activity 11.2

Keeping in mind these characteristics and the way in which slow twitch fibres derive their energy, write down a list of sports you think athletes with a high percentage of slow twitch fibres would excel in.

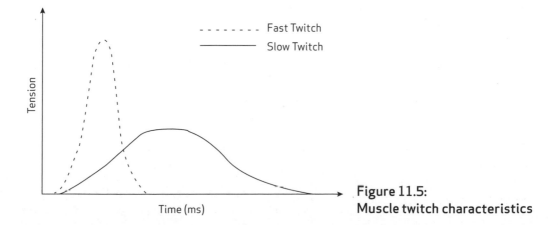

Figure 11.5:
Muscle twitch characteristics

Muscle fibre type IIb. Type IIb are the other extreme of fibre types: whilst type I are known as slow twitch and red, type IIb fibres are known as 'fast twitch' and 'white'. These fibres regenerate ATP anaerobically, which doesn't need oxygen to break down carbohydrate (the only substrate that can be broken down anaerobically; see Chapter 10). Because type IIb fibres have little need for oxygen, their blood supply is lower than that of type I fibres, which gives them their white colour. The twitch characteristics are also very different from those of type I fibres. As soon as the fibre receives the signal from a nerve, the force is generated very quickly and to a far higher level than in type I fibres. However, the fibre fatigues very quickly (see Figure 11.5).

Critical thinking activity 11.3

Keeping in mind these characteristics and the way in which fast twitch fibres derive their energy, write down a list of sports you think athletes with a high percentage of fast twitch fibres would excel in.

Check your answers to Critical thinking activities 11.2 and 11.3 using Table 11.3.

The amount of each fibre type changes from muscle to muscle so that postural muscles, which perform work for long periods of time, have a larger percentage of type I fibres, while muscles required to produce rapid movements will have more type IIb fibres. Not only does the balance of fibre types change from muscle to muscle within an individual but also in the same muscle from person to person. This is why some people are better at endurance activities while others are better at explosive, powerful activities; see Table 11.3. Fibre types can't be changed; your fibre type composition is determined genetically, so you are born with what you have. Table 11.3 summarises the differences between the two main fibre types.

Table 11.3: Fibre types from the quadriceps muscle group in different athletic populations

	% type I or slow twitch	% type IIb or fast twitch
Distance runners and endurance athletes	60–90	10–40
Sprinters and power athletes	25–45	55–75
Non-athletes	45–55	45–55
Sports students	40–80	20–60

Influence of speed of muscle action on force production and muscle performance

A muscle doesn't have the same capacity to generate force at all speeds (or velocities). This is evident if you try to lift a heavy weight; you can only do so slowly because muscle can generate more tension at slower velocities. When we examine speed of muscle action, we need to introduce three types of action; notice that this is not three types of muscle contraction, as during one of these the muscle doesn't change length and during another the muscle actually lengthens. The three types of muscle action are concentric, eccentric and isometric. The first two, concentric and eccentric, are sometimes collectively known as isotonic.

Concentric

This occurs when the internal force generated by the muscle is greater than the external force to be lifted. If you look at Figure 11.6, there is a load pressing the hand down, which is due to gravity and the mass of the object, in this example, a dumbbell. If the force generated by the arm flexors is greater than the load pressing down (IF > EF), the flexors will shorten, the dumbbell will be raised and the elbow will flex (reducing the angle at the elbow). Concentric actions result in shortening of the muscle and are termed dynamic, as movement occurs.

Figure 11.6: The relationship between internal and external forces during a biceps curl exercise

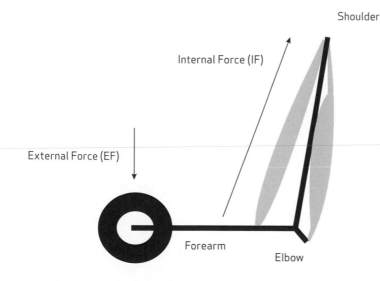

Key Point 11.4

Remember that the force generated is controlled by the number of motor units activated; more motor units = more fibres = more force.

Eccentric

In the same example, when you want to lower the dumbbell, you activate fewer motor units thereby reducing the internal force generated to the point where the external force is greater (EF > IF). At this point, the muscle lengthens under control and extension occurs at the elbow, but it is important to understand that it is the flexors working eccentrically not the extensors working concentrically. Since movement occurs during this type of muscle action, it is also termed dynamic. Can you remember the definition of flexors and extensors? If not refer to Key Point 11.1.

Isometric

If the internal force generated is equal to the external force (EF = IF), no movement occurs; thus this type of muscle action is known as static. While no movement occurs, the motor units are still activated as they are in any muscle action but the number of activated motor units at any one time is only enough to cancel out the external load.

Critical thinking activity 11.4

Pick up a weight of reasonable size, i.e. 5–10kg and hold it in your right hand with your arm by your side. Now flex your elbow and lift the weight. While doing this, feel the biceps brachii of your right arm with your left hand. The biceps brachii is tense and working concentrically to lift the weight. Now lower the weight so that the elbow is flexed at 90° and hold that position. Again, feel the tension in the biceps brachii as it works isometrically to hold the weight in position. Finally, lower the weight slowly; again, you will feel the biceps brachii is working to control the movement eccentrically.

Now perform a squat exercise:

Stand with your feet shoulder-width apart and bend the knee to lower your body. Stop when your knee is at 90°, then stand straight again. Now answer the following questions:

- What is the weight your muscles are working against?
- Which muscle group is working while you lower your body?
- Which type of muscle action is being performed?
- Which muscle group is working while you are at the bottom of the squat?
- Which type of muscle action is being performed?
- Which muscle group is working while you lift your body back to standing?
- Which type of muscle action is being performed?
- How could you make this exercise harder?

You can find the answers to these questions by clicking on the link to 'Critical thinking activity 11.4: Answers' in the internet chapter.

The muscle can generate more force when working eccentrically than it can when working isometrically. Similarly, more force can be generated during isometric than concentric actions. This is evident if you try to pull your body weight up during a 'chinning' exercise, where you start with straight arms hanging from a bar and then pull your body weight up so that your chin is level with the bar. People who can't perform a chin, which involves the elbow flexors working concentrically, are able to lower themselves under control to the ground from a bent arm position, i.e. the elbow flexors work eccentrically.

Influence of muscle position on force production and performance

When we discuss muscle position, we are interested in the position of the muscle in relation to its range of motion (ROM). The relationship between length, in relation to ROM, and force production, is referred to as the *length–tension relationship*.

> **Key Point 11.5**
>
> A muscle's range of motion (ROM) refers to the maximum range of movement a muscle can produce – from its shortest to its longest length (limited by flexibility). ROM is usually measured in relation to a specific joint, i.e. the ROM of the hip is usually limited by the flexibility of the hamstring.

Length–tension relationship

When the muscle is at its longest, there is very little overlap between the actin and myosin myofilaments, the Z lines are as far away from each other as possible and the H Zone and I Band are wide – see Figure 11.1(a). Thus the formation of cross-bridges and capacity for force production is limited. As the muscle shortens and the myofilaments slide past each other, more of the myosin heads can bind with the actin active sites, more cross-bridges can form and more tension can be generated. When the muscle is longer than its resting length, for example at the start of a biceps curl when the biceps brachii is lengthened, there is little overlap between the actin and myosin and it is difficult to generate force (see dashed line in Figure 11.7(a) and dashed box in Figure 11.7b).

However, at the muscle's optimal length there is greater overlap, more cross-bridges can be formed and greater force can be produced; this would be halfway through a biceps curl lift (see solid line in Figure 11.7(a) and solid box in Figure 11.7(b)). As you near the top of the lift the muscle is shorter than its optimal length and, while there is a lot of overlap between the actin and myosin, the end of the myosin myofilament is restricted by the Z Line, which limits any further sliding, and there is a rapid decrease in force production (see dotted line in Figure 11.7(a) and dotted box in Figure 11.7(b)).

Figure 11.7(a): Length–tension relationship

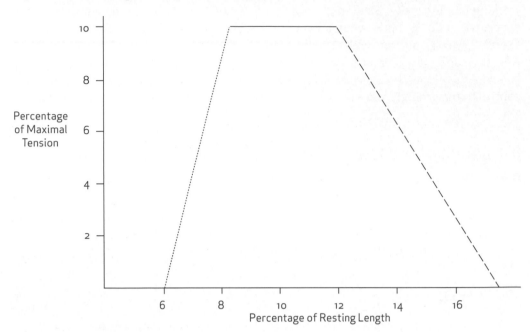

Percentage of Maximal Tension (y-axis)

Percentage of Resting Length (x-axis)

Figure 11.7(b): Actin–myosin overlap at various muscle lengths

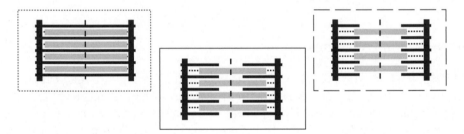

Elastic components

You will remember that one property of skeletal muscle is elasticity; so if you stretch muscle, without tearing it, it returns to its original length without the need for cross-bridges and metabolic energy. This property derives from the elastic nature of the protein, titin (see Figure 11.1), the connective tissue that surrounds the muscle fibres, the fascicle and the muscle. Within athletic throwing events, like the discus, this is used to great advantage; as the muscles involved in throwing a projectile are first stretched by rotating the body, leaving the throwing arm behind, the stretched muscle then returns to its original length while it is stimulated to shorten, adding to the force generated to throw the discus. For the most extreme example of this in action we have to look at the natural world and the kangaroo, which uses elastic energy to produce its characteristic hop. The kangaroo needs minimal energy to reach extreme speeds due to the elastic recoil in the tendons of the leg, which are stretched as the animal lands so that the next jump is powered by the stored elastic energy, with minimal need for metabolic energy.

Further reading (skeletal muscle)

Marieb, EN (2000) *Human anatomy and physiology*, 7th edition. Menlo Park, CA: Benjamin Cummings.
This is an excellent general anatomy and physiology text used by undergraduate medical students. Chapters 10 and 11 provide detail on the structure and function of skeletal muscle.

McArdle, WD, Katch, FI and Katch, VL (2006) *Exercise physiology: energy, nutrition, and human performance*, 6th edition, pp. 365–389. Baltimore, MD: Lippincott Williams and Wilkins.
This textbook is also written for undergraduate degree students and goes into some depth, but the quality of the figures can help with understanding some of the key issues. Chapter 18 (pp. 365–389) details the function of skeletal muscle during exercise.

Wilmore, JH, Costill, DL and Kenney, WL (2007) *Physiology of sport and exercise*, 4th edition, pp. 25–45. Champaign, IL: Human Kinetics.
This textbook is written for undergraduate degree students and goes into a little more depth than we have here. Again, the quality of the figures and graphs will help with understanding some of the key issues. Chapter 1 (pp. 25–45) examines the structure and function of skeletal muscle.

Jones, D, Round, J and de Haan, A (2004) *Skeletal muscle from molecules to movement*. London: Churchill Livingstone.
An advanced text that provides a great deal of detail on skeletal muscle in relation to physical activity.

Review

We began this chapter by examining the main functions and properties of skeletal muscle (LO 1). While most people would be expected to know that skeletal muscle is involved in producing movement, we also identified joint stability and the maintenance of posture and body heat as important functions of this muscle. These are possible due to the properties of skeletal muscle: excitability, extensibility, contractility and elasticity. Before muscle can perform any of its functions it must receive a stimulus, which comes from the nervous system and triggers the release of calcium into the muscle fibre, which in turn triggers muscle action (LO 2).

We then examined the macro- and micro-structure of skeletal muscle (LO 3) and related the proteins actin, myosin, titin, troponin and tropomyosin to the sliding filament model (LO 4). Numerous factors influencing muscle force production (LO 5) were identified, including activation, muscle structure, position of the muscle in relation to its length, speed of contraction, elastic components and the role of other muscles, including prime movers, synergists and antagonists. Finally, we examined the three distinct types of muscle action – concentric, eccentric and isometric – and related these to the muscle's ability to produce force (LO 6).

Work through the review questions in Study Skills Activity 11.3 in the internet chapter for an additional activity.

Chapter 12

Cardiovascular system

Rhys Thatcher

Chapter focus

This chapter introduces the structure and function of the cardiovascular system and examines its responses to sport and exercise.

All human movement, whether movement of the body around an athletics track or the movement of blood around the body, is dependent on energy. The body's ability to provide sufficient energy will limit the rate at which movement can occur, e.g. how fast an athlete can run or cycle. This energy is contained in the food we eat and is stored throughout the body until it is needed. The energy in these stores can be released via several metabolic pathways; a specific series of processes which result in energy that can be used by the body's cells; we examined this in Chapter 10. Which pathway is used depends on the substrate used (carbohydrate, fat or protein), the rate at which energy is needed and the availability of oxygen.

The main role of the cardiovascular system is to provide the oxygen needed in these metabolic pathways and to remove the by-products of metabolism such as carbon dioxide. In addition, it plays a vital role in the transport of many substances around the body, including hormones and substrates. In this chapter we examine the structure and function of the cardiovascular system, including the blood vessels and blood.

Learning outcomes

This chapter is designed to be able to:
1 Describe the anatomy and structure of the heart and blood vessels;
2 Describe the conduction system of the heart;
3 Identify the main features of an electrocardiogram;
4 Understand the control of cardiac output during physical activity;
5 Understand the terms systolic and diastolic blood pressure;
6 Identify the components of blood.

The heart

The heart, which is about the size of your fist, is the organ that is responsible for pushing blood around your body, which it does 24 hours a day, seven days a week for your entire life, potentially resulting in over three billion heart beats. At its most simple, the heart can be considered as a four-chambered organ that functions as two parallel pumps (Figure 12.1). The four chambers are the left and right atria (a tre-a) and left and right ventricles (ven tri-kel); the atria are receiving chambers, while the ventricles expel the blood from the heart. The right side receives blood from the body via the vena cava (great vein), which carries blood from the body's tissues. This blood is low in oxygen (O_2) and high in carbon dioxide (CO_2), as it has delivered the O_2 to the working cells and picked up the CO_2, which is a by-product of metabolism. Once the blood has arrived at the right atrium it travels via the tricuspid atrioventricular (a tre-o-ven-trik yu-lar) valve into the right ventricle, where it is ejected into the pulmonary artery, which transports the blood to the lungs. Here, CO_2 is removed and O_2 added. Once the blood has travelled through the lungs it is returned to the heart via the pulmonary veins, where it enters the left atrium.

Pulmonary – related to the lungs

The blood is now high in O_2 and low in CO_2; having entered the left atrium it flows through the bicuspid atrioventricular valve into the left ventricle, where it is pumped to the rest of the body (Figure 12.1) via the aorta. Since the left side of the heart has to pump blood to the whole body, the muscle here is far larger than that of the right.

Figure 12.1: Chambers, valves and main blood vessels of the heart

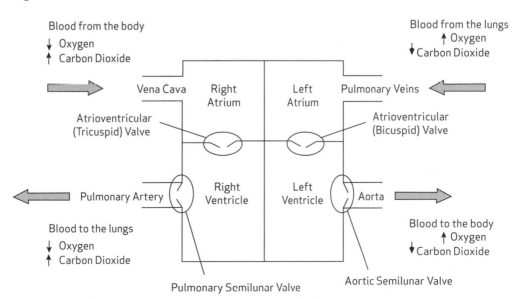

The heart wall

The heart is surrounded by a layer of connective tissue called the pericardium (per i-kar de-um; peri = around; cardium = heart), which protects and anchors it in position. The inner portion of the pericardium comprises two layers separated by the serous (ser us) fluid, which reduces friction to ensure the two layers glide over each other. This low friction environment is essential to protect the heart wall during the movement produced as the heart beats; without it the heart would rub against its surrounding structures, with every beat resulting in damage to the heart tissue.

Critical thinking activity 12.1

To highlight the importance of this low friction environment, make a fist with your right hand and then wrap your left hand around your right tightly. Now pump your right fist as if it were your heart; you will soon notice the heat generated as the skin of your hands rubs together and, if you do this for a couple of minutes, you could end up with a blister.

Inside the protective layer of the pericardium is the heart wall, which comprises three layers. The outer layer is the epicardium (ep i-kar de-um; epi = on); next is the myocardium (mi o-kar de-um; myo = muscle), which is the heart, or cardiac, muscle, forming the bulk of the heart; and finally there is the endocardium (en do-kar de-um; endo = within). The myocardium is the part of the heart which produces the beat and, like skeletal muscle, is striated or striped and has the same mechanism of contraction (see Chapter 11). There are, however, several key differences between the two. When you stimulate skeletal muscle you activate the number of motor units you need to produce the desired force. The heart, however, contracts all its muscle fibres in every beat. The reason for this is that, while skeletal muscle fibres are insulated from each other so that the electrical stimulation of one fibre does not stimulate the adjacent fibre, the fibres of the heart are connected by 'gap junctions' so that, once started, the electrical signal sweeps across the whole heart, resulting in a coordinated beat.

Key Point 12.1

The heart beat is said to be an all or nothing event at the organ level, i.e. the whole heart either beats or it does not beat at all; skeletal muscle, in contrast, is an all or nothing event at the motor unit level, i.e. while all the fibres in a single motor unit will be stimulated, other motor units within the same muscle are not necessarily stimulated.

Another key difference between skeletal and cardiac muscle is the way they re-form ATP. As discussed in Chapter 10, the body's tissues, and particularly skeletal muscle, can derive energy from both anaerobic (without O_2) and aerobic (with O_2) pathways. The heart muscle is, however, far more reliant on aerobic metabolism and it is vital that the blood supply, and therefore the O_2 delivery to the myocardium is maintained. If the blood supply is interrupted it can result in a myocardial infarction (mi o-kar de-al infark shun) or heart attack. The final layer of the heart wall, the endocardium, is in direct contact with blood as it passes through the heart chambers and it extends into the lining of the blood vessels which deliver the blood to, and carry blood away from, the heart.

Heart valves

Blood flows through both sides of the heart in one direction as a result of a series of four valves, two on each side. These valves are situated between the atria and the ventricles, the atrioventricular valves, and at the point at which blood leaves the ventricles and enters the main arteries, the semilunar valves (Figure 12.1). On the right-hand side of the heart, the atrioventricular valve has three flaps and is known as the tricuspid valve; while the left-hand side equivalent has two flaps and is known as the bicuspid or mitral valve. As blood flows through the atria and fills the ventricles, the pressure in the ventricles increases; the atria then contract, resulting in a final rush of blood into the ventricles, further increasing the pressure. The atria then relax and the ventricles contract; the increase in pressure in the ventricles snaps the valves shut, stopping blood flowing back into the atria.

This snapping shut of the atrioventricular valves results in the first of the heart sounds, the 'lub' of the 'lub-dub' you can hear when you place your ear against someone's chest or when you use a stethoscope. The second sound, the 'dub', is caused by the semilunar valves snapping shut after the ventricles relax following their contraction, pushing blood from the heart. Once closed, the semilunar valves stop blood flowing back into the ventricles from the main arteries.

See Study Skills Activity 12.1 in the internet chapter for an additional activity.

Key Point 12.2

Sometimes the valves of the heart do not seal properly and blood can flow in the wrong direction; this can be due to a heart abnormality or heart disease. If this occurs, there is a surgical procedure in which the valves can be replaced with synthetic valves or the valves from a pig's heart.

Blood supply to the heart

One thing to remember about the heart is that, while there is always a large volume of blood travelling through it, it is not this blood that delivers O_2 to its own tissue. The blood supply (and therefore O_2 and nutrient supply) to the heart's tissue is delivered by a special set of blood vessels that make up the coronary circulation. The arteries of the coronary circulation leave the aorta as soon as it leaves the left ventricle; they then wrap around the heart, delivering blood to its tissue.

Arteries – blood vessels that take blood away from the heart

After the blood has delivered its O_2 to the heart tissue, it is taken directly back to the heart chambers via the cardiac veins, which empty directly into the right atrium.

> Veins – blood vessels that take blood toward the heart

Key Point 12.3

The term coronary heart disease (CHD) refers to damage and deterioration of the heart's blood supply or, if the arteries are damaged, this is known as coronary artery disease (CAD). In the UK, 25 per cent of men and 17 per cent of women die from CHD, making it the country's biggest killer.

Conduction system

For the heart to pump effectively, contraction of the myocardium needs to be coordinated; this is orchestrated by the heart's conduction system. While skeletal muscle needs to be stimulated by a nerve, the heart's ability to contract is intrinsic; this means that you could disconnect the heart from all nervous connections and it would continue to beat. Even so, it still has a large number of nerves connected to it that play key roles in regulating its activity.

There are specialist cells within the heart called autorhythmic cells and, as the name suggests, these cells have the ability to set a rhythm automatically. They are found in several clusters throughout the heart and each cluster has its own rhythm. It is this rhythm that sets the pace of the heart beat. Since the different clusters of these autorhythmic cells have different rates, it is always the cells with the fastest rhythm that will set the rate at which the heart beats, or the heart rate (HR).

In a healthy heart the cells with the fastest rate, or rhythm, are found in the sinoatrial (SA) node at the top of the right atrium. The rhythm of these cells would trigger a heart beat every 0.6 of a second and result in a heart rate of 100 beats per minute (bpm). However, the nerves that are connected to the heart slow this rhythm down so that the heart actually beats at a rate of approximately 75bpm when resting. Resting heart rate is, of course, very variable and depends on the fitness level and health of the individual. Resting heart rates of below 30bpm have been recorded in elite endurance athletes, while heart disease patients can have resting values above 100bpm. The SA node initiates the heart beat by sending an electrical impulse across the left and right atria (Figure 12.2), which causes them to contract, forcing the blood into the ventricles. The electrical stimulus can't travel across into the ventricles from the atria as there are no gap junctions in the cells which separate them, so the impulse has to be transmitted via the atrioventricular (AV) node. Once the impulse has reached the AV node it is transmitted down the AV bundle and the two bundle branches that run down to the bottom of the heart before splitting into the purkinje fibres, which carry the impulse into the myocardium to stimulate ventricular contraction.

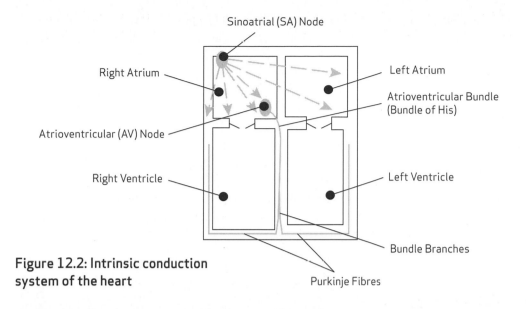

Figure 12.2: Intrinsic conduction system of the heart

Key Point 12.4

Since the SA node sets the rhythm of the heart, it is known as the heart's pacemaker. In some diseases the pacemaker can be damaged and stops working, so an artificial pacemaker is fitted surgically.

Electrocardiography (ECG)

The electrical impulse that causes the heart to beat can be detected on the surface of the body by a piece of equipment known as an electrocardiograph (e-lek-tro-kar de-o-graf). This plots the electrical changes during the heart beat, producing an electrocardiogram (ECG; Figure 12.3). The normal ECG pattern comprises three waves:

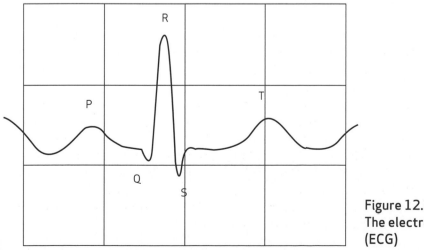

Figure 12.3: The electrocardiogram (ECG)

the P wave, QRS Complex and T wave, each of which is associated with specific events during a single heart beat. The SA node initiates the heart beat by sending a signal across the atria; this is seen on the ECG as the P wave. There is then a short pause while the impulse travels down the AV bundle, the bundle branches and finally the purkinje fibres. The QRS complex results from the contraction signal sweeping across the ventricles. Finally, the ventricles need to reset before the next beat; this results in the T wave.

Key Point 12.5

The ECG can be used in medical screening to identify numerous heart abnormalities. For example, a missing P wave indicates that the SA node is not functioning and the second-fastest set of autorhythmic cells, the AV node, instead sets the heart rate at 40–60bpm.

Cardiac output

We have so far examined the basic structure of the heart and how the heart beats to push blood around the body. We now examine how the amount of blood being delivered to the body can be manipulated. When you start to exercise, the amount of O_2 needed by your muscles will increase very rapidly, so you will start to breathe more deeply and move more air into the lungs so that O_2 can be taken by the blood and delivered to the working tissue around the body. The heart will also have to work harder to increase the rate at which blood is pumped around the body. The amount of blood leaving the heart in one minute is called the cardiac output (CO), which is a product of HR and stroke volume (SV). At rest, if an individual's heart rate was 60bpm and they pumped out 83ml of blood every beat, their CO would be 60bpm (83ml/beat = 4980ml/min). Cardiac output can therefore be changed by changing either HR or SV; so for a fixed CO, a larger heart with a larger SV would result in a lower HR. This is why endurance athletes have lower resting heart rates because one of the changes that occurs with training is an increase in heart size and SV (Table 12.1).

Table 12.1: Determinants of cardiac output in athletic and sedentary individuals

		Athlete	Sedentary
Heart rate	(bpm)	45	75
Stroke volume	(ml/min)	111	67
Cardiac output	(L/min)	5	5

Stroke volume – the amount of blood pushed from the heart in a single beat

> ### Key Point 12.6
>
> Units for cardiac output:
>
> $CO = 60 beats/min \times 83 ml/beat$
>
> $$\frac{Beats}{Minute} \quad \times \quad \frac{ml}{Beat}$$
>
> $$\frac{\cancel{Beats}}{Minute} \quad \times \quad \frac{ml}{\cancel{Beat}} \quad = \quad \frac{ml}{Minute}$$
>
> $= 4980 ml/min = 4.98 L/min$

The energy required when you start to exercise increases the demand for O_2, therefore the heart will have to increase CO. It can do this by increasing either the HR or the SV, but in practice both occur. The increase in CO is controlled very carefully so that it matches the increase in required O_2 and this is where the athlete and the sedentary individual differ greatly, as the athlete can increase their CO to a far greater extent, resulting in greater work capacities. After long periods of training athletes can increase their CO by five to seven times that at rest. So while at rest a typical CO value is 5L/min but during maximal exercise an athlete's heart can pump out 25–35L/min.

Heart rate

As already stated, resting heart rate is dependent on fitness level, and athletes have larger hearts and greater SV than sedentary individuals. Healthy individuals will have a resting HR of 60–75bpm and a maximal HR (HRmax) that is dependent on age. As we age, our HRmax will decrease by approximately one beat each year. A simple method of calculating your HRmax is to subtract your age from 220; so a 20 year old would have a HRmax of 200bpm. Care must be taken with this calculation as it is very approximate, and five per cent of all 20 year olds will have a HRmax of less than 180 or greater than 220bpm.

Heart rate increases with exercise intensity in a linear fashion (Figure 12.4). So as exercise intensity increases, so does HR, until you reach your HR, when you will be working extremely hard. Figure 12.4 shows the HR response of two 20 year olds during a treadmill exercise test. As you can see, the athlete has a much lower HR at all speeds but both individuals stop exercising at a similar HR: 200bpm. The main difference is that the athlete can run at 24km/h before they fatigue, while the sedentary individual can only manage 16km/h.

Anatomy of the blood vessels

There are three main types of blood vessel: the arteries, which carry blood away from the heart at high pressure; the veins, which carry blood back to the heart at a much lower

Figure 12.4: Heart rate response to increasing treadmill speed

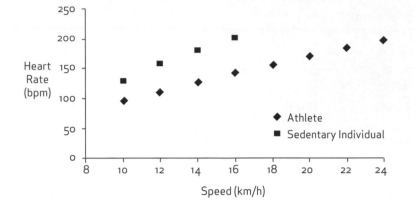

pressure; and the capillaries, which have very thin walls to allow the exchange of materials between the blood and the body's tissues. Arteries and veins have three layers or tunics; one of the differences between the two types of blood vessel is the way in which these three layers make up the blood vessel wall. The outer-most layer of a blood vessel is known as the tunica adventitia (ad ven-tish e-ah; coming from outside); it surrounds the blood vessel, protects it and anchors it to surrounding tissues.

The second layer, the tunica media (me de-ah; middle) is comprised of relatively large amounts of smooth muscle and plays an important role in the redistribution of blood flow via vasoconstriction. The final layer, the tunica intima (in ti-mah; intimate), is in direct contact with the blood and its cells have very smooth surfaces to minimise friction and allow the blood to flow easily. The hole that runs down the centre of the blood vessel, through which the blood flows, is called the lumen. While there are similarities between the three types of vessel, there are also many differences, as we will see below.

Vasoconstriction – reduction in the size of the blood vessel's lumen

Arteries

Arteries carry blood away from the heart; those leaving the right side of the heart carry blood low in O_2 to the lungs and those on the left carry blood high in O_2 to the rest of the body. As the heart beats it pushes blood into the arteries and, if you hold your fingers over an artery and press lightly on the skin, you will feel the pressure wave from the heart, known as the pulse. You can feel this at several places around the body; those most commonly used are the radial pulse on the inside of the wrist about two to three centimetres up from the thumb, and the carotid pulse in the neck on either side of the larynx.

Larynx – also known as the voice box or, in men, the Adam's apple

Critical thinking activity 12.2

Sit or lie down for five minutes, then find your own radial pulse and count the number of beats in 60 seconds to work out your own resting heart rate. Now walk around the room for a couple of minutes and check your heart rate again. Note if it has changed; if it has, think about why this might occur, based on what you have read above.

The artery walls are relatively elastic so that they can expand with the pressure created by the heart beat. They also have large amounts of smooth muscle to control blood flow to different organs. When an organ needs more blood, the artery walls relax to increase the diameter of the lumen, or when less blood is needed they contract to reduce the diameter. The amount of blood that an organ needs depends on the circumstances; for instance, following a meal when you are relaxing the stomach needs energy to digest your meal, so the arteries supplying the stomach relax and the ones supplying your muscles contract. However, if you begin exercising, the arteries supplying the skeletal muscle relax and those supplying the stomach contract, switching the blood flow from the stomach to the muscle.

Table 12.2 identifies the difference in CO at rest and during exercise, and the different tissues to which the blood is pumped. At rest, CO is five litres, with most of this going to the liver and kidneys; however, during exercise, CO increases to over 25 litres and is directed to tissues that are needed during exercise. These include: muscle; the heart, which has to work harder to increase CO; and the skin, which has to produce sweat to keep the body cool.

Veins

Veins return blood to the heart, so those supplying the left-hand side have high levels of O_2 as the blood has just passed through the lungs. The blood in the veins supplying the right-hand side is low in O_2 as the blood is returning from the body. The pressure in veins is much lower than in arteries, therefore the walls of the veins are much thinner, with relatively little smooth muscle. The low pressure also means that there is relatively little driving force to push the blood forward, so the veins have valves. These are functionally

Table 12.2: Distribution of blood flow at rest and during exercise in ml/min

	Volume of blood (ml/min)	
	At rest	During exercise
Muscle	1000	21000
Heart	200	1000
Skin	300	600
Brain	700	900
Kidneys	1100	250
Liver	1350	500
Other	350	780

similar to the ones in the heart, as they are one-way, meaning that blood can flow towards the heart but if it tried to flow in the opposite direction the valve would close to stop the flow until there was enough pressure to drive it forward again.

A mechanism that helps blood return to the heart is known as the 'muscle pump'. When skeletal muscle contracts concentrically (see Chapter 11), it shortens and widens; this presses against the vein, increasing the pressure and pushing the blood forward. This is an important reason why we warm down after exercise. During physical activity the arteries increase the blood supply to the muscles and blood is helped back to the heart via the muscle pump; however, if you stop exercise suddenly without warming down, the blood will not be able to return to the heart as effectively.

See Study Skills Activity 12.2 in the internet chapter for an additional activity.

Capillaries

Capillaries link the arteries and the veins. In the capillaries the blood exchanges the O_2 and nutrients it is carrying for CO_2 and other waste products produced by the body's tissues. For this exchange to occur the walls of the capillaries are very thin and have no tunica adventitia or tunica media. In the smallest capillaries the tunica intima can be made up from a single cell wrapped around the lumen, which is only wide enough for blood cells to pass through individually. Even though the cross-sectional area of the lumen of a single capillary is very small, there are so many more capillaries than arteries and veins that if you were to combine the cross-sectional areas of all the capillary lumens, the total area would be far greater than that of either the arteries or the veins. This is important as it allows the blood to slow down as it moves through the capillaries, giving time for the exchange of O_2 and CO_2.

Blood pressure

As the heart beats there is an increase in pressure, which pushes the blood out of the heart and into the arteries; this pressure is transferred to the artery wall and is known as blood pressure (BP). Blood pressure varies during the heart beat and two measures are normally taken when we record BP: systolic (sis tol-ik) and diastolic (di-as tol-ik). Systolic is the pressure exerted on the artery wall when the heart contracts, a period known as systole (sis to-le). Diastolic pressure is exerted when the heart relaxes to refill with blood between beats, a period known as diastole (di-as to-le). Typical values for a healthy adult are 120mmHg and 80mmHg for systolic and diastolic, respectively. It is important to note that these values are resting values and are only in the artery of the upper arm (the brachial artery). If BP was measured in an artery closer to the heart, the pressure would be greater; whereas if the measurement was taken in an artery further

---

Key Point 12.7

Units of BP: mmHg = millimetres of mercury
This unit expresses the pressure as an equivalent of the pressure that is exerted by a column of mercury of a given height in millimetres. For example, a typical systolic BP of 120mmHg means that the pressure the blood exerts on the artery wall is the same as that exerted by a column of mercury 120mm high.

from the heart, the pressure would be less. BP in the veins is very low in comparison, less than 20mmHg.

Blood pressure is very responsive to stress, posture and physical exercise. For example, if you stand up very quickly from lying down, you sometimes feel lightheaded. This is because while lying down your BP is low as the heart does not have to work hard to pump blood against gravity to your brain. When you stand up gravity has an immediate effect on the blood, pushing it down to your legs and it can take the heart several seconds to adjust to the change and increase the pressure to push the blood up to the brain; during this time you can experience dizziness. Similarly, when you start to perform exercise the heart has to work harder to pump more blood at higher pressure to the working muscles.

Blood

The typical male has five to six litres of blood and a typical female has four to five litres; this accounts for approximately 8 per cent of total body mass. Blood is the medium through which substances are moved around the body; this includes hormones, nutrients, proteins, cells and gases such as O_2 and CO_2. Blood has evolved some highly specialised methods of transporting these materials essential for life.

First, let's look at what blood is made up of. If you place a blood sample in a test tube and spin it in a centrifuge at several thousand revolutions per minute for several minutes the heaviest components of blood will be pushed to the bottom of the tube and the lighter ones will float to the top. If you then look at the tube, you will see that the blood has separated out into three distinct bands. In the bottom of the tube you will see a dark red substance; these are the red blood cells or erythrocytes (e-rith ro-site; erythro = red, cyte = cell). Next is a thin layer called the 'buffy coat', which is made up of platelets and white blood cells or leukocytes (lu ko-site; leuko = white). Finally, floating on the top, is a straw-coloured liquid called plasma.

The erythrocytes make up approximately 45 per cent of blood, although this does vary with training, and their job is to carry O_2 and CO_2 around the body. Oxygen is carried in the erythrocytes attached to a substance called haemoglobin (he-mo-glo bin); when O_2 is attached to haemoglobin it is known as oxyhaemoglobin (ok si-he mo-glo bin). The bond between O_2 and haemoglobin is very easily formed but also easily broken. When the blood cell is in an area high in O_2, i.e. the lungs, O_2 attaches to haemoglobin and the cells are then transported in the blood to the body's tissues that are low in O_2; at this point, the O_2 breaks away from the haemoglobin and can enter the tissue. At the same time, haemoglobin picks up CO_2 and transports it to the lungs to be expired.

Erythrocytes make up 45 per cent of blood volume but the buffy coat, which contains leukocytes and platelets, contributes less than 1 per cent. Leukocytes form an important part of the body's immune system; they travel around the body via the blood and if they encounter any tissue that they do not recognise as belonging to the body they will destroy it. They can recognise foreign tissue including viruses and bacteria, as all of your body's cells have protein markers on the cell wall which identify that cell as being a part of you; if the leukocytes can't find the markers, they destroy the cell. The platelets play a vital role in forming blood clots by sticking to damaged cells. If they didn't do this, the slightest cut wouldn't heal and bleeding wouldn't stop, with potentially fatal consequences. The final component of blood, plasma, typically makes up 54 per cent of blood and is itself 90 per cent water. Its main role is to carry substances and cells around the body, in addition to erythrocytes, leukocytes and platelets, plasma also carries nutrients, hormones, waste products, proteins and gases. Plasma can also act as a medium to store and transport heat away from metabolically active tissue, such as muscle during exercise. The heat can then be transferred to the skin as blood returns to the heart.

The effect of physical training on blood

Following a period of endurance training several changes occur to blood. One of the first is an increase in the volume of plasma, which occurs very rapidly, usually after only several training sessions. This increase in volume of plasma dilutes the number of blood cells, giving the false impression of anaemia; this is known as 'athletic anaemia' or 'sports anaemia'. A consequence of the increase in plasma volume is that the amount of blood pumped out of the heart in a single beat, the SV, will increase; this in part explains the lower resting HR seen in athletes. Following a slightly longer period of training of two to three weeks, the number of erythrocytes will start to increase; however, the increase in erythrocytes will never match the increase in plasma, giving athletes slightly anaemic blood. These changes together give athletes a greater O_2-carrying capacity, increasing the athlete's ability to produce energy aerobically.

Anaemia – low erythrocyte count

Further reading (cardiovascular system)

Marieb, EN (2000) *Human anatomy and physiology*, 7th edition. Menlo Park, CA: Benjamin Cummings.
This is an excellent general anatomy and physiology text used by undergraduate medical students. Chapters 17, 18 and 19 provide detail on the structure and function of the blood, the heart and the blood vessels, respectively.

McArdle, WD, Katch, FI and Katch, VL (2006) *Exercise physiology: energy, nutrition, and human performance*, 6th edition, pp. 313–363. Baltimore, Maryland: Lippincott Williams and Wilkins.
This textbook is written for undergraduate degree students and goes into some depth but the quality of the figures can help with understanding some of the key issues. Chapters 15, 16 and 17 (pp. 313–363) cover the cardiovascular system and its contribution to energy delivery.

Wilmore, JH, Costill, DL and Kenney, WL (2007) *Physiology of sport and exercise*, 4th edition, pp. 122–141 and pp. 160–184. Champaign, IL: Human Kinetics.
This textbook is written for undergraduate degree students and goes into a little more depth than we have here. The quality of the figures and graphs will help with understanding some of the key issues. Chapter 5 (pp. 122–141) provides information

on the cardiovascular system and Chapter 7 (pp. 160–184) examines the cardio-vascular system's response to exercise.

Bell, C (2008) *Cardiovascular physiology in sport and exercise*. London: Churchill Livingstone Elsevier.
An advanced text that provides a great deal of detail on the cardiovascular system in relation to physical activity.

Review

We started this chapter with the anatomy of the heart, including the heart wall, chambers and blood supply (LO 1), before we moved on to the heart's conduction system (LO 2) and the ECG (LO 3). We then spent some time examining cardiac output and specifically its control by increasing or decreasing heart rate and stroke volume (LO 4). Before taking a close look at blood, its constituent parts and the role each part plays within the body (LO 6), we spent some time examining blood pressure, specifically systolic and diastolic pressures (LO 5).

Work through the review questions in Study Skills Activity 12.3 in the internet chapter for an additional activity.

Chapter 13

Describing motion and quantifying kinetics

Matthew Portas and Simon Hood

Chapter focus

This chapter focuses on the biomechanical terms and concepts that are used to describe and analyse movement in sport and exercise, and the forces that are involved in straight line and rotational motion.

Have you ever wondered why sprint athletes spend so much time working on technique or how some football goalkeepers seem to throw the ball much further than others? These are the types of questions that biomechanists are interested in.

> *Biomechanics* is the discipline within sport and exercise that applies the science of physics to human movement.

Specifically, biomechanists consider how our interaction with forces influences human movement. These forces can act internally and externally. An example of an *internal force* is the amount of force produced by the biceps muscle to make your arm flex when performing a biceps curl, whereas an example of an *external force* is the force applied to your body by an opponent in a rugby tackle. If an athlete wishes to improve performance, the biomechanist may consider the action of forces (*kinetics*) or may consider the movement in terms of temporal and spatial factors without reference to the forces acting (*kinematics*). These concepts are covered in more detail throughout Chapters 13 and 14.

This chapter introduces the key theoretical concepts that underpin sport and exercise biomechanics. We introduce key definitions, provide written and diagrammatical explanations of the concepts and theories, and present worked examples and activities to check your understanding of the topics. The chapter begins by developing your understanding of how the body is designed to move and how we describe this movement. Concepts used to understand movement, including planes and axes of motion, are discussed and we help you to relate your knowledge of muscle contractions (from Chapter 11) to lever systems and force production. Once this is established, Newton's laws of motion and linear and angular kinetics are introduced.

> **Learning outcomes**
>
> **This chapter is designed to be able to:**
> 1   Identify linear and angular components of movement;
> 2   Identify and describe the main planes of motion and axes of rotation within the body;
> 3   Describe motion in terms of kinesiological and anatomical terminology;
> 4   Define and describe Newton's laws of motion;
> 5   Define and describe some concepts related to linear and angular kinetics.

If you feel a little baffled by some of the terms used in these learning outcomes at present, don't panic. By the time you read this chapter they should make much more sense and it will be a good test of your learning to refer back to these outcomes to check your understanding.

Basic biomechanical terminology

When analysing sporting movements, the terms linear and angular are used frequently and it is important to understand these terms from the outset. *Linear motion* refers to motion along a straight or curved line where the body or body parts are moving in the same direction at the same speed. *Angular motion* involves the body or body parts turning about a fixed point (axis of rotation). A tennis ball hit with top spin will travel in a *linear* fashion to the opposite side of the court, but the ball will also rotate (*angular motion*) at the same time.

Motion or movement is generated as the result of a body's interaction with forces and studying this is called *kinematic analysis*. We will go on to discuss kinematic variables in Chapter 14. Movement can either be static or dynamic. *Static* refers to objects that are in a constant state (such as in a stationary position or moving at a constant velocity). *Dynamic* refers to an object that is changing its movement state, such as a change in velocity due to acceleration. Imagine standing on a treadmill without the belt turning. This is an example of being *static*; now imagine you increase the speed of the belt to 8km/h. As the belt gradually gathers speed, you are in a *dynamic* state. Once you reach 8km/h you have returned to the *static* condition, as your speed is not changing.

Planes of motion

We are now going to look at how biomechanists describe body motion. The body is a complex multi-segmental structure (i.e. we are made up of many segments such as arms, legs, torso) that is capable of moving in three dimensions. Therefore, to simplify our analyses we often refer to movement in relation to three *planes of motion* (Figure 13.1), but it must be noted that the body can move in more than one plane at any one time. Therefore, we sometimes refer to the *principal plane of motion* to highlight the main focus of the movement.

Figure 13.1: Planes of motion

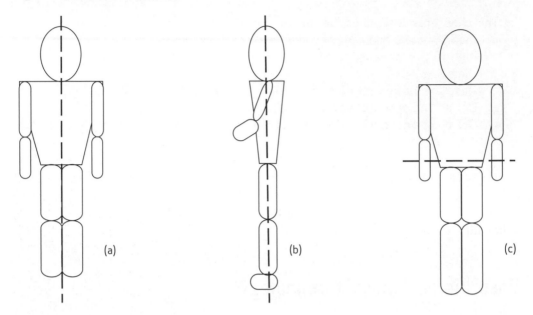

(a)   (b)   (c)

Axes of rotation

When discussing movements within the planes, we refer to imaginary points about which the body or body parts rotate, known as an axis of rotation. For whole-body movements we assume that the axis of rotation passes through the body's *centre of mass* (which will be discussed in more depth later in the chapter), perpendicular (at right angles) to the plane of motion. Flexion/extension movements in the sagittal plane rotate about the *medio-lateral/transverse* axis. Abduction and adduction movements occurring in the frontal plane will rotate about the *anterior–posterior* axis. Internal/external rotations within the transverse plane rotate about the *longitudinal* axis. With respect to a body part, such as the lower leg, an axis of rotation will pass through the knee joint at a right angle to the principal plane of motion (see Table 13.1 for further examples).

Table 13.1: Movement plane and associated axis of rotation with an example from an activity in sport and exercise

Plane	Axis	Example movement
Sagittal	Medio-lateral / Transverse	*At the hip when we perform a sit-up*
Frontal	Anterior-posterior	*Through the centre of mass when a gymnast is performing a cartwheel*
Transverse	Longitudinal	*Through the centre of mass when an ice skater performs a spin*

Critical thinking activity 13.1

For each image in Figure 13.2, can you identify the principal plane of motion and axis of rotation involved in a particular joint where motion is occurring? You can find the answers to this question by clicking on the link to Critical Thinking Activity 13.1: Answers in the internet chapter.

Figure 13.2: (a) during the left heel strike when walking, (b) performing a one-foot balance

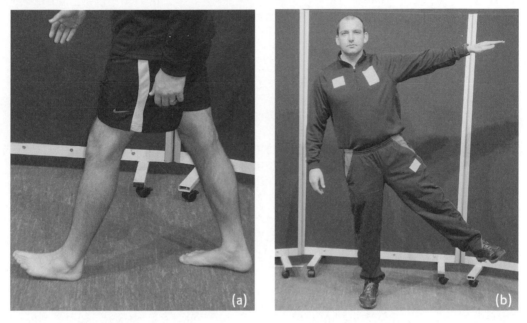

(a)   (b)

Describing movements anatomically

In addition to planes of motion and axes of rotation, we need to know the language we use to navigate around the body. Figure 13.3 highlights the descriptive terminology we use with diagrammatic representations.

Try this (it may be useful to complete this activity in pairs or in front of a mirror): begin by standing in the *anatomical position* (stand in an upright position with your feet shoulder-width apart, toes pointing forward, arms by your side with your arms slightly away from the side of your body and the palms of your hands facing forwards). From this position, bend your right arm at the elbow from a fully straight position into a 90° angle (the motion is called flexion). *Flexion* of a joint occurs when the angle between two segments decreases.

From the flexed position, straightening the elbow is called *extension* and occurs when the angle between two segments increases. When positioning the segment beyond its normal fully extended position (range of motion), we may say that the joint is in a position of *hyper extension* (but do not try to do this). Now re-position the elbow into the 90° bent position (flexed) and turn your palm so that it is facing the floor (this is called *pronation*); turning the palm back to its original position so that the palm faces upwards is called *supination*.

Figure 13.3: Anatomical terminology: frontal view (a) and sagittal view (b)

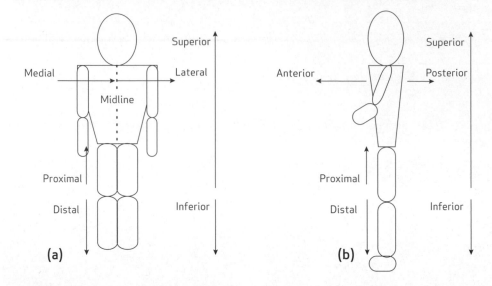

If you now hold your upper arm against your body with your elbow flexed to 90° (with the forearm parallel to the floor) and turn your arm at the shoulder so that your fingers point out to the side, the motion is called *lateral rotation* (taking the fingers away from the midline of the body). If you then rotate the arm back to its original flexed position with the fingers pointing in front of you, this movement is known as *medial rotation* (moving the fingers closer to the midline of the body). Lateral rotation is sometimes referred to as external rotation and medial rotation as internal rotation.

After all of that moving around you may need a rest, so find a chair and sit down. With your knees flexed to 90°, hold one of your feet slightly off the floor. From this position, move the ankle of your raised foot so that your toes are pointing towards the floor (this movement is called *plantar flexion*). Moving the ankle back to its original position is known as *dorsi flexion*. Now stand up and hold onto the back of your chair with your left hand to help you balance. Maintaining a straight leg, rotate your right leg about the hip laterally away from your body and position it as far as you can. This motion is called *abduction* (taking the leg away from the midline of the body). Rotating the leg back to its original standing position is called *adduction* (moving the leg towards the midline of the body). Note that throughout this short task you will have moved your arms and legs about different joints. The terms for flexion, extension, abduction and adduction can be used in different body regions. Try to think of some other movements and check your partner's learning by asking them to describe the motion.

Critical thinking activity 13.2

Complete Table 13.2 and insert an example of a movement from sport and exercise. Consider if this is a whole body movement or movement about a joint. Give as much detail as you can. After completing this exercise add additional rows where you can describe your own examples, including the principal planes and axes of rotation.

You can find the answers by clicking on the link to Critical Thinking Activity 13.2: Answers in the internet chapter.

Table 13.2: Plane of motion, associated movements, axis of rotation and practical examples

	Principal plane of motion	Principal movements along the plane	Axis about which movements occur	Example
1	Sagittal	Flexion/Extension		Sit-up
2	Frontal		Anterior–posterior	
3		Internal/External rotation	Longitudinal	
4				

See Study Skills Activity 13.1 in the internet chapter for an additional activity.

Lever systems

Knowledge of levers helps us understand how we move objects and why we move body parts in a certain way. They consist of three fundamental components: a *load* (what needs to be moved), an *effort* (the force required to move the load) and a *fulcrum* (the pivot point or axis of rotation about which the effort and load are acting). The arrangement of these components within a system will determine the classification of the lever system, either first, second or third class. Figure 13.4 outlines the arrangements of the components for the different classifications of levers. Third-class levers are most common within the body where muscle inserts (effort) are located in-between the joint's axis of rotation (fulcrum) and the load that is being moved. Refer back to the example of the biceps curl in Chapter 11 during the discussion of muscle contractions. The load is the dumbbell, the effort was applied at the insertion point of the biceps brachii and the fulcrum is the axis of rotation of the elbow joint (a third-class lever system).

Critical thinking activity 13.3

Can you think of any other sport or exercise examples where third-class levers exist? Now, what about second- and first-class levers? Try to provide examples of these too.

You can find example answers by clicking on the link to Critical Thinking Activity 13.3: Example Answers in the internet chapter.

Figure 13.4: Lever systems

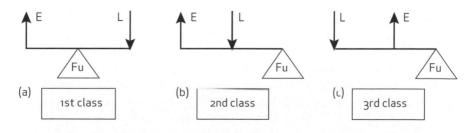

(a) 1st class   (b) 2nd class   (c) 3rd class

Newton's laws of motion

Sir Isaac Newton proposed laws that apply to the behaviour of forces and motion for both linear and angular movements. We first consider the laws in terms of linear motion. When *zero net force* is applied to an object, the object will remain stationary or moving at a constant speed in the same direction. Newton's first law is the *law of inertia*. Interpreting this law allows us to suggest that, in order for an object to change its motion path or speed, an external force must be applied. It must be noted that objects and bodies in sport and exercise are always exposed to the external forces of friction, air resistance and gravity.

Imagine a football sitting on the turf. The ball will not move unless it is kicked by the boot of a player or blown by a strong gust of wind. The boot and the wind in this example are both external forces acting on the ball. The ball will roll in the same direction but almost instantly it will start to slow down and eventually stop because of friction (an external force which will be discussed later in the chapter).

> Newton's first linear law: *a body will remain in a constant state unless an external force is applied.*

Newton's second law tells us that any movement created is proportional to the force that has been applied. This is known as *the law of acceleration* and may also be summarised as:

Force produced = mass x acceleration.

Try this: perform a Sargent jump up against a wall but do not push with full effort with your legs. Now do another jump, where you jump with everything you have. You should jump higher second time around. This is because on the second jump you have generated more force to move your body. Your mass has stayed the same from jump one to jump two but you have generated greater acceleration (see Chapter 14), resulting in a higher jump.

> Newton's second linear law: *a force applied to a body causes an acceleration of that body proportional to and in the direction that the force is applied.*

The third of the laws, the *law of reaction*, is often the most difficult to understand. The *law of reaction* occurs when two bodies exert a force on each other. Think back to your Sargent jump. When you pushed with your leg muscles to create the jump, you actually pushed your feet into the ground – the opposite direction to which you want to jump. It is actually the reaction force from the floor that accelerates your body, with equal but opposite force, up into the air.

> Newton's third linear law: *when one body applies a force to another body, the second object applies an equal and opposite force back to the first body.*

Newton's laws of angular motion

Newton's laws of angular motion follow the same principles as the linear laws; however, the terminology reflects the rotatory components associated with the movement. When discussing rotatory force, we must be aware that *the moment of force* or *torque* is the rotational equivalent of force. When performing movements our muscles exert torques, which cause body segments to move about the joint's axis of rotation, as in a biceps curl.

Torque is the product of the amount of force applied and the perpendicular distance from the point of application to the axis of rotation.

Newton's first angular law: *a rotating body will remain in a state of constant angular motion unless acted upon by an external torque.*

Consider a bike wheel freely rotating off the ground after an external torque has been applied. As the moment of inertia, the angular equivalent of mass, is evenly spread from the axis of rotation and cannot change (because the spokes are a fixed length), the angular velocity will remain constant until an external torque, such as the brakes, is applied.

Moment of inertia is the reluctance of a body to change its rotational state. It is dependent upon the mass of an object and the distance of the mass from the axis of rotation.

More torque is needed to rotate a wheel with longer spokes but the same mass because its moment of inertia is greater.

Newton's second angular law: *a net torque produces angular acceleration of a body that is directly proportional to the magnitude of the torque applied, in the same direction as the torque.*

Newton's second angular law can be summarised as:

Torque = moment of inertia x angular acceleration.

Think about our spinning bike wheel again. Greater angular acceleration given to the wheel by an external force will result in the wheel having greater torque.

Newton's third angular law: *for every torque exerted by one body on another there is an equal and opposite torque exerted by the second body on the first.*

Try this: to explain the third law of angular motion, lean backwards against a wall. By doing this you have created a torque and your body would rotate and you would fall flat on your back if the wall was not there. The reason you do not rotate is because the wall is producing an equal and opposite torque so you do not move.

Linear and angular kinetics

Mass, weight and gravity

To enable us to consider other basic concepts within biomechanics, we also need to think about *weight* and *mass*. In everyday life, we use these terms interchangeably but in fact they do have different definitions. Mass is the amount of matter (skin, bone, muscle, blood, etc.) a body possesses and is measured in kilogrammes (kg), whereas weight is a measurement of the effect of the gravitational force on a body and is measured in Newtons (N). Gravitational force pulls a body towards the centre of the Earth and the closer you are to the Earth's core, the greater your weight, but your mass will stay the same. In fact, because the Earth is not completely spherical (it is wider around the Equator than it is from Pole to Pole), your weight will be slightly greater at the Poles than at the Equator. When astronauts travel to outer space their bodies are too far away from the centre of the Earth's core to be influenced by its gravitational pull and they become weightless. However, their bodies still contain matter and so their mass is the same as it is on Earth.

When studying biomechanics, we often refer to a body's *centre of mass*, which is an imaginary point around which all of the body's mass is equally balanced. Try to balance a pencil on your index finger. When the pencil is balanced and is not moving, you have identified the pencil's centre of mass somewhere above your finger. With a human body, locating centre of mass is slightly more complicated due to its multi-segmental structure. The various segments that make up our arms and legs move in relation to our torso and this means that when they move our centre of mass moves too. When the centre of mass moves, it moves towards where the body's mass has moved. For example, stand with your arms by your sides and then raise your arms directly above your head. By doing this you have raised your centre of mass towards the raised arms.

In the images in Figure 13.5, see if you can locate the centre of mass (it is important to note that, because it is an imaginary point, the centre of mass can be located outside of the body in extreme body shapes).

Figure 13.5: Centre of mass examples

You can find answers by clicking on the link to Centre of Mass: Answers in the internet chapter.

Force and torque

From the outset of the chapter the concept of movement was outlined as the result of the effect of internal or external forces being applied to an object or a body. In sport, we know that to strike a ball we need to produce a force with our body that is then transferred to the ball during the contact phase. Also, during exercise it is important to use the correct technique so that forces and torques pass through joints correctly to prevent injury. From your previous physics education it is likely that you have referred to a force as a pushing or pulling action. It is important that you keep this idea in mind as you consider the following section in relation to human movement.

Measuring forces

Stand on a set of analogue bathroom scales and you will realise that, as you move on the scales, the needle will move depending on the severity of the movement. The bathroom scales record the interaction between you and the surface of the scales and you can interpret this information as your weight. We must be cautious however; as biomechanists, we know that weight is a force and should therefore be reported in Newtons. Weight is the product of *mass (kg) x gravity* (as we said earlier in the chapter) and should not be confused with an object's or person's mass. The force we apply to the bathroom scales is reported in one direction (vertically) based on the principles of Newton's third law of linear motion.

To measure the external kinetic data, as experienced between a person and a contact surface over time, a force platform can be used. Force–time data, particularly when combined with joint positions and body segment parameters, can be used to evaluate a wide range of movement patterns in sport and exercise. In effect, the force platform acts like a large, very accurate set of bathroom scales and it records reaction force to the subject's weight. However, unlike bathroom scales the force platform not only measures forces produced vertically (z-axis) but also in both directions horizontally (x- and y-axes) and the rotational force (torque) around these axes.

The theory of how the force platform works is best described using Newton's laws of motion. With respect to Newton's first law of motion, if the net force acting in a situation is zero, then there is either static equilibrium (i.e. stationary) or dynamic equilibrium (constant velocity). This means that, for any movement to occur, a net force of greater than zero must act. For the force platform to read a force there must be a net force greater than zero in at least one direction. We know that Newton's second law indicates that the magnitude (size) of the force (F) produced is equal to the product of the object's mass (m) and its acceleration (a) [F = ma]. This means that the reading from the force platform is a result of the mass of the body in contact with the platform, multiplied by the acceleration of that body. Newton's third law indicates that, if one object exerts a force on another object, then the second object exerts an equal and opposite force on the first object. Note that these forces acting on the second object should be discussed in this manner in accordance with this law (and not that both forces can be considered to act on the same object). This principle underpins the use of the force platform, where reaction force (R) to the subject's weight is recorded.

An athlete performing a standing vertical jump with countermovement and arm-swing produces various ground reaction forces throughout the movement. When analysing the ground reaction force data (in the z-axis), a number of key performance parameters can be identified (see Figure 13.6).

By analysing the ground reaction force curve generated from the force platform, we can begin to explain the movement. At point 'a', the athlete is standing still in an upright

Figure 13.6: Vertical ground reaction force for a standing vertical jump with counter-movement and arm swing over a four-second time period

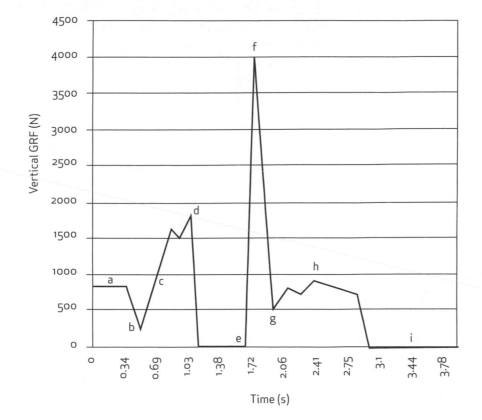

position preparing to jump; as the line is stable, we can assume that the force applied to the platform is the athlete's weight. As the athlete flexes his knees to begin a squat, the ground reaction force is reduced as the muscles relax to facilitate the squat, 'b'. The athlete then begins to apply a force to stop the knee flexion and begin the upward propulsive phase, 'c'. At point 'd', the athlete has produced his maximum upward force and takes off from the force platform. At point 'e', the force platform shows a zero force value; here, the athlete is in flight and is not in contact with the platform. On landing, a high ground reaction force is evident, 'f', so landing techniques are crucial to allow the force to be transmitted throughout the joints. At point 'g' it can be seen that the performer again goes into a squat position to allow the force to be distributed over a longer time period, thus reducing the impact on the joints. As the athlete regains a balanced position the force reading may fluctuate, 'h', until the value returns to the athlete's weight. If the athlete was then to step off the platform, the force trace would return to zero, 'i'.

A point to note when examining Figure 13.6, is that the force trace is displayed in Newtons; when analysing the performance we must refer to the force readings relative to the person's body weight. In this example, the athlete's body weight was 846N and the peak vertical ground reaction force was 4000N; this may not mean too much until we realise that the impact force was roughly 4.7 times the athlete's body weight on impact. Considering body weight, or normalising the force data relative to body weight as it is known, allows performances to be measured on an individual or group level.

Critical thinking activity 13.5

Create a suitable template/graph with the y-axis labelled 'force (N)' and the x-axis 'time (sec)'. Draw the vertical force (y-axis) trace you would expect to see for the movements below (remember Newton's first, second and third laws). You may wish to use a set of analogue bathroom scales when analysing the movements to get you thinking about the forces that are acting during each movement (e.g. when the needle on the scale decreases, vertical force has dropped below body weight).

1 Stand still on force platform.
2 Step on and stand still.
3 Step on, stand still, and step off.
4 Drop squat.

You can find the answers by clicking on the link to Critical Thinking Activity 13.5: Answers in the internet chapter.

Friction

> Friction is a force (measured in Newtons) that acts at the interface of two surfaces that are in contact and opposite to the direction of motion of the object.

Friction must be taken into account during sport as for performance can be a contributing factor to successful performance but can also be detrimental. When we think of physical activity, maximum *static friction* refers to the greatest friction force that is opposing motion before the movement begins. Once an object begins to move we might assume that the friction force has disappeared; however, this is not usually the case and a friction force is often present, but the applied force is greater than the friction force and therefore movement occurs. The friction force acting between two surfaces with one surface moving across another is referred to as *kinetic* or *dynamic friction*.

Dynamic friction remains constant during movement as long as the structures of the two surfaces that are in contact with each other remain constant. Friction values are often referred to as *friction coefficients* and lie between zero and one, with higher values indicating greater friction. Tennis players can deceive opponents by placing top spin or back spin on a passing shot. When the spinning ball contacts the ground, friction acts on the ball in different ways compared with shots without added spin and causes the ball to 'stand up' from back spin or 'kick' from top spin.

Try this: hold a tennis ball and throw it underarm across the room, allowing it to bounce off the ground. Now throw it twice more, once with back spin and once with top spin. Watch how the ball bounces differently. Can you use your understanding of friction to explain the behaviour of the bouncing ball?

Friction is often seen as a force that restricts movement. However, we must realise that, without friction forces, movements would be limited. If friction did not exist between our feet and the floor we would not be able to apply forces in an appropriate direction to propel us forward. Friction forces can however be potentially damaging during joint movement. Repetitive contact of two smooth surfaces can cause the surfaces to break down, ultimately reducing the range of motion, limiting movement and causing pain. It is therefore crucial that we think about friction when discussing movement and note both the positive and negative aspects during our analyses.

Impulse and angular impulse

In order to initiate motion of a body, an individual needs to produce a force over a period of time by contracting their muscles (see Chapter 11). This is known as *impulse*.

Impulse = Force (N) x Time (sec)

Impulse has a whole range of applications to sporting performance. Imagine an athlete performing the high jump. She needs to position her body and take-off leg on the last step to enable maximal vertical distance. To do this, she generates the highest possible force over a long period of time, i.e. maximising the impulse. She does this by making the last stride longer than normal by stepping her foot further in front of her, planting the heel and leaning back. This maximises the time available to her to produce force, whilst also enabling her body to be in a mechanically efficient position to maximise force production. This combination allows the high jumper to maximise vertical take-off velocity and subsequent jump height.

Another application of impulse in sport is when a gymnast lands when dismounting apparatus. When his feet hit the ground, the gymnast automatically bends at the knees and hips. This is a safety mechanism the body uses to prevent a high amount of force passing through it in a very short period of time, which would happen if the gymnast remained straight and stiff on landing. By bending the knees and hips, he increases the amount of time over which the impact force is absorbed by the body. Here, altering the impulse is a way of the gymnast protecting his body from injury.

Try this: take a tennis ball and stand with the ball in your hand and your feet together. Now, using only your arm, throw the ball overhand as far as you can and measure the distance. Next, take the ball in your hand again but this time stand one foot in front of the other, bend at your knees and lean back before throwing the ball as far as possible. You should find that the ball goes further when thrown from the second position. This is because you have maximised force production by positioning your body in a way that force can be applied over a longer period of time, i.e. you have increased impulse.

See Study Skills Activity 13.2 and 13.3 and the review questions in Study Skills Activity 13.4 in the internet chapter for additional activities to work through.

Review

We began by explaining that movement can be described in terms of linear and angular motion (LO 1) and how the terms static and dynamic relate to movement analysis. Further explanation of how the body can be referred to during motion was also introduced in terms of planes of motion (LO 2). The use of the terms linear and angular was then built on to allow you to begin to break movement down and consider movement as a whole, in addition to the movement of body segments about joint axes of rotation. Further descriptive terms were introduced through various figures and activities and hopefully you can now outline the different ways of describing a movement in relation to kinesiological terms and definitions, such as flexion and extension (LO 3). It must be noted that this text does not provide extensive descriptions of movements, so you will need to apply the basic definitions to practical scenarios in addition to completing further reading into movement analysis to advance your knowledge. The chapter then explained Newton's laws of motion and how they apply to sport and exercise (LO 4).

Finally, the main focus of the chapter described linear and angular kinetics. A number of variables were introduced and hopefully you will now be able to define Newton's laws of motion in terms of linear and angular interpretations (LO 5). Practical examples have been used where possible; however, additional thought is required to further your understanding. We will refer back to this chapter and your understanding of kinetics (forces) in Chapter 14, when the focus will move to quantifying motion in relation to space and time (kinematic analysis).

Analysing motion and quantifying kinematics

Simon Hood and Matthew Portas

Chapter focus

This chapter builds on the biomechanical principles discussed in Chapter 13. With knowledge of how the body moves in terms of force production (kinetics), we now consider how movement can be measured and quantified in terms of *temporal* (time) and *spatial* (space) factors. The study of motion in relation to time and space is known as *kinematic analysis*. We introduce key terms and equations used to describe and analyse movement, along with worked examples and activities to check your understanding of the topics.

The chapter begins by developing your understanding of qualitative and quantitative analysis. Here, techniques such as temporal and phase analysis are introduced, with a greater focus placed on the quantification of movement using kinematic variables such as distance, displacement, speed, velocity and acceleration. We also recap on your knowledge of the use of vector and scalar quantities.

Learning outcomes

This chapter is designed to help you be able to:
1 Define and describe movement using qualitative and quantitative terminology;
2 Perform a phase analysis of a sporting movement;
3 Describe the difference between vectors and scalars;
4 Define and utilise kinematic variables;
5 Analyse motion using linear and angular kinematic variables.

Again, many of these terms may be unfamiliar, but the chapter includes plenty of real-life examples and activities to help you to understand them.

Describing movement

A popular method to analyse movement in applied contexts is to qualitatively describe the movement that has taken place. This is common practice in gait analysis to give an early diagnosis before more complex quantitative measures are taken. It is also a popular method used by coaches when working with their athletes to provide immediate feedback after performance.

If you have ever been coached you will probably recall the coach saying something about your technique; possibly your leg was too straight or your body too upright, which are both examples of basic qualitative analyses. However, within biomechanics we can use the terms outlined in Chapter 13 to describe the motion. For example, consider the person in Figure 14.1b preparing to catch a ball.

The person is positioned in the ready stance used in goalkeeping; in coaching terms we may say that the feet are shoulder-width apart (although this is not clear from the image). A coach may say that the performer is ready, as he is 'on his toes' with knees bent, weight forward and hands forward. To use the terminology outlined in Chapter 13, we could say that, when viewed in the sagittal plane, the performer in Figure 14.1b is preparing to catch. There is flexion of the knee, slight plantar flexion at the ankle and the heel is not in contact with the floor. Both descriptions outline the position of the body segments using subjective views and without quantification of the positions.

To allow the description of the 'ready' position above, the movement was broken down into stages or phases in relation to time (*temporal analysis*). As many techniques in sport are complex multi-directional movements across performance planes using various limb segments, it is useful to break the movement down into a series of phases so that the mechanics involved become less complicated. This process is referred to as a *phase analysis*. It is important to realise that, when the phases are defined, they must have biomechanical significance in relation to the production of the movement as a whole and all of the phases must be necessary to carry out the movement. The identification of phases during analysis is important as it allows the analyst to identify

Figure 14.1: Goalkeeper catch broken into three phases: (a) the goalkeeper is in an upright position, (b) the goalkeeper takes up a 'ready position' to make a catch, (c) the goalkeeper performs the catch

(a) (b) (c)

if there are flaws within a technique at one of the phases, which subsequently may have a detrimental effect on the overall performance of the movement. Adaptations to the technique can then be made at different phases to see if they bring about improved performances. It may also be necessary to quantify biomechanical variables at the phases to try to improve movement efficiency (e.g. time of foot contact during sprinting or the range of motion of the hip during walking). We must note here that phase analysis is a useful tool but it is the overall movement pattern and the outcome which is most relevant when analysing performance and we should not attempt to make changes to a phase without considering the effects this will have on the rest of the movement.

Critical thinking activity 14.1

Referring back to Figure 14.1, conduct a qualitative analysis of the goalkeeper making a catch. The movement has been broken down into three phases: standing still, Figure 14.1(a), adopting a recognised goalkeeping start position, Figure 14.1(b), and then making the catch, Figure 14.1(c).

- Describe the body position at each of the phases and which joints are in use, and consider why the chosen phases are important to the movement as a whole. To help with your answer see page 200 and the further reading on page 210.
- Thinking back to Chapter 13, describe what will happen in relation to force production to move the body from one phase to the next. You may need to think about the type of muscle contractions that will occur at each phase and how the speed of the movement may need to change in different situations. Referring to information in Chapter 11, pages 165–166, may also help you answer this.
- Now consider a skill that you are familiar with from a sport and exercise activity you have done in the past. Try to break the skill down into its functionally distinct phases and describe what the contribution of that phase is to the whole movement (if you have a stop watch handy, you could time how long each phase lasts and so define the temporal boundaries too). Also, consider the key anatomical structures and movements involved in the movement.

See Study Skills Activity 14.1 in the internet chapter for an additional activity.

Quantifying movement

Variables associated with movement can be classified as either scalar or vector quantities. As we know, movements can occur at different rates and in different directions. When only the quantity of a variable is required, we can use *scalar* quantities to describe the motion. Speed is an example of a scalar quantity because we only receive information relating to magnitude, e.g. the car travelled at 30mph. If we require information on magnitude and direction, we use *vector* quantities.

A vector is often represented by an arrow, with the length and height of the arrow relating to the magnitude of the variable and the orientation of the arrow referring to the direction. Displacement, velocity and acceleration are examples of vectors and we discuss these in more depth later in the chapter. The kinetic variables force and weight, discussed in Chapter 13, are vectors, as we need information on the magnitude and the direction of the variable to fully understand how it affects movement, e.g. a force of 4000N was produced along the z-axis during a vertical jump. Movements can involve a number of vector quantities and when summed together produce a *resultant vector* that describes the total effect of the variable (e.g. force) on the movement. You may not think these variable are particularly relevant at the moment, however they will become important when discussing the movements of the body later in the chapter in terms of linear and angular movement.

> A scalar only considers the magnitude or amount.
> A vector considers both magnitude and direction.

What is meant by the study of kinematics?

To begin to quantify movement, kinematic analysis is often used. *Kinematics* is the study of movement in relation to *space* and *time*, without particular reference to force. Analysts may wish to consider a performer's position relative to other objects, the object's position in relation to space or the positions of the performer's joints or limb segments. The term position, as frequently mentioned in this paragraph, is used to identify the location of a point of interest (this may be the centre of a joint) on a person or object (centre of a ball) with reference to a known line or point, to allow changes in position to be quantified.

When quantifying motion, biomechanists use 2-D (two-dimensional) or 3-D (three-dimensional) motion capture techniques to find the position of known points on the body. The positions of these markers are then tracked over time, dependent on the length of the activity (a number of guidelines must be considered for 2-D motion capture; see Payton and Bartlett, 2008). This is also the case for 3-D motion capture, which uses retro reflective markers and infra-red cameras to track the positions of the joints/limbs in a 3-D space.

See Study Skills Activity 14.2 in the internet chapter for an additional activity.

Linear kinematics

Figure 14.2(a) shows a grid reference system that allows us to quantify the movement of an object on a flat surface (in this case, a ball moving across a pitch). In an applied setting, this may involve observing and quantifying the movement in one performance plane in two dimensions on a television screen, computer monitor or interactive multimedia board. We may also choose to scale the size of the screen based on real-life coordinates. In a scientific experiment, the biomechanist uses scaling objects to measure known distances within the field of view in both horizontal and vertical

Figure 14.2a

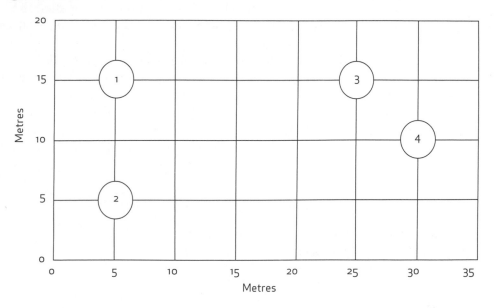

Figure 14.2b

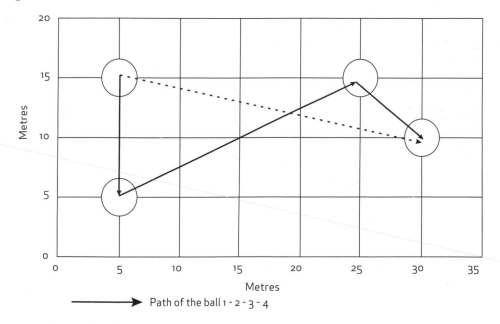

Path of the ball 1 - 2 - 3 - 4

directions. When looking at the image on a computer screen, specialist software can be used to measure the number of pixels (dots of colour that make up the screen) in relation to the known distances and a scaling factor is applied (for example, 10 pixels in the horizontal direction may be the equivalent of 0.01m in real life). Applying a scaling factor allows measures to be taken on screen using the software that are then reported in terms of real-life values. This process is commonly known as *digitising*. In the example above (Figure 14.2(a)), each small square is the equivalent of a 5m square in real life, although it is much smaller on the page.

The change in position of the ball during the movement can be seen via the numbers inside the balls. In the initial image (Figure 14.2a), we do not have any information about the direction of travel. Look at Figure 14.2 and consider how the ball moves from position 1 to position 4.

We can see in Figure 14.2(b) that the ball follows a motion path along the solid arrows from numbers 1 to 4. The change in position can be referred to as distance or displacement. The *distance* measured in metres (m) refers to the actual path taken by the ball to get from the start to the end position (1–2–3–4). *Displacement*, also measured in metres (m), refers to the shortest straight-line distance from the end to the start position (4–1). A point to note here is that, in some movements, displacement will equal zero if the performer starts and ends in the same position.

How quickly a person or object moves can be described in terms of *speed* and *velocity*, depending on which variable has been used to quantify the change in position. *Speed* is a term used in everyday life to discuss how quickly something is moving, and you probably used it during GCSE science lessons to describe how objects moved. You may discuss how quickly a car travels in terms of miles per hour (mph) or kilometres per hour (km/h). When we have information on the distance an object has travelled, we can use the following equation to calculate speed:

$$\text{Speed (m/s)} = \frac{\text{distance travelled (m)}}{\text{time taken (s)}}$$

The usual way to report speed in biomechanics uses the units of metres (m) to indicate distance and seconds (s) to indicate time. The normal units for speed in biomechanics are therefore metres per second (m/s); this may also be written as ms^{-1}. In everyday life we may see other units used; miles per hour, for example, is used to measure the speed of a car. Speed, like distance, is an example of a scalar quantity.

If we need information on the rate of change of position in relation to direction we use *velocity*, the change in position with respect to time. As velocity includes information on direction, it is a vector quantity. Therefore, when measuring velocity we may refer to the direction along the horizontal or vertical axis in which an object or body is moving. If we were referring to travelling in a car, we may say that the car has a velocity of 60mph in a northerly direction. Velocity is calculated using the following equation:

$$\text{Velocity (m/s)} = \frac{\text{change in displacement (m)}}{\text{change in time (s)}} \quad or \quad \frac{\text{final position–initial position}}{\text{final time–initial time}}$$

Velocity is also measured in metres per second (m/s, ms⁻¹). To measure the horizontal velocity of a long jumper on the run-up, we can use timing gates that are set at a known distance apart, say ten metres. When the jumper cuts the beam at the first gate a timer starts and it is stopped when she cuts the beam at the second gate. If the time taken through the gates was three seconds, we would know the jumper's mean horizontal velocity was 3.34m/s. We may not be happy however, with just knowing mean horizontal velocity because having more information on how the velocity is changing, i.e. increasing or decreasing over a period of time, may be useful. For this, we would need to measure acceleration.

Acceleration represents the rate of change of velocity and is calculated using the following equation:

$$\text{acceleration (m/s/s)} = \frac{\text{change in velocity (m/s)}}{\text{change in time (s)}} \quad or \quad \frac{\text{final velocity} - \text{initial velocity}}{\text{final time} - \text{initial time}}$$

Acceleration is also a vector quantity, as it takes into account direction (calculated using velocity). Acceleration can be calculated when the velocity of an object changes throughout a movement. If velocity remains constant, then acceleration is 0m/s/s. It is important to realise here that acceleration values may be positive or negative, depending on whether the velocity of the object is increasing or decreasing. The units of acceleration are m/s/s or ms⁻². In recent times, the advent of global positioning system (GPS) technology has allowed biomechanists to use satellites to monitor changes in velocity at a rate of five samples every second (5Hz), producing a new measure of velocity every 0.2 seconds. If we placed a GPS unit onto our long jumper, we would be able to measure her mean horizontal velocity over 10m, as we did previously with the timing gates, but the GPS unit also provides us with a measure of change in velocity every 0.2 seconds, i.e. we would measure her acceleration. For example, if between 2.2 and 2.4 seconds of the measure the velocity of the long jumper had changed from 3m/s to 3.2 m/s, then she would have a horizontal acceleration of 1m/s/s.

Critical thinking activity 14.3

The ball in Figure 14.2(b) takes ten seconds to move from position 1 to position 4. At position 1, the velocity of the ball is 0m/s. Calculate the following kinematic variables for the ball (you may need to use your answers from Critical thinking activity 14.2):

- Mean speed;
- Mean velocity;
- Mean acceleration

You can find the answers by clicking on the link to Critical Thinking Activity 14.3: Answers in the internet chapter.

Angular kinematics

We now move on to consider the kinematic variables that were outlined above in terms of angular movement (movement about a fixed point/axis of rotation). The images in Figure 14.3 are taken from an experiment where the biomechanists were interested in the lower limb kinematics in the sagittal plane during a standard two-footed landing from a 0.3m height. A high-speed camera set-up, positioned in accordance with BASES guidelines, was used to film the landing, sampling at 250Hz (the camera takes 250 pictures per second).

For the purpose of biomechanical analysis, and when you begin to read research papers from within the discipline, you will see that angles are measured in degrees or *radians*. You have probably measured angles in degrees previously but may not have heard of radians. At this stage, it is only relevant that you understand that angles can be expressed with either of these units, but radians are often preferred as they often result in smaller values: one radian is the equivalent of 57.3° (just as metres are often preferred to centimetres when measuring larger linear distances). The value for pi (π): 3.14159, is also often associated with radians, as it is used in calculating angular values such as half turns and full rotations (π radian = 3.14159 x 57.3 = 180° or half a turn, 2 π radians = 360°, one full turn).

Figure 14.3: Sagittal plane view of a performer completing a drop landing from a height of 0.3m onto a force platform; knee angle is the angle between the shank segment (lower leg) and a line projected down the length of the femur (thigh) and is measured in degrees

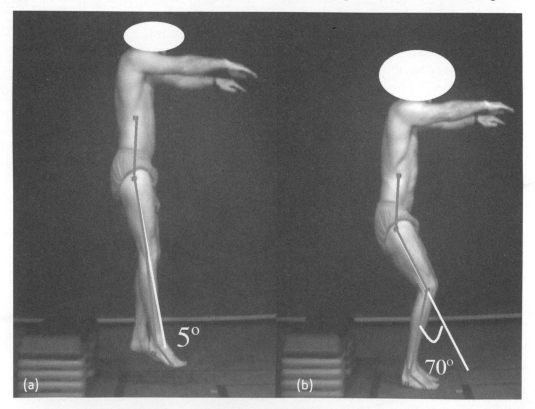

(a)　　　　　　　　　　　5°

(b)　　　　　　　　　　　70°

As you will see, the definitions of linear and angular kinematic variables are very similar, so hopefully you can grasp the concepts quite easily as you have an understanding of linear kinematics from the previous sections. *Angular distance* refers to the total of all angular changes measured following an object's/body segment's exact path. *Angular displacement* is the difference between the initial and final positions of the rotating object/body segment. In Figure 14.3, the initial knee position is 5° (Figure 14.3(a)) and the final knee position at the end of the movement is 70° (Figure 14.3(b)). As we can only see the final and initial images from the movement, we can't make comments on the angular distance the lower leg has rotated about the knee as we don't know anything about the path taken. We can however perform a simple subtraction to determine the angular displacement from the initial to the final position:

$$\text{angular position}_{final} - \text{angular position}_{initial} = 70 - 5 = 65°$$

The rate at which this rotation occurs or the angle turned through per second is known as *angular velocity*. It can be calculated using the following equations and is expressed in terms of degrees/second:

$$\omega = \frac{\text{angle turned through}}{\text{time taken}} = \frac{\theta}{t}$$

$$\omega = \frac{\text{angular position}_{final} - \text{angular position}_{initial}}{\text{change in time}} = \frac{\theta_{final} - \theta_{initial}}{t_{final} - t_{initial}}$$

ω – the Greek symbol omega is used to represent angular velocity
θ – the Greek symbol theta is used to represent an angle

Critical thinking activity 14.4

In Figure 14.3, the performer moves from an initial to a final position. The initial angle of the knee was measured as 5°. In the final image the knee is now positioned at 70°. The movement began at time = 0 and finished at time = 0.3 seconds. Using the equation above, calculate the angular velocity of the knee during the movement.

You can find the answers by clicking on the link to Critical Thinking Activity 14.4: Answers in the internet chapter.

See Study Skills Activity 14.3 in the internet chapter for an additional activity.

Linear and angular momentum

Sometimes in biomechanics we use measures where we need to combine kinematic and kinetic variables – when we measure the momentum of an individual or object we are doing just that. *Linear momentum* (M) is the amount of motion a body possesses and is measured by considering the mass, a kinetic variable, of a body and the amount of velocity it has, a kinematic variable (see earlier in this chapter for more on velocity and Chapter 13 for more on mass).

> Linear momentum is summarised as:
>
> M (Momentum) = m (mass) $\times$ v (velocity)
>
> M = mv

Linear momentum

Linear momentum is important in sport, especially in sports where impacts between individuals occur or where one object collides with another. In a rugby scrum, for example, where the masses of the two packs are equal, the team that generates the greatest velocity when the packs engage will have the greatest linear momentum and will therefore force the other pack backwards. Often in rugby, when one player tackles another the players are not the same mass. A small back player, for example, may sometimes successfully tackle a large forward player who has much greater mass than himself. In this case, the small back compensates for his smaller mass by generating velocity in his approach to increase his linear momentum, enabling him to knock a larger player off his feet.

Linear momentum is also evident on a snooker table and provides a good example of how linear momentum can be transferred from one object to another. The player initiates the linear momentum by moving the cue. The cue then transfers linear momentum into the cue ball and the ball rolls across the table. The cue ball then makes contact with one of the other balls on the table and the linear momentum is transferred to that ball. At each stage, here, not all of the linear momentum is initially transferred. This is because some of the energy created by the motion is lost when it is transferred into sound and heat – when the balls collide, for example. There is also linear momentum lost as the ball rolls across the table because of the effects of *friction* and *air resistance*. In addition, during collisions not all of the momentum is transferred from one object to the other. Here, when the cue ball strikes the coloured ball the cue ball may slow down but it keeps rolling. Therefore, the cue ball still has motion and so not all of its linear momentum has been transferred to the other ball.

Try this for yourself. If you have not got a pool or snooker table available try rolling a soccer ball at another across a floor area. Think about how linear momentum is initiated and how it may be transferred, wholly or partially, throughout the process. Also, see if you can note where linear momentum may be lost via energy leaks throughout.

Angular momentum

Angular momentum is generated when a force is applied to cause a rotation. Once an external force has been applied to cause a rotation, angular momentum is conserved until an external force acts to stop the motion (in many cases, the effect of friction). The higher the angular momentum, the greater the force needed to stop the rotatory motion. To highlight this further, note that angular momentum is the product of angular velocity and moment of inertia and can be expressed using the following equation:

Angular momentum = angular velocity x moment of inertia

The *moment of inertia* refers to the spread of mass from the axis of rotation. The higher the mass value and the greater the distance from the axis of rotation, the more resistance there is to rotation. Imagine a figure skater beginning to spin on the ice; as the limbs are positioned away from the body (increasing the moment of inertia as mass is positioned away from the axis of rotation) she rotates slowly. As the skater cannot apply an external force once the rotation has begun, angular momentum is conserved. The skater can reduce the moment of inertia (by pulling her arms and legs closer to the axis of rotation) and angular velocity increases (she spins faster). This can also be said for divers and gymnasts when they try to complete a number of somersaults during high difficulty level performances.

Review

Initially the chapter focused on the use of qualitative methods to analyse or describe movement and then, throughout the remainder of the chapter, you have seen and experienced ways to quantify kinematics performance (LO 1). This built on the know-ledge you acquired in Chapter 13, allowing you to use the most effective terminology to describe a movement. Phase and temporal analysis were also introduced, highlighting the importance of breaking movements down into stages when considering complex sporting movements. This allowed the analysis of different stages of the movement in relation to biomechanical concepts (LO 2).

To quantify motion, a number of kinematic variables were defined and described, categorising them into scalar or vector quantities (LO 3). Numerous practical examples of how to use the equations were provided to facilitate your understanding; however, the examples are far from extensive and further application of the concepts would be useful using your own examples (LO 4). The use of appropriate units when providing data from a kinematic analysis is essential, especially when analysing whole body linear movements and the angular movements of the joints within those movements (LO 5), and this chapter has provided a comprehensive list of units of measures associated with the kinematic variables that were introduced.

Work through the review questions in Study Skills Activity 14.4 in the internet chapter for an additional activity.

Further reading (describing motion and quantifying kinetics and analysing motion and quantifying kinematics)

Now that you have completed the two biomechanics-related chapters in this book, you have had a good introduction to some of the key topics that underpin the discipline. However, it would be a good idea to develop your understanding further by referring to some texts that focus purely on biomechanics in sport and exercise. This will help you to consolidate the areas covered within these chapters, as well as introduce you to new concepts and ideas that will help to further your understanding of biomechanics.

Floyd, RT (2008) *Manual of structural kinesiology*, 17th edition. Maidenhead: McGraw-Hill Higher Education.

Hamilton, N, Weimar, W and Luttgens, K (2008) *Kinesiology: scientific basis of human motion*. Maidenhead: McGraw-Hill Higher Education.

These two books will provide you with further reading around the anatomical principles we introduced at the start of Chapter 13. They both also contain further tasks and activities to help consolidate your understanding of the areas they discuss.

Carr, G (1997) *Mechanics of sport: a practitioner's guide*. Leeds: Human Kinetics.

Hall, SJ (2007) *Basic biomechanics*, 5th edition. Maidenhead: McGraw-Hill.

McGuinnis, PM (2005) *Biomechanics of sport and exercise*. Leeds: Human Kinetics.

These books are the best ones to refer to if you want to learn more about some of the definitions and concepts of biomechanics we introduced in Chapters 13 and 14. You will also find definitions relating to kinetics and kinematics that are not covered here, as well as new topics such as biomechanics in fluid mediums that will help to deepen your knowledge of mechanics in sport.

Bartlett, RM (1997) *Introduction to sports biomechanics*. London: Chapman and Hall.

Hay, JG (1993) *The biomechanics of sports techniques*. Englewood Cliffs, NJ: Prentice Hall.

If you think you are ready to extend your knowledge of sport and exercise biomechanics further, you should refer to these two books, but only after you have worked through some of the other texts above. These books are a little more in-depth but start to relate many of the biomechanical concepts and definitions to actual sporting skills.

Chapter 15

A multidisciplinary approach to sport and exercise science

Joanne Thatcher, Rhys Thatcher, Simon Hood, Matthew Portas and Melissa Day

Chapter focus

In this final chapter we show you how biomechanists, physiologists and psychologists can work together to help exercisers and sports participants to get the most out of themselves and their exercise and sport experiences. We've chosen to do this by using two hypothetical case studies which are quite common examples of applied work that sport and exercise scientists do. There's only one learning outcome for this chapter, and that's for you to begin to see how all the theory and research we've discussed throughout the book can lead to practical applications that can help people in real-life situations.

Case study one

John is a 42-year-old company director who has not done any exercise for the past 15 years. As a result, he is now somewhat overweight and finds he gets out of breath when he has to climb the stairs. He is unhappy with his current level of fitness and his weight and decides to do something about it. How can Sport and Exercise Science help him?

The physiological approach

What are the things a physiologist might want to know about John?
John has not exercised in a long time and he is somewhat overweight, so before he starts any form of exercise programme we need to establish several things. Since one of his goals is to lose weight, we need to know his typical diet and his calorie intake. We also need to know if his diet is sufficiently varied and includes a range of foods as identified in Figure 10.2. From Chapter 10 we know that a typical male should consume 2500 Calories (10450kJ) per day; analysis of a dietary recording sheet will tell us how many calories John does actually consume, if he is gaining energy from appropriate sources (see Table 10.4) and if he is reaching the RDA for all of the micronutrients (see Tables 10.2 and 10.3).

Next, before he starts an exercise programme we need to make sure he is healthy enough to perform the exercise by asking him to complete a questionnaire that identifies any symptoms that suggest he may be suffering from any illnesses that could be worsened or put him at risk of heart attack during exercise. Once we have ensured that John is healthy, if unfit, we can test his current fitness level. We can do this by checking his heart rate response to exercise; in Chapter 12 we saw that the fitter someone is, the lower their heart rate during exercise. We could ask John to walk or jog on a treadmill or cycle on an exercise bike and check his pulse, either using a heart rate monitor or manually by counting the number of heart beats from the radial pulse. Finally, since John wants to lose weight we can measure his BMI (Table 10.6) or, even better, check his body fat percentage by measuring skin-fold thickness.

What are some of the strategies or interventions that a physiologist might use to help John to exercise?
Now we have John's dietary information, have established that he is healthy and have an indication of his fitness level, we can think about interventions. If John is overweight he is probably consuming too many calories and we need to suggest ways he can cut down and improve his diet by consuming more foods from the bottom of the healthy eating pyramid (Figure 10.2). His exercise programme should focus on using large muscle groups, such as walking or cycling, to maximise the amount of energy he uses. He should aim to exercise daily for 30 minutes, although at the start of the programme this may be too long for him to complete at once. So, we may start him exercising for 10 minutes several times a day, so that the 30 minutes can be achieved in blocks. As he gets fitter we can increase the length of exercise bouts so that he ends up completing the 30 minutes in one session. We can make sure he is working at an appropriate exercise intensity by asking him to exercise at 70 per cent of his HRmax, as we discussed in Chapter 12.

What are some of the ways that a physiologist might use to evaluate the effectiveness of these strategies?
We can ask John to fill in the dietary recording sheet again every one or two months so that we can see if he has been successful in modifying his diet. Depending on the results of the analysis, we may need to continually check his diet and modify what he eats until he can achieve, and importantly maintain, a desirable food intake. We can check his fitness by using the same test we used in the initial fitness assessment and, if he is improving, we should see that his heart rate is lower than it was previously. This would indicate that his heart is becoming larger and stronger, increasing his CO as we discussed in Chapter 12. Finally, we can recalculate John's BMI; however, we would need to be careful as John may have lost fat but through exercise may have increased his percentage of muscle so his weight may show little change. This is why it is better to assess his body fat percentage using skin-fold measurements. The results of these tests will hopefully show John that he is getting fitter and losing fat.

The biomechanical approach

What are the things a biomechanist might want to know about John?
The biomechanist would start by considering John's posture. By performing a musculo-skeletal assessment we can check whether John's sedentary lifestyle has altered his

resting body kinematics (Chapter 14). Often sedentary individuals have rounded shoulders and a tilted pelvis because of insufficient exercise and lots of sitting on sofas and at desks. We considered anatomical terminology in Chapter 13 to help us with such assessments. We need to ask John whether he has any aches, pains or injuries to help decide what assessments may be needed later. We must refer individuals to a qualified physiotherapist or sports therapist to have any injuries assessed before we conduct exercise tests.

We would ask John to walk and jog up and down a room or on a treadmill to get an initial idea of his walking kinematics. This should only be done after the physiologist has assessed John's 'fitness' to run (see above). When observing John's gait we are looking at things such as his lower limb kinematics, how his feet interact with the ground, how he carries his arms and the motion of his shoulders during transit. We usually use at least one video camera so that we can review the performance from at least one plane of motion afterwards (Chapter 13). We could use a force platform or an isokinetic dynamometer to establish John's ability to produce force from the large muscles used during exercise. This enables us to establish baseline levels of power production before John begins his exercise programme. The psychologist may be interested in these measures to enable them to be incorporated into goal setting for the exercise programme, i.e. can John improve his scores through his exercise programme?

What are some of the strategies or interventions that a biomechanist might use to help John to exercise?
If John has problems with posture and ability to walk pain free or with poor kinematics, we may recommend that he start his training on an exercise cycle rather than the treadmill. This reduces impact and wear and tear on joints, whilst helping John to develop leg power and achieve training heart rates that the physiologist recommends. It also gives us time to use stretching and strengthening exercises to help John to improve his postural kinematics and develop strength so that he can walk and potentially jog pain free as part of his exercise regime in the future.

What are some of the ways that a biomechanist might use to evaluate the effectiveness of these strategies?
At regular intervals we would repeat the postural assessments and the kinematic gait analysis, as we want to know whether the exercises prescribed for stretching and strengthening have improved John's shoulder and pelvic positions. It is important that we remember to set the cameras up in the same position as we did the first time so that we can make direct comparisons between the two performances. We need to ask John about the aches and pains he had at the start of the process; has any discomfort subsided due to the exercise he has been doing? We would also re-evaluate John's ability to produce force during jumping on a force platform or performing exercises on an isokinetic dynamometer. This provides objective measures of his progress in developing power in the larger muscle groups and further evidence about the effectiveness of our programme. The psychologist, to help John develop his confidence and motivation, could again use results from such tests.

The psychological approach

What are the things a psychologist might want to know about John?
We would want to check John's stage of change: is he in the contemplation or the preparation stage? His self-efficacy to and perceived pros and cons of exercise will likely differ between these two stages, so knowing which stage he has reached will help us to decide which strategies we could use to help John to increase his exercise level (Chapter 9). We also identified that many people face barriers that prevent them from exercising, so we would want to know John's barriers and whether he has perceived control over his exercise. If we have low levels of perceived control we are unlikely to form strong intentions to exercise and are unlikely to exercise (theory of planned behaviour). This theory also suggests that attitudes and subjective norms will influence our intentions to exercise, so we would want to understand John's attitude to exercise and his perceived subjective norms. We would also want to know how self-determined John's motives are for exercising so that we can understand his motivation towards his exercise programme.

What are some of the strategies or interventions that a psychologist might use to help John to start exercising?
We might ask John to complete a decision balance sheet to understand his perceived benefits and costs of exercise; if he perceives fewer benefits than costs, we would try to modify his attitude towards exercise. We could make John aware of the physical and psychological benefits of exercise (see Chapter 9) to help him develop a more positive attitude towards exercise and help him to realise that everyone can do exercise, regardless of their age or experience. These strategies are based on cognitive processes of change (consciousness raising and self re-evaluation; Chapter 9). Once John has moved into the action stage, we might use social support and ask his friends and family to exercise with John (behavioural process of change: helping relationships) to help him stick to his exercise programme initially, as this is a vulnerable stage for new exercisers (Chapter 9).

To help John to develop self-determined motivation to exercise, we must ensure that his needs for autonomy, competence and relatedness are met (Chapter 6). Exercising with friends may contribute towards meeting his relatedness need, asking John to choose the exercise he participates in will help to fulfil his autonomy need and helping him to set achievable goals will help him to meet his competence need. By meeting these needs he is likely to develop more self-determined motivation to exercise and adhere to his programme. Feeling competent is also likely to lead to positive emotions and an increased motivation to demonstrate mastery (Harter's competence motivation theory; Chapter 6).

What are some of the ways that a psychologist might use to evaluate the effectiveness of these strategies?
We could re-administer the decision balance sheet to see if John's attitude towards exercise has changed. If our strategies have been effective, we would likely see more perceived benefits than costs of exercise and less barriers to exercise, as John is exercising more and has moved into the action stage. It would be useful to see if any perceived barriers need addressing to ensure that he doesn't suffer a relapse to the

contemplation or preparation stages (Chapter 9). We would want to identify if our strategies for fulfilling John's needs for autonomy, competence and relatedness have helped him to develop more self-determined exercise motivation. So, we would assess his levels of self-determination and consider new strategies to fulfil these needs if required to try to reduce the likelihood of drop-out later on. Thus, from a psychological perspective, whilst we examine John's exercise behaviour to measure effectiveness, we are also interested in whether John has experienced any changes in his attitude and motivation towards exercise, for example, as these are critical for maintaining his exercise behaviour over the long term.

Case study two

Claire is a 20-year-old trampolinist who currently competes at a national level. She has an important two-day competition coming up in two months' time, where the national squad will be selected for international competition. She is feeling stressed about the competition and is concerned about her technique during one of the moves she will perform during her routine. She is also seeking advice on how to manage her nutrition in preparation for and during the competition. How can Sport and Exercise Science help Claire to prepare for the competition?

The physiological approach

What are the things a physiologist might want to know about Claire and the competition?
Claire is competing at a high level so her fitness routine will be well established; thus a physiologist's main concern is that she is prepared to perform at her best on the day. We first need to determine the physical demands of the two-day competition, such as how long she will perform on each day, how long each routine lasts and how long she has to recover between routines. We would also ask Claire to record her normal diet for five days before her next competition; this is important as she may change her diet in the days before competition compared with what she normally eats. Finally, we need to know what Claire would normally eat during a competition.

What are some of the strategies or interventions that a physiologist might use to help Claire to deal with these competition demands?
From the dietary analysis we can identify if Claire is consuming sufficient carbohydrate; if not, she will need to increase her intake of complex carbohydrates in the days before the competition so that she is getting approximately 70 per cent of all her energy in this form (Table 10.4). This carbohydrate loading will ensure her glycogen stores are full at the start of the two-day competition. Since she could be asked to compete at any point, she can't eat large meals during either of the two competition days. So, when she eats, she must eat small amounts of carbohydrate during the day when she can; energy drinks can also be used to top up her stores between routines. At the end of day one she should

take the opportunity to have a carbohydrate-based meal with lots of bread, pasta or rice.

What are some of the ways that a physiologist might use to evaluate the effectiveness of these strategies?
As we stated at the end of Chapter 10, any sudden changes in diet can result in negative consequences, so Claire should try these foods in the months prior to the competition. When she implements these changes, it will give her the opportunity to see if she can maintain her performance over a two-day period when the stakes are not as high as they will be at the national championships. If the changes work, she should feel as fresh and full of energy at the end of the second day as she did at the start of the first day.

The biomechanical approach

What are the things a biomechanist might want to know about Claire's technique?
There are three main factors that would lead to Claire worrying about her technique. One is that she is not getting enough height in her rebound from the trampoline bed to give her sufficient time in the air to complete the skill she is attempting (caused by a lack of muscular power, poor technique and timing when contacting the bed, or a combination of these). We know from Newton's first law (Chapter 13) that a body only changes its velocity and direction when acted upon by an external force. Therefore the bed contact is really important because the height of the body during flight is set during the contact phase (see phase analysis in Chapter 14).

Another factor is body position during contact. To maximise height and spatial awareness, Claire needs to take off and land on the middle of the trampoline bed where the trampoline provides the most bounce. By consistently landing here she doesn't need to worry about re-adjusting her body during the next skill and can concentrate fully on the skill rather than staying on the trampoline. Poor body coordination and kinematics during landing lead to irregular flight phases and poor technical execution. Finally, we need to consider the aerial kinematics of the skills. Claire rotates about the transverse and longitudinal axes when somersaulting. As we know from the discussion of angular momentum in Chapter 14, poor positioning of the arms and legs during such movements can slow rotation.

What are some of the strategies or interventions that a biomechanist might use to help Claire to develop her technique during the move that is troubling her?
As Claire has only two months until the competition, there is not much we can do regarding power production; problems with this need to be addressed over the long term. After her competition we could quantify her jumping power using a force platform and use this information to determine whether there is a problem with Claire's ability to produce power with her lower limbs. Prior to her competition we can use video technology to help us to observe her body kinematics during the contact and aerial phases of her routine and subsequently make adjustments to her technique. We may need to quantify body and joint angles to try to help us to explain any inconsistencies. We should also set up cameras to observe the flight phases of the routine to look at the techniques used during rotation. For example, when rotating in the longitudinal axis,

arm position is very important. Holding the arms out sideways will slow rotation, so we need to check that Claire is pulling her arms in close whilst 'twisting'.

What are some of the ways that a biomechanist might use to evaluate the effectiveness of these strategies?
The measures we take from filming Claire performing skills in her routine can be used to evaluate the progression of her performance. We must ensure that we set the cameras up in exactly the same way and that the method used to measure joint and body angles is the same each time we repeat the assessment. This will guarantee that we can attribute any change we see to a change in Claire's performance rather than a change in measuring methods. Over time, we are looking for increased consistency in Claire's technical performance. We will hope to see improvements in her ability to consistently use the same take-off kinematics and achieve consistently high flight phases with improved limb positioning.

The psychological approach

What are the things a psychologist might want to know about Claire and the competition?
Claire has said that she is feeling stressed about the upcoming competition, so this would be the sport psychologist's initial focus. We know from Chapter 7 that stress is caused by an imbalance between the demands of the situation and the resources that the athlete feels she has available to her. This then has a negative effect on well-being. As a psychologist, we may be concerned that this stress could have a negative effect on Claire's performance, as it is likely to result in debilitative levels of arousal and anxiety. To help Claire deal with her stress, we need to know the underlying causes of it. Research that we presented in Chapter 7 has shown that the sources of stress may vary depending on the individual. To help Claire, we need to know the sources of her stress; these may be related to her environment, the move that she is finding difficult, or the selections that will be made. Using Lazarus and Folkman's model, we can then discuss the underlying properties of this stress, e.g. novelty, ambiguity, etc. with Claire.

What are some of the strategies or interventions that a psychologist might use to help Clare to deal with these competition demands?
In Chapter 7, we presented Lazarus and Folkman's model of stress, appraisal and coping. The appraisal section of this model shows us that an athlete can appraise a stressful situation as either harmful, threatening or challenging. It may be that Claire is appraising her upcoming competition as threatening; this means that she sees the situation as potentially damaging for her. As a sport psychologist, we want Claire to appraise the situation as a challenge. One intervention that may help Claire to change her appraisal is cognitive restructuring. This involves changing the underlying thought processes that Claire has regarding these stressors. Identifying the negative thoughts that Claire is experiencing about this competition and restructuring these to more positive ones may help her to appraise the situation as a challenge.

As a psychologist, we can also help Claire by ensuring that she is aware of the coping strategies available to her to deal with these stressors. As we saw in Chapter 7, there are four main categories of coping: emotion focused, problem focused, approach and avoidance. We may work with Claire to ensure that she is aware of the coping strategies that are available to her. It may not be possible to use problem-focused strategies that take physical action to remove the stressor but it would be possible to use emotion-focused coping to help Claire to manage her emotional responses to the stressor. Emotion-focused strategies may include imagery or relaxation strategies. By restructuring her thoughts and applying these coping strategies, Claire will hopefully reappraise the stressful situation as a challenge and subsequently experience facilitative, not debilitative, arousal and anxiety during competition.

What are some of the ways that a psychologist might use to evaluate the effectiveness of these strategies?
Our main method of evaluating the effectiveness of these strategies is through in-depth discussion with Claire about her experiences. We can monitor Claire's stress levels leading up to and during the competition, and after the competition we can discuss with Claire whether certain strategies were more effective and helped her to lower her stress more than others. Strategies such as cognitive restructuring may take longer to implement than teaching someone relaxation strategies, so we may need to help Claire to further develop her cognitive restructuring skills before her next competition. If Claire felt that neither of these strategies was effective, we need to find out why so that we can identify other strategies that may be more effective for her in future. Research has also found that coping strategies that are automatic will be more effective (Chapter 7). After evaluating the effectiveness of these strategies, we may ask Claire to continue to use them so that they become more automatic and are therefore more likely to be effective.

Final comments

In this chapter our aim was to help you begin to see how Sport and Exercise Science is a multidisciplinary subject where all three disciplines contribute towards our understanding of sport and exercise participation and participants.

Throughout this book our aim has been to introduce you to Sport and Exercise Science in an interesting and interactive way and to encourage you to think critically about the research and theory we have presented and how it can be applied to real-life situations. We hope that you are inspired to study this subject further and to start to answer your own research questions.

Bibliography

Adrian, MJ and Cooper, JM (1995) *Biomechanics of human movement*. Dubuque: Brown and Benchmark.

Bartlett, RM (1997) *Introduction to sports biomechanics*. London: Chapman and Hall.

Bell, C (2008) *Cardiovascular physiology in sport and exercise*. London: Churchill Livingstone Elsevier.

Carr, G (1997) *Mechanics of sport: a practitioner's guide*. Leeds: Human Kinetics.

Delavier, F (2006) *Strength training anatomy*. Leeds: Human Kinetics.

Floyd, RT (2008) *Manual of structural kinesiology*, 17th edition. Maidenhead: McGraw-Hill Higher Education.

Hall, SJ (2007) *Basic biomechanics*, 5th edition. Maidenhead: McGraw-Hill.

Hamilton, N, Weimar, W and Luttgens, K (2008) *Kinesiology: scientific basis of human motion*. Maidenhead: McGraw-Hill Higher Education.

Hay, JG (1993) *The biomechanics of sports techniques*. Englewood Cliffs, NJ: Prentice Hall.

Jonas, WB, Anderson, RL, Crawford, CA and Lyons JS (2001) A systematic review of the quality of homeopathic clinical trials. *BMC Complementary and Alternative Medicine*, 1, http://www.biomedcentral.com/1472-6882/1/12.

Jones, D, Round, J and de Haan, A (2004) *Skeletal muscle from molecules to movement*. London: Churchill Livingstone.

Jeukendrup, A and Gleeson, M (2004) *Sport nutrition: an introduction to energy production and performance*. Leeds: Human Kinetics.

MacLaren, D (2007) *Nutrition in sport*. London: Churchill Livingstone Elsevier.

Marieb, EN (2000) *Human anatomy and physiology*, 7th edition. Menlo Park, CA: Benjamin Cummings.

McArdle, WD, Katch, FI and Katch, VL (2006) *Exercise physiology: energy, nutrition, and human performance*, 6th edition. Baltimore, MD: Lippincott Williams and Wilkins.

McGuinnis, PM (2005) *Biomechanics of sport and exercise*. Leeds: Human Kinetics.

Muscolino, JE (2006) *Kinesiology: the skeletal system and muscle function*. St. Louis, MO: Mosby Elsevier.

Nigg, BM and Herzog, W (1999) *Biomechanics of the musculo-skeletal system*. Chichester: Wiley.

Payton, CJ and Bartlett, RM (2008) *Biomechanical evaluation of movement in sport and exercise: the British Association of Sport and Exercise Sciences guidelines*. London: Routledge.

Robertson, D and Gordon E (2004) *Research methods in biomechanics*. Leeds: Human Kinetics.

Walder, P (2001) *Mechanics and sport performance*. New Milton: Feltham Press.

Wilmore, JH, Costill, DL and Kenney, WL (2007) *Physiology of sport and exercise*, 4th edition, pp. 25–45. Leeds: Human Kinetics.

Winter, DA (1990) *Biomechanics and motor control of human movement*. New York: Wiley.

Zatsiorsky, V (2000) *Biomechanics in sport: performance enhancement and injury prevention*. Oxford: Blackwell Science.

References

Ajzen, I (1985) From intentions to actions: a theory of planned behaviour. In J Kuhl and J Beckman (eds) *Action control: from cognition to behaviour* (pp. 11–39). New York: Springer-Verlag.

Ajzen, I and Fishbein, M (1980) *Understanding attitudes and predicting social behavior*. Englewood Cliffs, NJ: Prentice Hall.

Andersen, M (2005) *Sport psychology in practice*. Leeds: Human Kinetics.

Anshel, MH, Jamieson, J and Raviv, S (2001) Cognitive appraisals and coping strategies among competitive male and female athletes. *Journal of Sport Behavior*, **24**, pp. 128–144.

Atkinson, JW (1974) The mainstream of achievement-oriented activity. In JW Atkinson and JO Raynor (eds), *Motivation and achievement*, pp. 13–41. New York: Halstead.

Bamber, D, Cockerill, IM, Rodgers, S and Carroll, D (2000) 'It's exercise or nothing': a qualitative analysis of exercise dependence. *British Journal of Sports Medicine*, **37**, pp. 393–400.

Barker, JB and Jones, MV (2006) Using hypnosis, technique refinement, and self-modeling to enhance self-efficacy: a case study in cricket. *Sport Psychologist*, **20**, pp. 94–112.

Baumgartner, TA, Strong, CH and Hensley, LD (2002) *Conducting and reading research in health and human performance*, 3rd edition, Chapter 1, pp. 56, 82. Maidenhead: McGraw-Hill.

Biddle, SJH (2000) Emotion, mood and physical activity. In SJH Biddle, KR Fox and SH Boutcher (eds), *Physical activity and psychological well-being*, pp. 63–87. London: Routledge.

Biddle, S and Bailey, C (1985) Motives toward participation and attitudes towards physical activity of adult participants in fitness programs. *Perceptual and Motor Skills*, **61**, pp. 831–834.

Biddle, SJH and Mutrie, N (2008) *Psychology of physical activity: determinants, well-being and interventions*, 2nd edition. London: Routledge.

Blamey, A, Mutrie, N and Aitchinson, T (1995) Health promotion by encouraged use of stairs. *British Medical Journal*, **311**, pp. 289–290.

Blaxter, L, Hughes, C and Tight, M (2005) How to research. In D. Burton and S. Bartlett, *Practitioner research for teachers*. London: Paul Chapman.

Blaydon, MJ, Lindner, KJ and Kerr, JH (2004) Metamotivational characteristics of exercise dependence and eating-disorders in highly active amateur sport participants. *Personality and Individual Differences*, **36**, pp. 1419–1432.

Breus, MJ and O'Connor, PJ (1998) Exercise-induced anxiolysis: a test of the 'time out' hypothesis in highly anxious females. *Medicine and Science in Sports and Exercise*, **30**, pp. 1107–1112.

Buchler, J (ed.) (1973) Philosophical writings of Pierce, Chapter 2. In FN Kerlinger, *Foundations of behavioral research*, p. 6. New York: Holt, Rinehart and Winston (first published 1955).

Burton, D and Bartlett, S (2005) *Practitioner research for teachers*, pp. 18–23, 76–77. London: Paul Chapman.

Canadian Fitness and Lifestyle Research Institute (1996) *Progress in prevention*. Ottawa, Ontario.

Carron, AV and Chelladurai, P (1981) Cohesion as a factor in sport performance. *International Review of Sport Sociology*, **16**, p. 2–41.

Carron, AV, Bray, SR and Eys, MA (2002) Team cohesion and team success in sport. *Journal of Sports Sciences*, **20**, pp. 119–126.

Carron, AV, Hausenblaus, HA and Eys, MA (1998) *Group dynamics in sport*. Morgantown, WV: Fitness Information Technology.

Carron, AV, Widmeyer, WN and Brawley, LR (1985) The development of an instrument to assess cohesion in sports teams: the group environment questionnaire. *Journal of Sport Psychology*, **7**, pp. 244–366.

Cerin, E and Barnett, A (2006) A processual analysis of basic emotions and sources of concerns as they are lived before and after a competition. *Psychology of Sport and Exercise*, **7**, pp. 287–307.

Chi, L (2004) Achievement goal theory. In T Morris and J Summers (eds), *Sport psychology: theory, applications and issues*, 2nd edition, pp. 152–174. Brisbane: Wiley.

Clews, GJ and Gross, JB (1995) Individual and social motivation in Australian sport. In T Morris and J Summers (eds), *Sport psychology: theory, applications and issues*, 1st edition, pp. 90–121. Brisbane: Wiley.

Creswell, JW (1998) *Qualitative inquiry and research design: choosing among five traditions*. London: Sage.

Crocker, PRE, Kowalski, KC and Graham, TR (1998) Measurement of coping strategies in sport. In JL Duda (ed.), *Advances in measurement of sport and exercise psychology*, pp. 149–161. Morgantown, WV: Fitness Information Technology.

Dale, GA (1996) Existential phenomenology: emphasising the experience of the athlete in sport psychology research. *Sport Psychologist*, **10**, pp. 307–321.

Deci, EL and Ryan, RM (1985) *Intrinsic motivation and self-determination in human behavior*. New York: Plenum.

Deutsch, M and Krauss, RM (1965) *Theories of social psychology*. New York: Basic Books.

Duda, JL (1989) The relationship between task and ego orientation and the perceived purpose of sport among male and female high school athletes. *Journal of Sport and Exercise Psychology*, **11**, pp. 318–335.

Duda, JL and Whitehead, J (1998) Measurement of goal perspectives in the physical domain. In J Duda (ed.), *Advances in sport and exercise psychology measurement*, pp. 21–48. Morgantown, WV: Fitness Information Technology.

Elliott, J (ed.) (2001) *Oxford dictionary and thesaurus III*, p. 565. Oxford: Oxford University Press.

Eys, MA, Carron, AV, Beauchamp, MR and Bray, SR (2003) Role ambiguity in sport teams. *Journal of Sport and Exercise Psychology*, **25**, pp. 534–550.

Fahrenwald, NL and Walker, SN (2003) Application of the transtheoretical model of behavior change to the physical activity behavior of WIC mothers. *Public Health Nursing*, **20**, pp. 307–317.

Fazey, JA and Hardy, L (1988) *The inverted-U hypothesis: a catastrophe for sport psychology*. Leeds: British Association of Sport Sciences Monograph No. 1 National Coaching Foundation.

Folkman, S and Moskowitz, JT (2004) Coping: pitfalls and promise. *Annual Review of Psychology*, **55**, pp. 745–774.

Fox, KR (1999) The influence of physical activity on mental well-being. *Public Health Nutrition*, **2**, pp. 411–418.

Gauvin, L and Rejeski, WJ (1993) The exercise-induced feeling inventory: development and initial validation. *Journal of Sport and Exercise Psychology*, **15**, pp. 403–423.

Giacobbi, P, Jr, Foore, B and Weinberg, RS (2004a) Broken clubs and expletives: the sources of stress and coping responses of skilled and moderately skilled golfers. *Journal of Applied Sport Psychology*, **16**, pp. 166–182.

Giacobbi, P, Jr, Lynn, TK, Wetherington, JM, Jenkins, J, Bodenhorf, M and Langley, B (2004b) Stress and coping during the transition to university for first-year female athletes. *Sport Psychologist*, **18**, pp. 1–20.

Greenlees, IA, Graydon, JK and Maynard, IW (1999) The impact of individual efficacy beliefs on group goal selection and group goal commitment. *Journal of Sports Sciences*, **18**, pp. 451–459.

Hagger, MS, Chatzisarantis, NLD, Barkoukis, V, Wang, JCK, Hein, V, Pihu, M, Soós, I and Karsai, I (2007) Cross-cultural generalizability of the theory of planned behavior among young people in a physical activity context. *Journal of Sport and Exercise Psychology*, **29**, pp. 2–20.

Hagger, MS, Chatzisarantis, NLD and Biddle, SJH (2002) A meta-analytic review of the theories of reasoned action and planned behavior in physical activity: predictive validity and the contribution of additional variables. *Journal of Sport and Exercise Psychology*, **24**, pp. 3–32.

Hanin, YL (1980) A study of anxiety in sport. In WF Straub (ed.), *Sport psychology: an analysis of athletic behavior*. Ithaca, NY: Mouvement Publications.

Hanin, YL (2000) *Emotions in sport*. Champaign, IL: Human Kinetics.

Hanrahan, S (1995) Attribution theory. In T Morris and J Summers (eds), *Sport psychology: theory, applications and issues*, 2nd edition, pp. 122–142. Brisbane: Wiley.

Hanton, S and Jones, G (1999) The effects of a multimodal intervention program on performers: II. Training the butterflies to fly in formation. *Sport Psychologist*, **13**, pp. 22–41.

Hart, C (2003a) *Doing a literature review* (pp. 1–2, 27, 126). London: Sage.

Hart, C (2003b) *Doing a literature search* (pp. 1–2, 27, 126). London. Sage.

Harter, S (1981) A model of intrinsic mastery motivation in children: individual differences and developmental change. In WA Collins (ed.), *Minnesota Symposium on Child Psychology*, Vol. 14, pp. 215–255. Hillsdale, NJ: Erlbaum.

Hausenblas, HA and Carron, AV (1999) Eating disorder indices and athletes: an integration. *Journal of Sport and Exercise Psychology*, **21**, pp. 230–258.

Hausenblas, HA and Giacobbi, PR, Jr (2004) Relationship between exercise dependence symptoms and personality. *Personality and Individual Differences*, **36**, pp. 1265–1273.

Heider, F (1958) *The psychology of interpersonal relations*. New York: Wiley.

Hoffmann, P (1997) The endorphin hypothesis. In WP Morgan (ed.), *Physical activity and mental health*, pp. 163–177. Washington, DC: Taylor and Francis.

Holmes, D, Moody, P and Dine, D (2006) *Research methods for the biosciences* (pp. 9–10). Oxford: Oxford University Press.

Holt, NL and Sparkes, AC (2001) An ethnographic study of cohesiveness on a college soccer team over a season. *Sport Psychologist*, **15**, pp. 237–259.

Huxley, H and Hanson, J (1954) Changes in the cross-striations of muscle during contraction and stretch and their structural interpretation. *Nature*, **173**, pp. 973–976.

Hyllegard, R, Mood, DP and Morrow, JR (1996) *Interpreting research in sport and exercise science*, pp. 3–27, 131, 134–135, 139–140, 150–153, 161, 274–275. London: WCB, McGraw-Hill.

Jonas, WB, Anderson, RL, Crawford, CC and Lyons, JS (2001) A systematic review of the quality of homeopathic clinical trials. *BMC Complementary and Alternative Medicines*, www.biomedcentral.com/1472.6882/1/12.

Kalasountas, V, Reed, J and Fitzpatrick, J (2007) The effect of placebo-induced changes in expectancies on maximal force production in college students. *Journal of Applied Sport Psychology*, **19**, pp. 116–124.

Kerlinger, FN (1973) *Foundations of behavioral research*, pp. 6, 17, 306. New York: Holt, Rinehart and Winston.

Krane, V, Greenleaf, CA and Snow, J (1997) Reaching for gold and the price of glory: a motivational case study of an elite gymnast. *Sport Psychologist*, **11**, pp. 53–71.

Kremer, J, Trew, S and Ogle, S (1997) (eds), *Young people's involvement in sport*. London: Routledge.

Kuhn, TS (1970) *The structure of scientific revolutions*, 2nd edition. Chicago: University of Chicago Press.

Lavallee, D, Kremer K, Moran, A and Williams, W (2004) *Sport psychology: contemporary themes*. Basingstoke: Palgrave Macmillan.

Lazarus, RS (1990) Theory based stress measurement. *Psychological Inquiry*, **1**, pp. 3–51.

Lazarus, RS (1999) *Stress and emotion: a new synthesis*. London: Springer.

Lazarus, RS (2000) How emotions influence competitive performance. *Sport Psychologist*, **14**, pp. 229–252.

Lazarus, RS and Folkman, S (1984) *Stress, appraisal and coping*. New York: Springer.

Lewis, BA, Marcus, BH, Pate, RR and Dunn, AL (2002) Psychosocial mediators of physical activity behavior among adults and children. *American Journal of Preventive Medicine*, **23**, pp. 26–35.

Lincoln, YS and Guba, EG (1985) *Naturalistic inquiry*. Newbury Park, CA: Sage.

Locke, EA and Latham, GP (1984) *Goal setting: a motivational tool that works*. Englewood Cliffs, NJ: Prentice Hall.

Maehr, ML and Nicholls, JG (1980) Culture and achievement motivation: a second look. In N Warren (ed.), *Studies in cross-cultural psychology*, pp. 221–267. New York: Academic Press.

Marshall, SJ and Biddle, SJH (2001) The transtheoretical model of behavior change: a meta-analysis of applications to physical activity and exercise. *Annals of Behavioral Medicine*, **23**, pp. 229–246.

Martens, R, Burton, D, Vealey, RS, Bump, LA and Smith, DE (1990a) Development and validation of the Competitive State Anxiety Inventory, 2. In R Martens, RS Vealey and D Burton (eds), *Competitive anxiety in sport*. Champaign, IL: Human Kinetics.

Martens, R, Vealey, RS and Burton, D (1990b) *Competitive anxiety in sport*. Champaign, IL: Human Kinetics.

Mason, J (1998) *Qualitative researching*. London: Sage.

McAuley, E and Blissmer, B (2002) Self-efficacy and attributional processes in physical activity. In T Horn (ed.), *Advances in sport psychology*, 2nd edition, pp. 185–205. Leeds: Human Kinetics.

McClelland, D (1961) *The achieving society*. New York: Free Press.

Mellalieu, SD (2004) Mood matters, but how much? A response to Lane and Terry (2000). *Journal of Applied Sport Psychology*, **15**, pp. 99–114.

Miles, MB and Huberman, AM (1994) *Qualitative data analysis: an expanded sourcebook*. London: Sage.

Mutrie, N (2000) The relationship between physical activity and clinically defined depression. In SJH Biddle, KR Fox and SH Boutcher (eds), *Physical activity and psychological well-being*, pp. 46–62. London: Routledge.

National Health Service Information Centre (2008) *Health survey for England 2006: CVD and risk factors adults, obesity and risk factors children*. Leeds: Information Centre.

Neutens, JJ and Rubinson, L (2002) *Research techniques for the health sciences*, 3rd edition, Chapter 1, pp. 31–32, 48, 86, 140, 142. San Francisco: Benjamin Cummings.

Nicholls, AR and Polman, RCJ (2007a) Coping in sport: a systematic review. *Journal of Sports Sciences*, **25**, pp. 11–31.

Nicholls, AR and Polman, RCJ (2007b) Stressors, coping, and coping effectiveness among players from the England under-18 rugby union team. *Journal of Sport Behavior*, **30**, pp. 199–218.

Noblett, AJ and Gifford, SM (2002) The sources of stress experienced by professional Australian footballers. *Journal of Applied Sport Psychology*, **14**, pp. 1–32.

Oskamp, S and Schultz, PW (1998) *Applied social psychology*, 2nd edition. Upper Saddle River, NJ: Prentice Hall.

Osterberg, KL, Zachwieja, JJ and Smith, JW (2008) Carbohydrate and carbohydrate plus protein for cycling time-trial performance. *Journal of Sports Sciences*, **26**, pp. 227–233.

Patton, MQ (2002) *Qualitative research and evaluation methods*. Thousand Oaks, CA: Sage.

Payton, CJ and Bartlett, RM (2008) *Biomechanical evaluation of movement in sport and exercise: the British Association of Sport and Exercise Sciences guidelines*. London: Routledge.

Prochaska, JO and DiClemente, CC (1982) Transtheoretical therapy: toward a more integrative model of change. *Psychotherapy: theory, research and practice*, **19**, pp. 276–288.

Rees, T and Hardy, L (2000) An investigation into the social support experiences of high level sports performers. *Sport Psychologist*, **14**, pp. 327–347.

Rees, T, Smith, B and Sparkes, A (2003) The influence of social support on the lived experiences of spinal cord injured sportsmen. *Sport Psychologist*, **17**, pp. 135–156.

Roberts, GC (ed.) (1992) *Motivation in sport and exercise*, pp. 3–29. Champaign, IL: Human Kinetics.

Ryan, RM and Deci, EL (2007) Active human nature: self-determination theory and the promotion and maintenance of sport, exercise and health. In MS Hagger and NLD Chatzisarantis (eds), *Intrinsic motivation and self-determination in exercise and sport*, pp. 1–20. Leeds: Human Kinetics.

Ryan, RM, Frederick, CM, Lepes, D, Rubio, N and Sheldon, K (1997) Intrinsic motivation and exercise adherence. *International Journal of Sport Psychology*, **28**, pp. 335–354.

Scanlan, TK, Stein, GL and Ravizza, K (1991) An in-depth study of former elite figure skaters. III: Sources of stress. *Journal of Sport and Exercise Psychology*, **13**, pp. 103–120.

Senécal, JL, Loughead, TM and Bloom, GA (2008) A season-long team-building intervention: examining the effect of team goal setting on cohesion. *Journal of Sport and Exercise Psychology*, **30**, pp. 186–199.

Smith, RE, Ptacek, JT and Smoll, FL (1992) Sensation seeking, stress and adolescent injuries: a test of stress buffering, risk taking and coping skills hypotheses. *Journal of Personality and Social Psychology*, **62**, pp. 1016–1024.

Smolak, L, Murnen, SK and Ruble, AE (2000) Female athletes and eating problems: a meta-analysis. *International Journal of Eating Disorders*, **27**, pp. 371–380.

Sparkes, A (1992) *Research in physical education and sport: exploring alternative visions*. Oxford: Routledge.

Spence, JT and Spence, KW (1966) The motivational components of manifest anxiety: drive and drive stimuli. In CD Spielberger (ed.), *Anxiety and behavior*, pp. 291–326. New York: Academic Press.

Spence, JC, McGannon, KR and Poon, P (2005) The effect of exercise on global self-esteem: a quantitative review. *Journal of Sport and Exercise Psychology*, **27**, pp. 311–334.

Sports Council and Health Education Authority (1992) *Allied Dunbar National Fitness Survey: main findings*. London: Sports Council.

Spray, CM, Wang, CKJ, Biddle, SJH and Chatzisarantis, NLD (2006) Understanding motivation in sport: an experimental test of achievement goal and self-determination theories. *European Journal of Sport Science*, **6**, pp. 43–51.

Stagno, KM, Thatcher, R and van Someren, K (2005) Seasonal variation in the physiological profile of high-level male field hockey players. *Biology of Sport*, **22**, pp. 107–115.

Steiner, ID (1972) *Group process and productivity*. New York: Academic Press.

Taylor, AH (2000) Physical activity, anxiety and stress. In SJH Biddle, KR Fox and SH Boutcher (eds), *Physical activity and psychological well-being*, pp. 10–45. London: Routledge.

Taylor, AH, Daniel, JV, Leith, L and Burke, RJ (1990) Perceived stress, psychological burnout and paths to overturn intentions among sport officials. *Journal of Applied Sport Psychology*, **2**, pp. 84–97.

Thatcher, J and Day, M (2008) Re-appraising stress appraisals: the underlying properties of stress in sport. *Psychology of Sport and Exercise*, **9**, pp. 318–335.

Thelwell, RC, Weston, NJV and Greenlees, IA (2007) Batting on a sticky wicket: identifying sources of stress and associated coping strategies for professional cricket batsmen. *Psychology of Sport and Exercise*, **8**, pp. 219–232.

Thomas, JR and Nelson, JK (2001) *Research methods in physical activity*, 4th edition, pp. 3–24, 309–318. Leeds: Human Kinetics.

Thompson, RA (1987) Management of the athlete with an eating disorder: implications for the sport management team. *Sport Psychologist*, **1**, pp. 114–126.

Tuckman, BW (1965) Developmental sequences in small groups. *Psychological Bulletin*, **63**, pp. 384–399.

Uphill, MA and Jones, MV (2004) Coping with emotions in sport: a cognitive motivational relational theory perspective. In D Lavallee, J Thatcher and M Jones (eds), *Coping and emotion in sport*. Hauppauge, NY: Nova Science Publishers.

Wang, CJK and Biddle, SJH (2001) Young people's motivational profiles in physical activity: a cluster analysis. *Journal of Sport and Exercise Psychology*, **23**, pp. 1–22.

Weiner, B (1985) An attributional theory of achievement motivation and emotion. *Psychological Review*, **92**, pp. 548–573.

Weiss, MR and Ferrer-Caja, E (2002) Motivational orientations and sport behaviour. In T Horn (ed.), *Advances in sport psychology*, 2nd edition, pp. 101–184. Leeds: Human Kinetics.

Weiss, MR and Petlichkoff, LM (1989) Children's motivation for participation in and withdrawal from sport: identifying the missing links. *Pediatric Exercise Science*, **1**, pp. 195–211.

Widmeyer, WN and Loy, JW (1981) Dynamic duos: an analysis of the relationship between group composition and group performance in women's doubles tennis. Paper presented at the Conference on the Content of Culture, Constants and Variants, Claremont, CA.

Williams, C and Wragg, C (2004) *Data analysis and research for sport and exercise science*, pp. 12–13, 34, 40–41, 60–61. London: Routledge.

Yerkes, RM and Dodson, JD (1908) The relation of strength of stimulus to rapidity of habit-formation. *Journal of Comparative Neurology and Psychology*, **18**, pp. 459–482.

Index